Walk to Remember
The Karakoram Highway

Naba Basar

A Travel Journey from Chipursan to Rakaposhi

Copy Right © 2020 by Naba Basar.

ISBN: 978-969-7851-17-1

First Edition: July 2020.
All rights reserved. No part of this book may be used or reproduced in any manner whatsoever without written permission except in the case of brief quotations em- bodied in critical articles or reviews.
Photographs Copyrights @ Naba Basar.

Reach The Author: nababasar@hotmail.com

Printed and Designed By: **Thazbook.**
www.thazbook.com

"Travel isn't always pretty. It isn't always comfortable. Sometimes it hurts; it even breaks your heart. But that's okay. The journey changes you; it should change you. It leaves marks on your memory, on your consciousness, on your heart, and on your body. You take something with you. Hopefully, you leave something good behind."

- Anthony Bourdain

Contents

Foreword

This book has been compiled for the benefit of those who share the same passion as this passionate traveler who loves and appreciates nature in all forms.

All stories and events, accommodations and dwellings, sites and conversations compiled are from my memories and experiences of them. I treasure the memories and personal exchanges during my journey to the beautiful land of Gilgit-Baltistan. In order to maintain the anonymity in some instances I may have changed the names of individuals, some identifying characteristics and details such as physical properties, occupations and places of residence. I would also take this opportunity to thank the real-life members of the families portrayed in this book for taking me into their home and accepting me as one of their own. I recognize that their memories of the events described in this book may differ from my own. They are each humble, cultured, and hospitable people who enjoy playing host. Travel and you will realize that whatever physical, emotional, and financial challenges you face, there's someone halfway around the world that struggles similarly or more intensely. This book does not intend to hurt any individual or family. Both my publisher and I regret any unintentional harm resulting from the publishing and marketing of my travelogue. My sincere apologies if I have misspelled names of people, villages, valleys, mountains, rivers, waterfalls and edibles.

Note of Thanks: I would like to thank my limited savings that allows me to travel. I would also take this opportunity to thank everyone I travelled with; they made my journey a joyous memory. I would also like to thank my son Rayyan in particular, who models for me in every picture with a slight puff & phew!

Thank you Zumer Basar for suggesting a beautiful title for my first publication 'Gateway to Serenity The Karakoram Highway' and going through my endless photographs to help me choose the best cover photo.

Special Thanks to: Team Climax Adventure Pakistan – CEO – Muqeem Baig and Mujahid Ali for an amazing experience since 2016.

I would also like to take a moment to thank a few people who believed in me when my first book was published. I am thankful for your support, trust and encouragement.

Zahid Ali Khan (Manager at Borith Lake Hotel & Resort – Borith Lake)
Amir Khan sahab (North Gems & Handicrafts Karimabad Hunza)
Karim Khan Saka (CEO Café' de Pamir Aliabad Hunza and Pizza Pamir Karimabad)
Amin Xon (Pizza expert at Pizza Pamir Karimabad Hunza)
Ahmed Ali Khan (Apricot man / Owner/Manager at Glacier Breeze Restaurant Passu)
Nawazish Ali (at Café' de Hunza Karimabad Hunza)

Handy tips especially if you are travelling to Northern areas of Pakistan

- Always carry tissues / wipes / sanitizer (all 3 make a perfect combo up in the mountains with little or no water!)
- Zip lock bags (small & big) / preferably paper bags – to store or disposal of trash
- Medicines especially fever / flu / tummy ache / anti-allergy / headache / nausea / for acute mountain sickness etc.
- Bandages (for cuts) and crepe bandages (for strains & sprains) / alcohol swabs
- Repellent / Polyfax (skin ointment used to treat infected wounds, burns, skin grafts, skin ulcers, itching and rashes. Used to treat multiple skin infections)
- Blister pads / cotton flannel patches / gel bandages flex are easily available at drug stores (to be used if you are planning to trek / hike or walk longer)
- Olive oil / Honey comes in handy for multiple purposes (to heal wounds and for stomach and throat problems)
- Biscuits or cookies which won't easily crumble / dry fruits / nuts / trail mix / mouth fresheners / sugar free gums / candies / chocolate preferably with nuts
- Travel fork and spoon set / Swiss knife / Swiss Army knife / Leatherman multi-tool
- Coffee beans / tea bags if you fancy black or sugarless. Sachets of 3 in 1 tea or coffee as a backup for instant caffeine craving
- Milk / cereal sachets if you are travelling with toddlers
- Cash – ATM's are not easily available and even if they are, there may be major power or technical issues or non-availability of cash in certain areas

- A sturdy water bottle preferably double insulated steel flask– nothing like enjoying fresh spring / glacier / waterfall water (no matter what people say!)
- Flashlight / Torch / Headlamps for emergency situations after sun sets
- Warm piece of clothing even during summers for it may get chilly after hours
- Raincoat / Mackintosh / Windbreaker (prevents you from severe weather conditions) / Fleece / Thermals / Down Jackets (light, warm & water resistant) – if you plan to trek to high altitude areas during summers or winters
- Hat / Cap / Woolen Caps / Knit hat / Scarf / Sunglasses / Sunscreen / Lip balm – the weather conditions may intensify during daytime
  Note: Pack less but pack right!
- Trekking poles / Hiking poles / Walking poles (single or a pair but it must be lightweight aerospace aluminum - collapsible and adjustable with telescoping shafts). They increase your stability and boost your walking if you plan to trek
- Power bank / extra phone battery / additional camera battery
- If you happen to be around a market place when on a vacation buy half kg rice! Tried and tested remedy for when your cellphone accidentally falls in the water. Just submerge and leave your phone (and the disconnected battery) in a bowl of grains overnight. If you're worried about rice dust getting inside your phone, you can instead use the packets of silica gel)

- **Caution:** Electricity, hot water, clean washrooms and luxurious hotels on the way towards your destination are not guaranteed – so before starting to complain be prepared to leave your comfort zone for the best time of your life!

Good to know

Abbreviations you come across when travelling to Northern Areas of Pakistan
KPK – Khyber Pakhtunkhwa
KKH – Karakoram Highway
BTTP – Billion Tree Tsunami Project
GB – Gilgit Baltistan
NLI – The Northern Light Infantry is a light infantry regiment in the Pakistan Army, based and currently headquartered in Gilgit, the capital of Gilgit–Baltistan.
NATCO – The Northern Areas Transport Corporation
NCP – Non Custom Paid car service
AKRSP – Agha Khan Rural Support Programme
AKCSP – Agha Khan Cultural Service Pakistan
- A sign on the mountain slope commemorates the time in 1987, when the Ismaili Imam, the Agha Khan, visited the remote region
RISE – Rural Initiative for Societal Evolution

Rivers in Gilgit District
Main rivers in the Gilgit District are:

- Khunjerab River - flows south along the Karakoram Highway from the Khunjerab Valley and is known as the Nagar River, Hunza River south of Sust.
- Nagar River - flows further south and enters the Gilgit River by touching Hunza River to Gilgit
- Hunza River - flows further south and enters the Gilgit River just to the northeast of Gilgit town.
- Gilgit River - enters the Gilgit District from the west, south of the Bichhar Pass (Naltar Valley), and flows west through Gilgit town.
- Indus River - enters the Gilgit District from the Skardu District about six kilometers north of

Jaglot, where the Indus River is joined by the Gilgit River. From there, the Indus flows south along the Karakoram Highway.

Recommended Places to stay in Gilgit-Baltistan

- Café de Pamir – Upper Link road Aliabad Hunza
- Borith Lake Hotel & Resort – Gojal Hunza Contact: 0345 – 6900428
- Gulmit Tourist Inn – Upper Hunza Contact: 0346 – 0030255
- Passu Tourist Lodge – Passu, Gojal Hunza Contact: 0355 – 5449927
- Heaven Lodge – River view road Sonikote Gilgit Contact: 0315 – 6667117
- Capital Lodge Gilgit – Shahrah Quaid-e-Azam Jutial, Gilgit Contact: (05811) 455901

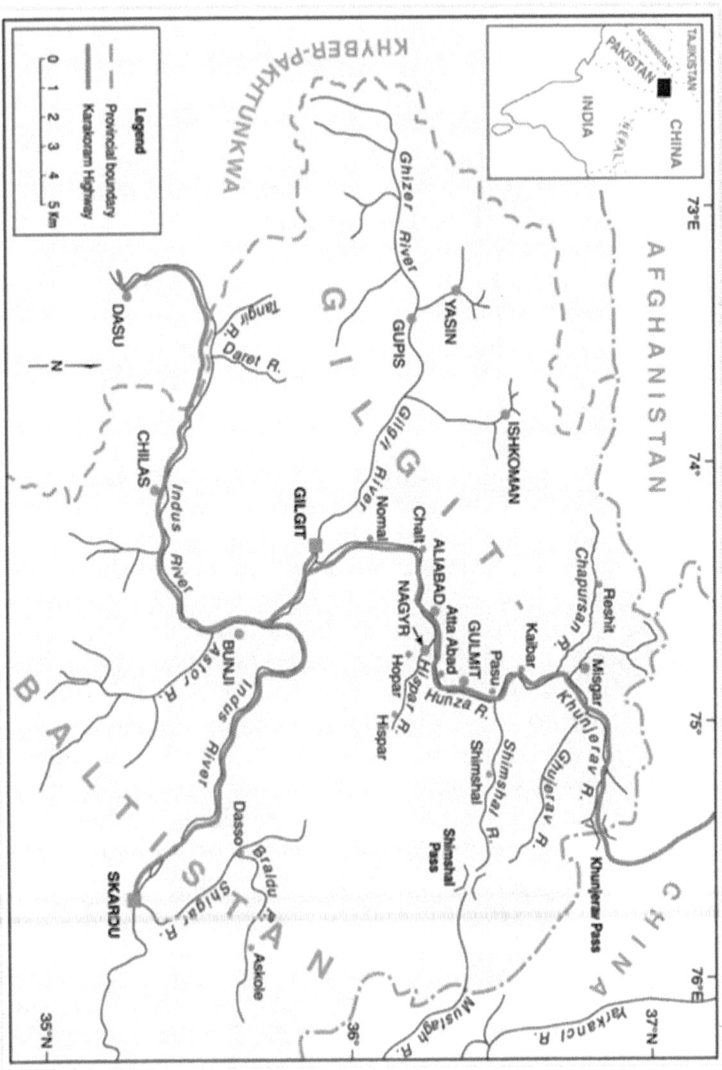

Gilgit-Baltistan, Pakistan (Map by David Butz)

The Departure

I always wondered if I could pack my bags and take everything with me — everything except a concrete travel plan. It may just be the best adventure of my life! And that's what was cooking in my mind since the last time I travelled to Fairy Meadows to Hunza and all the way to Khunjerab.

Skimming through one of the travel reads in my bookshelf I came across this line; "I guess sometimes the greatest memories are made in the most unlikely of places..." Spontaneity may be more rewarding and for travellers who love surprises, the excitement never ends. In all these years I have travelled, this year (2018) I just yearned to go on a journey unprepared, unpredictable and less repetitive. It materialized to be one of the best that I have ever had. During my journey I had random yet meaningful conversations with strangers who I feel are waiting to become your new friends and acquaintances. Even a simple encounter of you asking for directions can help you gain a friend for life, and asking for a recommendation for the best place to get *kehwa* in the mountains can end up with you having tea and a local snack. The possibilities are endless!

Normally I choose to travel right after Eid; it is not the best of the times but is the only time for me and my 7-year-old. We started totally unprepared and uncertain, leaving our comfort zone for the next 4 weeks. This was going to be my son's fifth expedition towards the Northern part of Pakistan and every year we tend to become more adventurous. The inner-peace I have been seeking all my life, I found it in nature, in what Allah has created, in the mountains of Gilgit Baltistan.

*** Tip:** Never underestimate your children based on their age and physical health. They are flexible, intuitive, responsible and confident. Therefore, make the best out of their potentials and strengths especially when you are travelling.

The Karakoram Range is the most fascinating mountain ranges in the world. The range is one of the finest, most magnificent and jaw-dropping creations of nature. The Karakoram is a network of mountain ranges in the heart of Asia, including the Hindu Kush (west), the Pamirs (northwest), the Kunlun Mountains (northeast) and the Himalayas (southeast). The word Karakoram is derived from the Turkic word that means 'black gravel or black mountain or black rock'. The European travelers used the term Muztagh for this range which means "Ice Mountain". Granites, metamorphic rocks, lime stones, marbles (schists, phyllites), micaceous slates and the sedimentary rock cut by the intrusions of granite, dominate the geologic composition of the Karakoram range. Over the period of time the Karakoram was characterized by great tectonic changes and emerged as the result of intensive geologically recent disruptions. There is still frequent 'seismic activity' in the region; often triggering massive rock and ice avalanches. Hot springs are also found in several parts.

18th June 2018 – Monday 6:30 p.m.

As I boarded the plane and switched off my cell phone I had no clue what I will be doing as soon as I land at the Islamabad Airport. Even writing about it I can feel a little adrenaline rush coursing through my veins. Absolutely oblivious to what our next step would be. My freedom begins from this runway here each year – my platform to explore adventure in all its dimensions. My travels leave such deep imprints in and on me that I must on occasion deliberately take time to unpack them, much as I might my backpack upon concluding a trip. Upon landing at the Islamabad Airport I was relieved to find out that a guesthouse booking was made and I was to leave for Hunza early morning at 4 a.m. I squealed with joy and was eagerly looking forward to a dazed restless night.

We followed the crowd into the luggage terminal. Not yet a complete backpacker but I have always believed that a traveller must be ready to carry their own bags effortlessly. Booking a local car service is a sensible secure selection than the local Taxi cabs in the capital, especially on the 4th day of Eid! When I landed at the Islamabad International Airport I happened to book my ride with one and was twice as much happier to come across a decent driver. I didn't know he was headed home after a tough day of driving, and seemingly was dropping his last ride at the airport before I booked him. A friendly, good-humoured gentleman who kept laughing at his own jokes, talked non-stop for almost an hour until we finally located the Suwana Guesthouse in F/6-1 Islamabad. He asked everything from where I came to where I was headed to and when will I return to Islamabad and back home to Karachi. He had all suggestions and opinions ready and was not even a tad bit hesitant to express them. He told me, "Baji (sister) I run a Rent-a-car service. Please save my name and number in case you need to go anywhere in Islamabad or surrounding areas. Save it under Khurram Shehzad Rent-a-car." And that's what I did. I started telling him about the rough plan I had mentally sketched, places I have planned to visit. "I plan to revisit Khewra Salt Mines, the last time I went was in 2007 and my son really wants to see the salt mine," I told him. He quickly responded, "Baji, I will take you. Just tell me the day and place to pick you." I asked him the most important question, "How much will you charge for a day trip?" He claimed his rates were reasonable, but like a professional he assured me, "Baji, my proposed plan will InshaAllah be the best, reasonable and satisfying. You can check with others and decide." I ensured that I will contact him once I am back from my trip. We had little trouble finding the guesthouse at night but he did not lose his patience. Once I checked in I was eager to call again and find out if I was leaving for Hunza tonight. I was told again that, "you must be ready by 4 a.m. or else they will leave you." I felt a frisson of excitement until the clock struck 4:00. Empty stomach, anxious and wide awake I made mental notes, charged my phone, repacked our backpacks and woke up my son. Half-awake, groggy eyes he wore his shoes and dozed off again.

An hour later than 4 a.m. a car full of strangers pulled up outside our guesthouse in F6 Islamabad.

Note: My stay here was not the best and the most comfortable, therefore I would not personally recommend it.

Day 01 – Hunza – here I come again 19th June 2018

Plan: *Departure from Islamabad 5 a.m., arrival in Hunza (don't know when), Dinner (most probably) & overnight stay (definitely).*

As soon as my son and I settled in the Toyota with the three ladies and the man driving speaking incessantly in Wakhi language, I smiled to myself that undoubtedly this seems like the perfect beginning. Watching the sun rise over Kashmir Highway, trying not very hard to understand the happy conversation, enjoying the landscape, leaving Margalla hills behind in the midst of the morning glow, dreaming of my day in Hunza once again; my heart couldn't help but beat fast with delight. At first I thought they were a family, but turned out the two elderly women were returning home to Hunza from Islamabad. The young girl was studying in Islamabad and going home for vacations and the guy Abdul Wahid runs a dry fruit shop in Karimabad Hunza. Not completely related! After 6 hours of continuous drive we stopped at Parhena Cottages and Resort Bella Naran. The hotel is 14 kilometers away from Saif ul Muluk and 5 kilometers from Naran bazaar. The ladies told me this place is run by people of Hunza and they serve the best doodh patti chai (milk tea). The young girl baked a local bread phitti a day before and it was the best combo with namkeen chai (salt tea). The bread was slightly hard than it should be, but very rich. Hunza bread is delicious, dense and chewy and is very nutritious and almost impervious to spoilage. A 2-inch square, high in protein, vitamins and minerals, can be kept for days at room temperature, even longer in the fridge and indefinitely in the freezer. Made from natural buckwheat or millet flour, this bread is rich in phosphorous, potassium, iron, calcium, manganese and other minerals, as nothing has been destroyed in the preparation from the wheat. Thus it contains the essential nourishment of the grain. This is why you must only use natural buckwheat or millet flour to make your own Hunza Diet Bread as it is popularly known. (*Hunza bread recipe can be found towards the end of the book*)

The view from this hotel is spectacular; you can relax in the gardens along the river and enjoy solitude while immersed in the constant soothing sound of the flowing Kunhar River. It started drizzling while we were clicking pictures and the beauty of this place amplified. A group picture here was a must, with the perfect backdrop of lush green mountains and roaring river.

A 40-minute drive from Naran, you can also take a day trip to Lake Saif ul Muluk. Situated around 5 miles north from the town of Naran in the northern end of Kaghan Valley, in Khyber Pakhtunkhwa, the lake is considered as the fifth most popular tourist destination in Pakistan. The greenish-blue perfectly clear and solidifying water, encompassed by massive ice sheets, including Malika Parbat, mirrors the magnificence of Saif ul Muluk. At an elevation of 3,224 metres (10,578 feet) above sea level, the lake is said to be one of the highest lakes in Pakistan. It is home to wide-ranging brown trout, which weighs up to 7 kilograms. Lake Saif ul Muluk additionally gives a glorious perspective of Malika Parbat, which is the most significant peak of Kaghan Valley. The lake is named after a legendary prince – a fairy tale called Saif ul Muluk, written by the Sufi poet Mian Muhammad Bakhsh, talks of the lake. It tells the story of the prince of Persia named Prince Saif ul Muluk who fell in love with a fairy princess named Princess Badri-ul-Jamala at the lake.

It took us 11 hours from Islamabad to Babusar Pass which is normally an 8-hour drive. Samina Bano and Shamim aunty, the ladies I was travelling with, found out that Hunza was overbooked and Karimabad was over flowing with local tourists since the first day of Eid.

* **Tip:** My advice, do not travel to popular tourist destinations during Eid holidays or be prepared to be wedged in between cars – unless you enjoy incredibly long

drives like me. Also make sure to pre-book a hotel for yourself.

On the way you will notice how locals have made use of glaciers to keep their beverages cold and fruits fresh. Caught sight of 'sonami shajar kari' – billion trees tsunami project across Khyber Pakhtunkhwa in different places. The Billion Tree Tsunami Afforestation Project in Pakistan's northern Khyber Pakhtunkhwa (KPK) province has surpassed its target by restoring and planting trees in 350,000 hectares of degraded forest landscapes. Launched by Imran Khan, the then Chairman of Pakistan's Tehreek-e-Insaf party and now the Prime Minister of Pakistan. Commenced in 2015 the Billion Tree Tsunami Project (BTTP) aims to turn the tide on land degradation and loss in the mountainous, formerly forested KPK province in the Hindu Kush mountain range. The campaign simultaneously helped KPK province achieve its 348,400-hectare commitment to the Bonn Challenge – a global effort to bring 150 million hectares of deforested and degraded land into restoration by 2020 and 350 million hectares by 2030. This marks the first Bonn Challenge pledge to reach its restoration goal. (*Taken from various descriptions over the Internet*)

My son and I enjoyed watching children sitting comfortably in wheelbarrows; one inside and the other dragging him around, taking turns gleefully, a young boy had a plastic chair over his head when it started raining, men selling ember-roasted corn that fills the air with its charcoal smell, little young girls and boys waving at us or selling fresh fruit with big welcoming smiles, a herd of domestic animals crossing the road at their own pace, men sitting by the edge of the mountain top enjoying a cup of tea with gorgeous views. Occasionally you will spot a group of local men cooking food or just making tea on mountain tops. By midafternoon Abdul Wahid chose to stop for lunch before continuing to drive towards Hunza. It started drizzling and the weather turned cold as we stepped out at Trout Park Restaurant Burawai. Burawai is a beautiful valley before you reach Babusar top. We decided to pool in and order lamb karahi (an appetizing mix of meat, lamb fat, green chilies, tomatoes, ginger, salt and black pepper). My journey with these strangers in high spirits had turned into a very pleasant unforgettable experience. They kept joking and laughing in Wakhi language which I was trying my best to understand and occasionally they would decode for my benefit. Abdul Wahid scrapping ice from the glaciers while the cars were clogged in, changing one traditional song to another, chitchatting with men driving away with lighthearted humour; besides playing tour guide was quite entertaining. For a while we got stuck near Lulusar lake too.

Babusar Pass is at a distance of 80 kilometers from Naran. Battakundi is at a distance of 16 kilometers from Naran and provides access to Lalazar Plateau, Dodiputsar Lake and Lulusar Lake which is the biggest natural lake in Hazara and the source of Kunhar river. On our way towards Batakundi we stopped at Lulusar Lake. One of the most scenic lakes I have witnessed so far. The place was so serene, so peaceful in the midst of high mountains and serene meadows.

Lulusar is a group of mountains near the Naran Valley. It is famous for the large lake situated there which is a popular tourist attraction. The lake is at 3,410 meters in height. This lake is the main source of the Kunhar River, which flows through the entire Kaghan Valley through Jalkhand, Naran Valley, Kaghan, Jared, Paras and Balakot until it joins the Jhelum River. The lake is much bigger than other lakes around the valley, and is surrounded by snowcapped hills, making it a natural tourist attraction. It has a baby lake beside it too. The word "sar" means "lake" in Shina language. At Batakundi a Hiace tried to overtake and add to the traffic jam, the KPK Policeman stopped the driver and just took the keys away and cleared the way before dealing with the driver.

By 9 p.m. we reached the famous Raikot Bridge alongside Indus River. The famed natural Sulphur Spring flows from here, locals call it tatta pani. These hot water springs are located at about 2 hours' drive from Gilgit to Rawalpindi. Due to presence of Sulphur underground, the water of the spring is hotter than boiling water. As suggested by some medical experts, bath in hot water springs lowers blood pressure due to dilation of blood vessels by hot water, and reduces insomnia. Also said to improve joint mobility, beneficial for arthritis sufferers and eliminates toxins from the body because of sweat. Abdul Wahid told me, "Baji do you know 18 wheelers pass from the narrow road here, which can be life threatening. Also you can easily boil eggs in this spring water!" We couldn't stop here both because of non-stop traffic and night time. We reached the crowded market place of Aliabad around midnight – an almost 20-hour drive later I was still all smiles. Found a comfortable place to stay here the night and had my second cup of namkeen chai (salt tea) before dozing off.

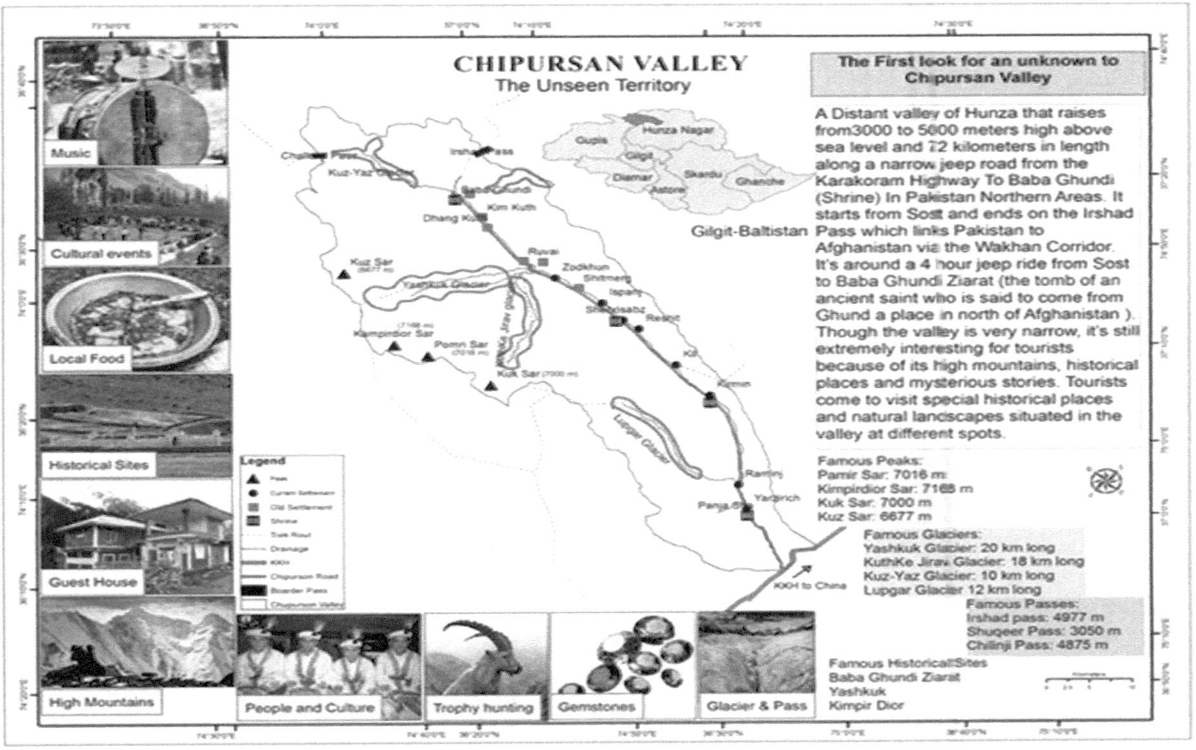
CHIPURSAN VALLEY
The Unseen Territory

The First look for an unknown to Chipursan Valley

A Distant valley of Hunza that raises from3000 to 5800 meters high above sea level and 72 kilometers in length along a narrow jeep road from the Karakoram Highway To Baba Ghundi (Shrine) In Pakistan Northern Areas. It starts from Sost and ends on the Irshad Pass which links Pakistan to Afghanistan via the Wakhan Corridor. It's around a 4 hour jeep ride from Sost to Baba Ghundi Ziarat (the tomb of an ancient saint who is said to come from Ghund a place in north of Afghanistan). Though the valley is very narrow, it's still extremely interesting for tourists because of its high mountains, historical places and mysterious stories. Tourists come to visit special historical places and natural landscapes situated in the valley at different spots.

Gilgit-Baltistan

Famous Peaks:
Pamir Sar: 7016 m
Kimpirdior Sar: 7168 m
Kuk Sar: 7000 m
Kuz Sar: 6677 m

Famous Glaciers:
Yashkuk Glacier: 20 km long
KuthKe Jirav Glacier: 18 km long
Kuz-Yaz Glacier: 10 km long
Lupgar Glacier 12 km long

Famous Passes:
Irshad pass: 4977 m
Shuqeer Pass: 3050 m
Chilinji Pass: 4875 m

Famous Historical Sites
Baba Ghundi Ziarat
Yashkuk
Kimpir Dior

Legend
Peak
Current Settlement
Old Settlement
Shrine
Trek Road
Drainage
KKH
Chipurson Road
Boarder Pass
Chipurson Valley

Chilinji Pass
Irshad Pass
Kuz-Yaz Glacier
Baba Ghundi
Dhang Kuth
Kim Kuth
Ravai
Zodkhun
Sintmerg
Ispanj
Shikarisabz
Reshit
Kil
Kirmin
Ramin
Yardrinch
Panja/Sr
Kuz Sar
Yashkuk Glacier
Kampirdior Sar
Pomn Sar
Kuthka Jirav glacier
Kuk Sar
Lupgar Glacier
KKH to China

Hunza Nagar
Gupis
Gilgit
Diamer
Astore
Skardu
Ghanche

Music
Cultural events
Local Food
Historical Sites
Guest House
High Mountains
People and Culture
Trophy hunting
Gemstones
Glacier & Pass

Day 02 – Chipursan – 20th June 2018

Plan: *Departure from Aliabad, Hunza (slightly indefinite when and how). Reach Sost by 2:00 p.m. sharp. An adventurous jeep-ride towards Chipursan village (almost 4 hours to reach Zoodthkhoon last village of Chipursan Valley) & overnight stay.*

The next morning after a delicious breakfast of non-greasy roti and daal (lentil), we went out to search for a warm jacket in the market place. It is surprising how early the markets come to life here, as compared to my hometown Karachi. I was under packed for Chipursan and I realized my sole full length jacket wasn't enough. After making the purchase, we checked out of the hotel. A short walk to the bus stand we had to find a ride from Aliabad Hunza to Sost, which is the last town inside Pakistan on the Karakoram Highway before the Chinese border. There are regular buses from Hunza bus stop at Aliabad which is on the KKH below Karimabad - to Sost every morning. This was my first ever ride to an unknown valley in a public transport chock-a-block with friendly strangers. With the sudden rush of excitement, I closed my eyes and prayed. Once the small coaster was packed with people we set off. We were to cross Attabad Lake, Shishkat, Gulmit, Gulkin, Hussaini, Passu and Khyber and reach Sost in 2.5 hours. Sost dry port is the first formal port at the China-Pakistan border where immigration and customs offices are also based. Numerous money transactions are made in this town every day being the epicenter of Pak China trade. In addition to commercial and trading activities, Sost and its surrounding areas hold great potential for developing the tourism industry. From Sost, the Karakoram Highway climbs through the nature sanctuary where markhor, snow leopard are said to roam. The only animals I have seen here are herds of shaggy, domesticated yaks. These strong hairy beasts mostly found in highland pastures due to their tractability and tolerance to the harsh climate. They are valued highly for carrying loads, pulling ploughs, providing fibre, milk and meat. Its hair is widely used for making coarse rugs, ropes, their tails are used as dusters.

*** Tip:** If you want to withdraw cash this is the best place considering the number of functional ATMs in this area and none ahead.

Travelling in a local bus was my first ever experience and so far the best. Non-stop conversations in local languages, strangers exchanging smiles, Shina song playing in the background and a bunch of young boys going back to Chipursan started singing and playing their instruments. One of them carrying a *tumbak – tumbakh* in wakhi (a single-headed goblet drum) another with his flute started playing along.

*** Tip:** Normally I record sounds of different places to hear them later as it brings back lots of memories while skimming through pictures.

Unlike other parts of Pakistan, you certainly feel safe in this part of the country (as I reckon). A lady travelling home to Hussaini village from Hunza invited me to stay at her place before leaving for Chipursan, which I politely turned down. We waved goodbye as we dropped her with her sacks full of fresh vegetables near her village. As we drove towards the Passu cones I spotted fresh fruits along the roadside. I screamed, "Cherries! Fresh cherries!" The driver turned, looked at me and was kind enough to stop near Passu so I could make my purchase of fresh juicy cherries. I just stared in awe at the Passu cones on my left as I savoured every bite of the luscious black ripe cherries. Tupopdan (20,033 feet), also known as "Passu Cones" or "Passu Cathedrals", a set of great mountain peaks. It lies to the north of the Passu village and believed to be the most photographed peak of the Passu region. The inhabitants are wakhi and speak the wakhi language. The village of Passu is located among the towering peaks of the Karakoram Mountain Range. A peaceful retreat in the very heart of magnificent mountain scenery. Pointed unclimbed and un-scale able rock peaks, ice-demes with sharp fluted ridges; stand like knife blades. The village is surrounded by a huge wall of mountains and is the base of three important valleys: Shimshal, Khunjerab and Batura, as well as the short valley of the Passu Glacier.

*** Tip:** Consume as much fresh fruit whenever, wherever possible. They keep you happy and hydrated!

Upon reaching Sost we had to wait an hour for the next jeep ride to Chipursan. This may happen if you reach even slightly late or if the rides are unexpectedly jam-packed. It was almost 3 p.m. as we got off at Baba Ghundi Hotel Sost, Affeyatabad, Sost, Gojal District Hunza. A desolate parched looking place had not much to offer, except a much needed hot cup of tea. Fond of exploring Rayyan and I headed out. The landscape and scenery is quite different; the mountains become barren with little to no green patches. A few dozen steps away we met Mofeed Shah, an elderly but cheerful man who was putting a large piece of Poplar wood through the machine. Poplar tree commonly known as sufaida (locally) involves less labour and money in return for greater profit. Mofeed Shah owns Nadir and Sons and has been in this business for over 30 years. He tells me, "This place is named after my father. MashaAllah by Allah's will, I have 6 daughters and a son but my son works in Khyber. He doesn't want to cut and chop wood like me. I came to Karachi in 1990, stayed and worked there. But I returned to my business here and this is all I know," showing his blistered hands proudly. All praises for Karachi, he calls it a "poor man's abode", which is very true.
Pakistani people are very generous and you will be offered ridiculous amounts of free food and chai. And that's what he insisted upon and I declined politely asking for permission to leave, as the jeep had arrived. I always try and click pictures of people I meet with my son, so he remembers the stories behind those charming smiles.

Settled in the front seat with a jeep full of people all headed to Chipursan, which is 80 kilometers from here. We drove for an hour on a rocky road towards the village, until we took a stretch break near a small stream of fresh water. These small breaks are very refreshing and you get to enjoy natural water. No matter what people say my son and I love drinking and splashing flowing water on our faces, especially if it is freezing cold! Back on the road, I realized every time I travel to the Northern areas especially Gilgit Baltistan I fall in love with the place a little deeper. Predominantly has to do with the people of GB who are respectful, generous, genuinely warm and hospitable.

*** Tip:** Remember you may not reach your destination at the given time due to unexpected road conditions. This is conditional to traffic jams, road blocks due to landslide, rain and snowfall, punctured wheel or frozen engine.

By the time we reached Zoodthkhoon, the ultimate settlement of Chipursan, it was 7 p.m. With a warm welcome we entered the traditional Gilgit-i home. The traditional Wakhi greeting is to greet by kissing each other's hands, regardless of the gender. It's a sign of respect but this trend is decreasing lately. People are liberal in nature and don't hold extreme views.
A number of old houses in Hunza and Nagar still preserve the more ancient form of posts with two step-like transitions to the capital (similar to Baltit Fort). You will notice variations in the form and decoration of the base and of the adjoining bulbous, often fluted part. Bricks as well as wooden slabs are used for the boundary and such houses are called *Thather*. They are considered to be very strong as this is the demand of the climate of this region. *Swastika* is also used for carving on the wooden planks and this design is considered to bring luck for the people and not everyone believes that. The homes are not very tall and many are made of wood. The different levels of working, resting, sitting, and sleeping platforms around the common space of a traditional house are sometimes

bordered by low railings decorated with floral patterns. The central roof opening above the space, composed of an overlay of decreasing, diagonally superimposed squares of small beams, constitutes an essential carpentry task and marks, structurally and symbolically, which is the navel of the house and the place of the fireplace.

A wakhi *khana* meaning home is built with three elements in mind; economy of space to fit a large number of household members, maximum protection again chilly weather and the cost and availability of building material. The Wakhi-Pamiri house design is said to be more than 2,500 years old. To reach the entrance to the main room in a wakhi house where the main fireplace is, one has to go through a maze-like passage including 2 or 3 low wooden doors. Around the core structure of the home, extra construction such as washroom, stable, sheds for the cattle, verandah and summer rooms with a couple of windows can be added. That external door does not open directly into the main room. People have to go through a mazelike corridor, closed by an additional door. The main room has a single direct opening, like a skylight that equips the room with light and allows smoke to escape. The sitting area is a square place around the fire place. The males sit on the right side and the females on the left. All cooking is done on the clay hearth which is a brick- or stone-lined fireplace, without an oven and is mainly used for heating and for cooking food. Furnished with a wooden trapdoor, framed by panels it can be opened or shut using small stick. The opening is not vertical as traditional windows but horizontal, therefore the layer of warm air that sits below the window acts as a buffer and prevents cold air from entering the home. As a matter of fact, the cold air is pushed away from the home by the interior warm air and is a very energy efficient means of keeping the home insulated. Traditional fire oven in wakhi is called '*qamachdoon*'. The bread baked in it is called Qamooch or Pitok – a thick bread made out of sprouted grain and stored away, baked in the cast iron oven. These are the finest and coziest homes that I always yearned to live in. Wish granted!

We sat by the fire while the head of the family made tea for us in a small cozy room by the stove used as a fireplace too. Pleasant smiles of the 3 little girls and their older son made me feel at ease instantly. My son handed the bag of half-eaten cherries to one of the little girls as a token of gratitude for opening their home and hearts to us. The lady of the house had gone to see a girls' football match with the other villagers, while their 6 children were home. As the tea boiled, one little girl went out carrying a big round platter another carried a large pot of oil. They were preparing local wheat bread for us. A few minutes later a lady greeted us with a generous dish of freshly cooked roti (local bread). She was a neighbour who came down when she heard guests were over. A proud happy mother of two adorably bubbly kids, she taught as a teacher in the nearby school. Every village (*diyore* in wakhi), we passed by had a school, a vocational center and a health care center. In large parts of GB education for girls is more prevalent and encouraged than many parts of Pakistan to this date. Women working in the fields, shops, playing sports or working in schools is also common. In 2005, a great new initiative was taken to educate the older generation. Now even the older people are taught how to read and write unlike most parts of Pakistan.

All through the night until dinner time and after, between several cups of tea we were entertained by the rubab and the duff playing. *Rubab – raboob* in wakhi, is a lute-like musical instrument originating from central Afghanistan. Duff is also a musical instrument and its frame is usually made of hardwood and the membrane is usually fish skin but other skin types such as cow, goat, and horse are also used. The girls helped their mother clean up, wash up, before sitting down with us to enjoy the live music. Surprisingly they don't seem troubled with house work. They do things consciously, without constant reminders or instructions. It's a quiet home with just the rubab and duff breaking the silence.

The Unseen Splendor of Chipursan Valley

The magnificent landscape of Chipursan Valley is yet to be explored by tourists. Located west of Sost, it ends on Irshad Pass which links Pakistan to Afghanistan via the Wakhan Corridor. This valley is a network of villages, and features a shrine to a Sufi saint. An adventurous 45-minute jeep ride takes you to the first village of the valley. Upon entering the valley, the snow-capped mountains, mighty glaciers and fresh water fountains leave the visitors mesmerized with its overwhelming beauty, historical places and mystical stories. The population of Chipursan is roughly about 4000 (these statistics may not be accurate). Gojal is a chain of large and small valleys bordering with Hunza in the south, China in the north-east and Afghanistan in the north-west. Shishkat is the first village of Gojal. Except for Shimshal, Misgar and Chipursan valleys, all the villages of Gojal can be seen from the Karakoram Highway, which crosses Gojal, entering China at the Khunjerab Pass. People of Chipursan and Gojal valleys and upper Hunza have ancestral cultural ties with the people of Wakhan.

Chipursan is a distant valley of Hunza that rises from 3,000 to 4,925 meters above sea level and 72 kilometers in length along the KKH. Chipursan River flows through the valley which then merges into Hunza River at Khudabad on Karakoram Highway. The regions' most important shrine to a Sufi saint Baba Ghundi (old man from Ghund), located after the last village Zoodthkhoon, is at 3,500 meters. The popular pilgrimage site in Hunza-Gojal, the shrine is surrounded by meadows that host herds of sheep in summer. Periodically from June to September, Kyrgyz traders from Afghanistan who conventionally cross the Irshad Pass with horses, yaks and sheep to trade with the Chipursan villagers. Places worthy of visit are the Irshad Pass 4,979 meters, Wakhan, Badakshan, the Chilinji Pass 4,630 meters and the Ishkoman valley. It is a

4-hour drive to Chipursan valley from Hunza. With the improved Karakoram Highway, now able to host vehicles such as Jeeps and 4x4s, thus, visiting remote areas is easier and accessible.

Farman Karim, a resident of Gojal, says that, "the people of Chipursan and Wakhan had been carrying out barter trade for centuries. In summers Kyrgyz and some Tajik Pamiri traders from Afghanistan cross the Irshad Pass and exchange household commodities with local livestock or their products from the markets in Hunza and Gilgit. This exchange takes place near the shrine of Baba Ghundi."

Before reaching the first village **Yarzarich**, which takes approximately 45 minutes from Sost, you will come across Punja Shah where you will find many ancient symbols too. The valley contains eight prominent villages and three clustered ones, which makes a total of 11 villages – Yarzarich is significant because of its rare splash of green vegetation and low stone-and-mud dwellings, a distinctive feature of the valley. Fifteen minutes further and an hour from Sost, is the large village of Raminj, mostly unseen above the road.

Raminj village is 3,095 meters high above sea level on the upper side of the Chipursan link road. The next three villages **Aminabad, Rahimabad and Nurabad** are clustered and are collectively known as **Kirmin**, which is 1 hour 40 minutes from Sost. Ten minutes from Kirmin, massive slopes of grey rubble are separated from the green wheat terraces and irrigation canals of **Khill**, a village that spans the river and is linked by a fragile suspension bridge and almost 2 hours from Sost. There is also a beautiful water fall across the river called Sumayar surrounded by greenery and beautiful grassland. The stream flows from the top of a nearby mountain called Khill-a-dur. The next villages along the valley road are **Reshit** and **Sher-e-Sabz**, which will take 2 hours 15 to 20 minutes to reach from Sost. Both the villages have a guesthouse. Further ahead there is **Ispanj**, a 2-and-a-half-hour drive from Sost and **Shuthmarg**, which is another 10 minutes from Ispanj. And the last village of **Zoodthkhoon** at about 3,500 meters is lmost 3 hours' drive from Sost. Reshit is the oldest village of Chipursan. Known to be the central village, the story of Chipursan begins from Reshit when the three people from Gulmit migrated to this valley. The breathtaking meadow is called Rashtigar. This stunning beauty spot is also a well-known peak for climbing. After the last village the meadow area is called Yishkok at 3450 meters (an ancient village, capital of Gojal). Large part of this region speaks the Wakhi language, but the villagers of Raminj town speak Burushski language. Wahki language is spoken in Wakhan (Afghanistan) Tajikistan and Kashgar (China). The language has a history of over 2500 years.

Nazir Sabir, the famed Pakistani mountaineer who summited Everest and K2, was born in Raminj. He started his climbing career with a Japanese expedition to the 7,478 meters high Passu peak in Gojal back in 1974. On May 17, 2000 he stood on the summit of Everest becoming the first Pakistani to scale the roof of the world. He has climbed four of the five 8,000 meter peaks in Pakistan, including the world's second highest mountain K2 in 1981, Gasherbrum II 8,035 meters, Broad Peak 8,050 meters in 1982 and Gasherbrum I 8,068 meters in 1992. He runs an adventure tourism company by the name of Nazir Sabir Expeditions and says, "As a mountaineer who has watched the day dawn after lonely nights of terror and have had close brushes with death on the world's highest peaks, I can say that there is nothing like going back for a new encounter with the unknown. I have the honour to be elected unanimously on October 10, 2004 as a President of the Alpine Club of Pakistan. I have also earned the prestigious President's Award for Pride of Performance in 1982 and The Sitara-i-Imtiaz (Star of Distinction) in 2001 for my outstanding achievements in mountaineering. The preservation of the natural habitat, its flora and fauna is closest to my heart. I am a naturalist by inclination and a vegetarian by choice!" he summed up his story.

As a reward of years of services rendered to the people of Hunza, Nazir was elected as their representative to the Northern Area Legislative Council in the October 1994 elections and appointed Advisor on Education and Tourism to the government.

The valley's incomparable beauty makes it a trekking paradise offering endless opportunities for exploration and relaxation, which many are still unaware of. It encompasses small treks, picturesque meadows, scenic fresh water springs, clean air and green pastures brimming with a variety of wild flowers. One can find many unusual flowers famous for their distinctive fragrance, Banafsha, Shadunbet, Sosan, Gul Morvoy (Gul Mohar, I assumed), to name a few. The meadow is for the grazing cattle only. The valley has a blooming cultural feeling that is very appealing for the tourists. Rocks found in this valley contain precious minerals such as quartz, coal and crystals. More valuable minerals can be explored in the area with the help of geologists and latest exploration techniques. One can just sit or walk for hours without getting bored in the lush pastures of Chipursan. Someone walking by told me, "We have many natural herbs here and they cure many diseases including jaundice, skin diseases and several eye infections etc. Of the many herbs found here, the most famous is Chumuro which can be brewed as a tea". Chumuro may be similar to Tumoro (Hunza special wild-thyme tea). It is slightly flavourless but has a pleasant appealing fragrance to it. He continued, "Other herbs can also be brewed to cure many diseases known to afflict residents such as flu or gastric issues. They include Bozlanj, Yinath (to cure jaundice), Naghurdum wosh (for eye treatment), Youm wosh, Mandirich, Nilterk and many others". To this day no significant research has been made regarding the properties of these Himalayan herbs. Therefore, none of these can be medically prescribed or believed to be hundred percent fit for consumption.

*** Tip:** Investigate before you consume anything unknown or lesser-known.

I personally enjoy all sorts of herbal teas especially those scarcely available in cities. This time I brought back home lots of Bozlanj (green tea), not easily available though and Tumoro (wild-thyme tea) quite easily available now.

Last year in summers I visited Fairy Meadows and collected fresh wild thyme from the deep forest and dried it myself. An interesting tea for non-Gilgitis, who don't think of thyme as an herb used for tea. In Hunza, it is valued for its medicinal properties: It is said to alleviate headaches, calm nerves and soothe sore throats. I drink it because it just reminds me of the mountains!

Prominent cultural and historical sites are Baba Ghundi ziyrat (shrine), Kumpir Diyore, and Reshit Fort along with the Reshit Polo ground, Yeshkok, the meadows at 3,450 meters near Zoodthkhoon and Punja Shah Shrine on the way to Chipursan. The Reshit Coal mine is also an important tourist point, which is 5 kilometers from Reshit village. Kumpir Diyore is a small village – *Kumpir* means 'old woman' and *Diyore* means 'village', situated in Shitmerg the second to last village has the famous legendary flood and old woman's village story. Besides traditional Buzkashi and Polo are played in the valley and local festivals are organized annually. The polo field is used for Buzkashi too.

Speaking to Mirza Aman Shah from Sher-e-Sabz Chipursan, now living in Karachi says, his village Sher-e-Sabz has a guesthouse, a cricket ground and a famous peak not many know of; *Dastaana* (glove) peak which is approximately 5,600 meters above sea level, probably a 2-hour trek. No one knows if anyone climbed it. Studying and working as an assistant accountant for a construction project, he told me about *Buzkashi*, "*Buzkashi* is a Persian word. In wakhi language it is called *Cheigh Khushakh* – *Cheigh* or *Buz* means 'baby goat / kid' and *Khushakh* or

Kashi means 'grab or pull'. It's like a headless goat polo. The baby goat is slaughtered first and then used as a ball. The players on horses try and drag the kid to the goal." "It's brutal," I was appalled beyond words. He continued, "The sport is Pamirian / Wakhan central Asian sport and is still popular especially at Baba Ghundi festival. Teams from Kirghiz tribe from Pamir Afghan participate as well who are animal traders and we import yaks and goats from them."

I am not a huge pet lover but I am against zoological gardens, wildlife and safari parks and keeping animals in confined quarters as pets outside their natural habitats. We live in a world that not only turns a blind eye to animal cruelty but condones it. We need to stop these ruthless acts for these poor creatures, especially in places where they are being used for sports and pleasure.

Mirza Aman Shah also told me about *Kuchkhamak* which is a traditional festival, "where herds from the pastures return to the village in late autumn. It is quite a delightful event for tourists and a joy for local youth, women and children. There are also many seasonal tournaments organized every year, such are polo, cricket, football, volleyball etc. Not very popular as it used to be, as the animals are now not taken to the pastures and we don't have enough animals to take." A few words he taught me are, *pul* – means money / rupees – *polpol* means starring at someone / looking longer – *pil* means bowl – *palpal* means trance/ traverse – *pitkh* means peak. That covers a little bit of /p/ vocabulary for the day!

Chipursan – Valley of Saints and dragons

Yishkok or Ishkok is famous for the legend of a nine-headed dragon, which was slain by a holy man– story narrated by my host – an eminent Wakhi poet, singer and artist (Shireen Sada):

The people of Yishkok village were all farmers and earned a living off their cattle; yaks and other livestock including camels. They clothed themselves from the sheep wool, crafted their own shoes using the yaks or other livestock skin and ate a simple diet of meat and wheat chapatti (unleavened bread). Not only was the colony independent it was also protected by seven large Iron gates. It was surprising, considering this was a poor colony without a strong, well-developed economy. Where did this Iron come from? Who prepared the gates and how? Since there was no road at that time towards Yishok, there was no way they carry such materials. Did it come from China, Russia or Afghanistan? These questions largely remain unanswered. No one knows. The people of Yishkok village were known to be immoral and uncivilized at that time. They had little or no respect for others and were involved in many unacceptable activities. Ruvai hill situated on the west side of Yishkok village had a large deep lake, Ravai Lake which has dried up now. Years ago, a gigantic Dragon appeared in that large lake that had eight small heads and one large head and it could speak like a human. The dragon demanded food from the villagers, which they refused and so the dragon threatened them. If the villagers do not feed it daily, it will eat the villagers one by one. It claimed to consume one human being, a large sheep or goat, plus 40 kilograms of traditional ghee and over 200 chapattis. The villagers made sure that all the food was in one place without triggering anger. The situation dramatically changed when it was a little girl's turn to be eaten. Fastened with a sheep and waiting at the eating spot, the girl sat restlessly, weeping uncontrollably. A young man passed by, concerned, as the girl recount the story. The man listened intently and calmed her. As the dragon's lunchtime approached, the young man stood firm and pulled his sword from its sheath, to battle the dragon. As the dragon rose from the lake the man lashed out and cut off his head one by one with a single stroke until finally the dragon died.

The lake was red with the blood and the dead body float on the surface. The girl returned to the village but no one believed her story. When the villagers saw the slashed heads of the dragon, they believed and were relieved. The man told them they were now free. This young man *reminded them to go back and be gentle, remember God and give up their immoral activities. But that didn't last long. You can still see the dried lake and fossil remains as you travel towards Baba Ghundi shrine. Many other stories are linked with this area and people have firm belief in them as well.*

The history of Baba Ghundi is written in Persian language. He first came to Chipursan from Ghund in Northern Afghanistan with his luggage on a camel. He was a religious teacher and had many students. Chipursan was a green and wealthy valley where the people lived in sin. He went from house to house, asking for alms, but only one old woman offered him food. Baba Ghundi told her to leave her house and climb the hill. As she did, she saw him riding at the head of a great flood that wiped out the valley and its people in punishment for their sinful ways. Evidently a great outburst from the Yishkok glacier did cover most of the valley with boulders and mud.
Baba Gundi's real name was Muhammad Baqar, the saint migrated from Afghanistan to Gojal Valley in GB to preach Islam centuries ago. His mission took him to many places and he finally settled in Chipursan and was buried in the village. There are many different versions of his story, everyone will tell you the account one believes in.

Note: Legends and myths may differ in details and I narrated what I heard.

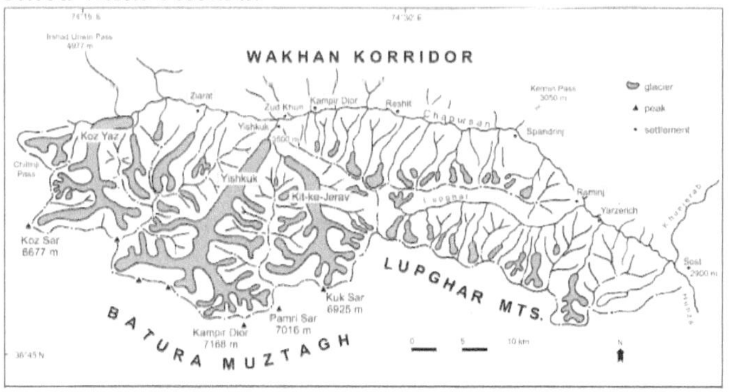

Day 03 – Chipursan still – 21st June 2018

Plan: *Stay and explore Chipursan village (Zoodthkhoon and adjoining villages). Visit Baba Ghundi shrine. Overnight stay.*

The night was chilling and numbing, as I stepped out in the dark to walk to my room next to the common place of the house, that is normally used as a guest room with an attached washroom. The lady of the house had very nicely set our beds on the floor with one blanket below and 2 layers of blankets on top with a set of hand embroidered pillows. These are rolled back up during the day and spread out at night. The platform floor, where people sit and sleep, is usually made of wood or mud and is covered with thick carpets. The walls are either plain or painted or covered partially with a thin fabric of coloured patterns.

Note: Seemingly, the Tajik-Wakhi way (probably influenced by the Russians) of hanging heavy wool carpets on the walls is not a tradition from Gojal.

Rayyan and I were loving our vibrant snug accommodation. We lay watching the art work on the plain whitewashed walls, rubab on one side where the real rubab lay hanging. On the other side a markhor, ibex, hoopoe bird with a backdrop of mountains, sun shining in a clear blue sky with grassy patch. We were interpreting the hidden sentiments behind the artistry that they most likely enjoy bright sunny days over cold snowy ones or longing for more such days. I turned off the light and the room turned completely dark with no extra lights around.

*** Tip:** Torch / solar powered lamp would come handy here.

Waking up in the quiet peaceful village in a cozy bed was perfect, as one of the boys comfortably barged in to inform us that breakfast is ready. The early hours of Chipursan are bright, chilly and full of life. If you find yourself up early you won't be alone. You will come across locals, children going to school in a world full of chirpy birdsong.

Soak up the morning glory by getting up as early as possible and go outside. The air is crisp and clear; brilliant green leaves stand out in sharp contrast against a sky of deep blue, the quiet meadows where butterflies flit above the wildflowers. The soaring mountains loom in the distance. The houses here are scattered throughout the oasis to be closer to the plots where, in addition to barley and wheat, potatoes, lentils and some other vegetables are grown. Since each crop is irrigated by canals bringing water from the melting glaciers, therefore, agriculture and housing are closely intertwined.

The family I astayed with, their children study in the village school and doing very well. Not educated himself the father builds houses for a living and very proudly told me how he built his own house brick by brick. Education being their primary focus they need nothing else. Modest, simple and honest these people will make you reflect on what you are missing out in the city life.

Early morning after we greeted each other I was told about the special rug I removed my shoes on. It was a handmade yak *plos* (rug). Said to last a food 100 years, no maintenance no wash required. In Burushaski it is called *sharma.* Yak skin/hides are used locally for flooring and some use the skin to cover and support yurts against wind and snow. Some Kyrgyz people make reins for horses and *maghsi* (very soft socks made from yak skin) after proper treatment. Yak cashmere is usually collected in May and June. The fibers are often collected in a mixed manner and used mainly for rugs, tents, and rope making. On an average 500–600 grams of cashmere is collected from a mature yak per season. Regrettably there is no popular market for the fine cashmere, thus the combed fiber is not further sorted or processed for marketing.

Asmat Ullah Mushfiq sahab, a resident of Chipursan, a famous wakhi poet, historian and author of Hazrat Baba Ghundi, told me that, "There are two types of plos. One is called Xugaj that lasts for 2 – 3 human lives. The second is called Tugaj that lasts for 60 – 80 years. Xug means yak and Tugh mean goat".

For breakfast we had fried roti, plain omelet and Phitti served with pale salt milk tea. Tradition here is that they will keep re-filling your cup until you tell them that you are done. So after my third cup of namkeen chai (salt tea) I had to politely tell her I did not want more. Our breakfast was followed by rubab playing and my son started beating the duff alongside. I sat watching the dust particles floating through the air through the roof window. Rayyan was enjoying every minute of the village life and decided he wanted to stay longer, more so because he found children his age, the freedom to play outdoors and flexible bedtime. Later that day, my host proudly showed his awards and achievements which he kept hidden away in the guest room. He received a High Achievers Award in 2016 from the Gojal Educational and Cultural Association. Another Hunza Arts and Cultural Council presented him with an award in 2015 in recognition of his magnificent services for promotion of Wakhi Adab & Art. They give him the title of Shreen Sada for being an eminent Wakhi poet, singer and artist.

We decided to leave for the shrine at 12 p.m. as soon as the jeep arrived. As we left we came across this really elderly man who I was told has never sat in a vehicle ever and walks 72 kilometers from here to Sost (the 4-hour jeep ride that we took from Sost to Zoodthkhoon)! We waved him goodbye as we started our rocky ride towards Baba Ghundi. 40 minutes later we reached the Dragon Lake where the jeep driver bhai told us that you can still find remains of the dragon here. With no permission to descend to the lake it left me curious and puzzled but I did not want to sound intrusive to their beliefs and understanding.

In about an hour we reached a meadow, the grassy expanse at Baba Ghundi ziarat which offers ample room to camp. These pastures host crowds of cattle including yak, in summers. To protect the food crops between planting and harvesting time, animals stay in remote pastures. In summer, just a small number of them graze, in the village, for domestic purposes.

A number of local women dressed in their local dresses and caps adorned with their traditional beaded jewelry were taking group pictures with a handful of men in the group. These women seemed extremely happy on a warm sunny day. Most of them shook hands and started talking and wanted me to share my experience living in the village. They briefed me about the place, the flowing river and the sacred stream. Close to the shrine, near the river, is a spring adorned with ibex horns; its mineral water is called aab-e-shafa, and the people here believe that it bestows health on those who drink it. I was introduced to Pyar Ali, the care taker of the shrine, who was exceptionally respectful and courteous. This responsibility was transferred to him after his grandfather and father. Everyone here seems thrilled when you tell them you are travelling all the way from Karachi.

The meadows are beautiful, with large flocks of black Alpine Chough birds (crows with bright yellow beaks – qarghah in Wakhi language as I was told) hovering the blue skies, gushing river on one side, beautiful rock formations and fairly clean washrooms. You can walk around, follow little streams, chase butterflies and sheep, dodge wild flowers and enjoy the soaked grassy patches... sheer freedom from ringing phones and popping messages – a great place to unplug!

* **Tip:** You must visit all sorts of washrooms to start counting your blessings. You end up realizing the agony of people living in the mountains with lack of facilities like properly made washrooms, clean water, sometimes cold or no water at all. Hot water is considered a luxury in most places.

For tea we went to this cozy little kitchen (*Khoun* in wakhi) near the shrine, a hushed snug place where we met Hamidi sahab and Shuwa begum, calm, collected and simple couple. Hamidi sahab has been running this little café since last 23 years and his wife Shuwa begum for the last 16 years. Very quietly she served us tea and different types of breads and rotis – Arzoq (bread made from flour, eggs, butter and milk) – Fitri (they put real ghee in the middle and roll it into a roti) – Phitti (a type of leavened bread baked by Hunzakutz People of Hunza, GB) – Chilpak (paratha like roti). I had the maximum number of namkeen chai (salt tea) here in this village and it blends well with all sorts of local breads. Once again we had a round of rubab and duff playing, the faint sound of it echoed as I walked around the meadow with little streams flowing, tiny wild flower patches of yellow and purple and light summer breeze. I just sat there on the soft damp grass, the warm gleaming sun, the cold water dripping between my fingers, the birds and the distant sound of music until I was asked to come back. Part of me wanted to stay a little longer and camp that night, but sadly I wasn't prepared well enough to sleep outdoors in the wild. Sit back and enjoy the jeep ride with the sheep crossing, the birds chirping and the rocky road that takes you back to Zoodthkhoon. Happy, chit chatting and full of questions we stopped at the river side to freshen up, clicking pictures, savouring the fresh river water; glistening like specs of gold under the scorching sun. It was evening when we reached home. The children were back from school, quickly all the children took their positions, found a ball, a wooden slab and started playing cricket instantly. I sat by the fields, under the intense sunlight, the long blades of maize swaying to the light wind; a moment you want to cease forever. I was called for lunch but I did not want to leave the picturesque sight. Every moment of being here, I simply wanted to take in the light breeze, soak up this feeling of being connected with nature, feeling free of all the worldly materialistic things, thoughts and worries…but I was called in again and I didn't want to sound rude.

Inside it was quite because the children refused to eat. The lady of the house had cooked delicious sochal saag for lunch with flat non-oily roti. Sochal is a wild vegetable found anywhere on the road sides, parks, playgrounds, grazing lands and similar places. I love the way they keep the vegetables crispy and use very little spice so as to savour its earthiness. The first time I had sochal in its raw and cooked form was last year at Fairy Meadows.

After lunch I went for a stroll, children giggling and squealing in the distance, men and women working the fields, waving, smiling and greeting as you pass by. Here, the farmable ground and the grass are too precious to be trampled. I was hoping to visit the library in that area but it was closed. The village is amazingly calm and peaceful. You see many different birds in this area; the most prominent of all is the Baltistan Magpie, an attractive and friendly bird larger than the English Magpie. It is a black-and-white bird with a foot-long tail, but if you look closely you see it has the deep blue-green iridescence.

While wandering around Zoodthkhoon I visited Dilawar Baig sahab's home, who was a renowned and highly respected teacher in the valley. He has been teaching since 25 years before he decided to retire. He welcomed me in his home and we sat in a room that apparently was a guest room. Furnished with thick carpet and donned with bright long round bolster pillows. Dilawar Baig sahab started talking about him-self, "I have been teaching from 1986 – 2010. I have lived in Karachi for almost 17 years. I did my Masters from Karachi University and lived in Karachi from 1870 – 1986. I worked in different factories there and completed my education on self-help basis. I visited Karachi in 2011 again and witnessed no changes especially in the Saddar area. When I was staying there back in the days there were parts of Karachi with no population but now there is immense traffic and its sadly highly populated. Karachi is a lovely city." He started asking me where I live and what I do. I asked him if he could tell me the history of Chipursan but he politely refused. After tea I bid farewell to him and the lady who served tea.

Back home to the quite house, the children were still out playing and rest of the people were at the Jamatkhana (the word comes from the Persian language that literally means 'congregational place'). Tea was served as soon as the lady of the house returned. Generally, there are frequent power cuts here and amazingly each house has their own solar panels for basic light. I realized this when I had to charge my cell phone. I never knew remote valleys and villages in Pakistan were equipped with solar panels. You will see numerous satellite antennas, however, phone and internet connections are almost non-existent, which is a break from the outside world. Everything in this house seemed very methodical. The girls were back to helping their mother without being told to, while my son taught tic-tac-toe to Juniad the 12-year-old boy, he grew really fond of. Later I found out he taught the game to all 3 girls as well. Very excitedly Rayyan told me, "I taught them how to play tic-tac-toe and now they keep beating me to it!"

It was surprising how the children would all sit down together with their homework in the family area of the house; again no adult nagging, ordering or repeating instructions. My son joined in. He started writing about the children, his experience, games he played with them and the food he ate. After dinner they played with the push-back blue Lamborghini my son brought with him. The children later decided to play football and cricket in the house until they knocked my tea over and it was bedtime.

Chipursun

I had a lot of fun on the jeep ride. At first I was a little scared because of the flowing river and the steep jeep trek. I was excited that I was going back to Zood Khun village. I was doing excellent balling when I was playing with Shaila, Junaid bhai, Karishma and Shafia. I hit enormous sixes and didn't drop a single catch. When we were going back I was sad. I played volley ball too. I would like to go back to Chipursun and Hunza.

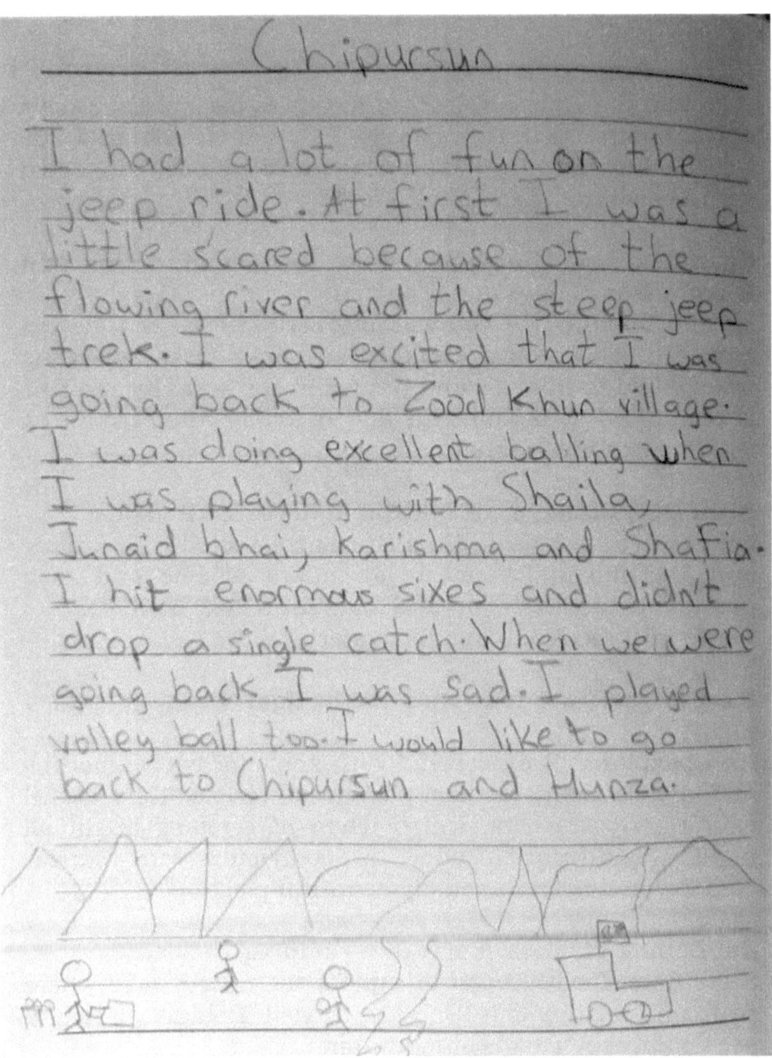

The Undiscovered Trekking options in the Valley

Kirmin Pass (2 – 3 days)
Junction of Pamir & Karakoram, this is possible in 3 days and 2 nights. Visit Vuin Sar see Klik and Mintika and Sue Qeer, a beautiful fresh water lake and wildlife, connected with Misgar and Qalandarchi fort.

Spandrin Sar, Khrid Sar, Sekr Peak behind Goz and Kirmin Dur (3 days and 2 nights)
Behind Shikore Goz you will find many herbs and flowers and see a beautiful Peak called Sekr Peak which is unexplored to this day and unique in the area. Kirmin Dur is connected with Khill Dur and is a very interesting trek with tremendous wildlife.

Khill Dur, Sumayar, Mashthin (2 days and 2 nights)
Unexplored high peak, Khill Dur is connected with Lupgar and its interest lies in its abundant wildlife and good pasture area. Sumayar and Mashthin are both easy to reach with nice camping and waterfalls.

Rashthigar (meadow) and Rashthigar Peak (2 days 1 night)
An unexplored Peak covered with snow for twelve months and a holy point (osthoon) for local people. Here an oil exuding stone exists, which when lit remains bright all night. Rashthigar meadow is connected with Lupgar Meadow and is an incredibly beautiful place.

Jui Sam & Yishkok (Easy, nice camping)
Start from Zoodthkhoon to explore the nearby lake where you can swim or fish. Be sure to visit Yishkok glacier to see Chapurson's highest mountain.

Access to Baba Ghundi (3.5hrs from Yishkok)
Easy walk along a jeep road to see the shrine of Baba Ghundi and the Dragon Lake. Along the way meet shepherds and Kyrgyz coming down from Afghanistan to

trade. Baba Ghundi makes a great base for other small explorations in the area. You can alternatively reach Baba Ghundi by Jeep (45 min) or trek along the opposite side of the road (beautiful camping).

Baba Ghundi to Kuz Sar (Moderate, unexplored)
Camping out on a glacier with views of the Pamir Mountains, Kuz Sar Peak and more.
Pamiri (Easily reached by Yak)
Visit Chipursan's favorite high point which is especially nice in June through September with many flowers, wildlife and multi-coloured mountains. Experience the Wakhi hospitality and a shepherd's life!

Irshad Vuin (Moderate/strenuous, reach by horse)
This 4925m Pass marks the border with Afghanistan in the Wakhan Corridor, with an incredible variety of scenery, multi-hued mountains and Kyrgyz traders.

Ghulam Ali's Pass (Moderate/strenuous, unexplored)
Experience the Red canyon, glacier crossing and natural stone bridge and view the Afghan Pamirs at the end of it all.

Lupgar Pir Pass (Moderate)
Cross a glacier, summit the Lupgar Pir Pass (5190) and trek from Yishkok to Raminj to see two famous snowy Peaks: Saker Sar and another at Lupgar Sar.

Zoodthkhoon Pass to Misgar Valley (Moderate)
Enjoy the view on Yishkok Glacier and Dilisang Sar Peak during your crossing from one valley into the next. It's possible to extend the trek to see Mintaka Pass (Chinese border).

Chilinj An (Strenuous, reach by yak)
Dare a glacial crossing with ropes, experience stunning views and see Karambar Lake & Valley during your crossing from Gojal to Chitral.

Yuksh Goz (Strenuous, technical)
Trek opened in 2001 takes 12-15 days. Cross a glacier
with ropes and trek from Chapurson to Passu via the
Batua Glacier which is rarely visited and an excellent
chance to see wildlife.

Note: For the treks you can, rent a yak or horse. You may
either ride them or use them to transport luggage. Women
can trek to the high pastures with local Wahki women. Mr.
Alam Jan Dariyo is known to escort many on treks in and
around Chipursan.

Guest Houses you will have access to in Chipursan:

1. Family Guest House Kirmin owned by Mr. Muhammad
Wafi
2. Sumayar Guest House Khill owned by Mr. Sher Ahmed
Khan who is also a tourist guide
3. Village Family Guest House Reshit owned by Mr. Iqbal
Khan and sons.
4. Village Guest House Sher-e-Sabz, owned by Mr. Rasool
Khan.
5. Family Style Guest House owned by Ahmed Khan at
Ispanj
6. Mr. Alam Jan's Family-style Guest House "Pamir Sarai"
at Zoodthkhoon and Baba Ghundi Ziarat
Note: I haven't stayed in any of these, therefore can not
personally recommend them.

Day 04 – Farewell Chipursan – 22nd June 2018

Plan: *Explore adjoining villages in Chipursan and see how the day unfolds. Dinner & overnight stay (don't know when and where).*

I loved how we were living in the moment, unplanned, unsure how the day would proceed and end. At this point we weren't even sure if we were staying the night here or leaving the same day. Leaving for? No clue!

The joys of breathing and walking on a rainy hazy village morning, the murmuring winds, smelling the fresh air and listening to the sweet sound of various birds gracefully flying swiftly across the open pastures; that moment can only be felt and not captured. Hence I decided to go out for a walk, spend time alone, seize the panorama and meet people. The valley flanked by the 5,000 meters high mountain range, with wheat, maize and barley fields scattered around. I noticed walls around were made out of round pebbles and stones, that always appeal to me. The canals built to drain the hand-sculpted headwaters of streams and bring water down to the fields and village. Each house is now pipe-supplied with drinkable running water. I noticed no fruit trees around except the locally grown wild sea buckthorn – the powerhouse of nutrients is a very thorny bush, quite common in Hunza Valley. The village is too high for apple and apricot trees like the ones growing in the first lower hamlets. Not new to sea buckthorn, I have had dried ones and the jam that tastes slightly tart and bitter. These are small round orange berries and considered to have rich healing properties containing more vitamin C than most citrus fruits. Additionally, an important dietary supplement wild sea buckthorn berries are sometimes harvested to be sold, in small bottles, as a local energizing juice as well. Used for skin glow, slow aging process, boost immunity, lower cholesterol and numerous other anti-oxidant properties.

Groups of children chattering as they walk to the school seemingly unaware of large raindrops falling, skipping puddles, as they walked past me some greet with a smile others' simply nodded a salaam but no one was curious to stop and talk. Or probably too shy and not used to having visitors around. You will observe local men roaming around wearing their local caps, leather jackets and rough loafers usually over shalwar kameez or track pants and shirts. Except for the noise of some occasional motorbike on the main road, there is the permanent smooth roar of the mighty river, sometimes accessorized with the bird chirping and the gentle wind blowing through the poplar branches. For a while I sat near the homes where I could see a couple of women feeding their cattle, waving or smiling, gesturing or asking why I was sitting there all by myself. An elderly local woman walked straight towards me with a cheerful smile, dressed in the local colourful dress trousers (shalwar, phirwal, tumboon, chanalay), shirt (kameez, kurtani, peeran, cheelo), shawl (dupatta, phatek, cheel) and traditional embroidered cap. The most distinctive feature of the male and female dress of Glgit Baltistan is the traditional cap. A range of caps are used by women and the most popular is the beautiful embroidered Iraghi cap with traditional piece of jewel called silsila. Many other types of caps are used in various regions. The elderly woman shook hands and started talking in Wakhi and smiling knowing I couldn't understand a word she was saying. It was a delightful moment for me, I was talking in my own language trying to explain using hand gestures and so was she. Maraana begum held my hand and took me home where there was another identically dressed elderly lady Mehrunnisa begum. I could decode a little that this house belonged to Aslam Shah and both graciously offered me to have breakfast and tea with them. These ladies were amazingly friendly, happy-go-lucky individuals who enthusiastically posed for me to click pictures of them. I tried telling them I was staying at a nearby home with a family, she cried with joy saying "bhai...bhai..." (brother! brother!). A known fact that everyone knows everyone.

*** Tip:** Never take pictures of locals (adults, children, their homes) unless you take permission and they gladly agree. Never share pictures on social media unless you have taken permission to do so. Respect peoples' privacy.

Maraana begum held my hand and we started walking towards the home and on the way she told me she was taking chai and breakfast to their Jamatkhana today and some other things in Wakhi that I could only smile at. We reached the place and she went in to meet the family. While I started packing – today's plan unknown.

*** Tip:** Wherever and whenever you get a chance to take a bath with warm/hot water avail it. Just don't say no!

Rayyan was awake but not ready to brush or wash up, since he knew the water must be freezing cold. Most rural areas of Pakistan have very simple looking washrooms with a squat toilet. It has essentially a toilet pan or bowl at floor level which is also called a "squatting pan". It requires an individual to squat with bent knees. My son has mastered the art of sitting since his first trip to Muree in 2013.

I regret not taking a bath but to this day I do not regret going out and exploring instead. I just could not get enough of this valley and went out yet again. It wasn't just the sight that pleased the senses. The sounds, the fresh crisp clean weather were out of this world. The poplar trees framed the field's perimeter. The sky above the meadow was a feast for the eyes. It stretched as far as the eye could see in a dome of fluffy clouds. As I made my way back to the host family's house one last time I closed my eyes to click a mental picture of this arresting beauty. My last morning in Chipursan was undoubtedly enthralling – the cloudy, foggy, almost misty morning in the literal sense. My son came running to me and said, "I want to give this car to Junaid." And when he gave it to his mother she cried with joy at the little gesture and promised to give it to him after he returns from school. She held my hand

and kissed it and I instantaneously hugged her, I couldn't find words to thank her for her sincere hospitality.

The pleasant weather ended before midday. As we drove towards Reshit village which is 45 minutes' drive from Zoodthkhoon the ride was spectacular; wild flowers growing along the low stone-and-mud dwellings, the jeep path lined with silver birch and poplar trees and swaying fields stretched out. Some people have started planting fruit tress here such as apricots, cherries, apples and mulberries and also looking into a simple greenhouse design to extend the growing season for vegetables; although it's difficult to grow them here due to severe weather.

We stopped for tea and then headed off to see the Public Library under construction, for which a month earlier, I had voluntarily donated books. This library will run under RISE – Rural Initiative for Societal Evolution and aspires to facilitate students, teachers and general public of Chipursan with books, newspapers and other sources of non-digital information. I was told, "In the early 90s a library was built in Reshit named Reshit Public Library, which did not survive for long due to lack of awareness and resources. The people of Reshit have decided to renovate the existing structure of this Public Library and rename it to 'The First Public Library Chipursan'. Reshit being the central village of Chipursan is convenient and accessible for all other adjacent villages. Teachers and senior students will monitor and operate this library voluntarily. There is another public library in Zoodthkhoon". We passed by the ruins of an earlier fort and the restoration of this fort will start soon too. Legend has it that there was also a fort with twelve gates of gold, before a great flood devastated the entire town. No one knows the real story.

* **Tip:** The weather is unpredictable in the mountains therefore make sure your light and warm clothes are handy.

It was such a quiet place and three shy kids were curiously following us since I don't know when. It was quite a task to communicate with them. Hesitantly they told me their names Fareeha, Arfa and Shahzain all study in grade 1 at the Government School in Rishet. Arfa's favourite subject is English; Fareeha's is Math and Shahzain enjoys Urdu. Off they went saying they are going home. This was an ideal place for photography, as you can see the entire village from Library community center. Mud houses and dry stone walls lined with tall slender trees was growing on me. The sound of the leaves rustling as the wind blows through the trees. It was a nice walk. The weather here keeps fluctuating from sunny to cloudy. The children were going back home and finally four girls stopped to talk; Usnia and Rubi who study in class 3 and Hira and Kiran who are in class 4. With not much to say or ask they told me they had an exam and our now walking back home. I was told that, "These stone walls are dry mounted without using any mortar, except for enclosures and field terraces. The spaces between stones are filled in with mud as it provides the insulation required when the temperatures are low."

We then visited Javed Ahmed sahab's home who insisted we have lunch with them. So we promised we would return in an hour as we wished to explore, walk around the village and meet more people around. We passed a huge ground which is used for helicopter landing, skipped between puddles and photographed streams, wooden bridges, many solar panels when we met a young guy who invited us to his home. A cozy quiet home with the fire burning and we were greeted by two very cheerful young women chattering non-stop in Wakhi. It was interesting to see how these people recycle, reuse and burn everything as all unwanted waste disappears in the burning fire. I had to take a picture of how this lady had collected every piece of scrap and waste on a plastic sheet; pieces of all sorts of wood, an elastic band, a strip of used up medicine, match box, papers, wrappers and even small pebbles. It is always fascinating to observe how people do their daily chores differently; in this case it was making rotis (flat wheat bread). From the way they roll it around the rolling pin, cook it on a flat metal pan, to using the bat-like utensil to flip the roti and the way they serve it. The other lady started making omelet for us. Here in the village you will notice they don't use a lot of cutlery and crockery. They will use a tea cup and spoon to whisk an egg, pour the mixture in the pan and use the same spoon to flip the omelet. They don't use strainers to strain the tea, perhaps because they use very little tea leaves. Keeping cooking simple and hassle free! Also I was wondering how the kitchen is in the family area so the women do not feel lonely when cutting, chopping, whisking and cooking or brewing a big pot of tea or was it so the home remains warm or the wisdom to keep the family together in one place, unlike what has happened in the cities. Some elderly men joined us for the midday breakfast and tea. I am not sure why but everyone stood up and for a while the house went silent. Up in the mountains you will observe how anyone just walks in and the people in the house will serve anything as simple as roti, bread, yogurt or fried egg. My son has never enjoyed a fluffed up omelet as he did in this valley every single day. I kind of had to stop him as he ate nonstop. We finished off with a cup of salted milk tea. With our second breakfast of the day done, we bid farewell to this very friendly family. From here we went back to Javed Ahmed sahab's house for our promised lunch. En route Javed sahab's house I found a rather unusual crumpled lonely orange leaf which had a distinct smell. Instinctively I picked it up and started flashing it… "Look what I found!" but unfortunately no one was interested. All they said was "oh" and started making fun of me by pointing at stuff on the ground saying, "Look! Look! Look! …take it home Naba!" I heard someone say "oh we eat this." I thought to myself 'that's not possible!' This was dried rhubarb leaf. Rhubarb is an enduring, easy to grow vegetable, though it is generally used as a fruit in desserts and jams. Most commonly cooked with sugar and used in pies, crumbles and other desserts. The whole plant is not consumed only the stalks are eaten, which is rich and sharp-tasting. The leaves of the rhubarb plant are poisonous and not to be ingested. Rhubarb needs cool weather to thrive. Alam Jan Dario sahab, a resident of Zoodthkhoon told me that, "the locals here make savoury deserts out of it. *Shepodh* is the wakhi word for rhubarb – when there is no food in cattle rearing areas for shepherds they eat this for lunch – not the leaves but stems and make dessert without using sugar", says Alam sahab. Had I known earlier I would've requested someone for a sweet treat. Better luck next time! My brittle looking rhubarb leaf accompanied me to Javed sahab's house for lunch. Kids were playing outside with a hand pump and my son joined in. They gave him a handful of completely unripe apricots which he devoured saying, "It's fruit from the tree!" Flavoursome rice and gravy with home grown potatoes was served with orange juice. After lunch the kids started playing football in the huge ground close to the house. Javed sahab started telling me about his stay in Karachi back in 1997, where he worked in S. Zia Ul Haq & Sons Oil and Gas Company and they offered catering services as well. "The company has bases in Hyderabad, Multan, Sukkur, Quetta and I was working as the store keeper at the Head Office, from where the food was supplied to other parts of the country", he added. A very soft spoken gentle man he is. Expressing his love for Karachi with a smile he said, "Karachi is a good place and people are also nice, especially the ones I have worked with and I have interacted with all kinds of people. It's been 10 years and I am sure a lot has changed – the place and the people. I still know the people who work at the Head Office in Gulshan-e-Iqbal in Karachi. Earlier I used to work at a restaurant on the Highway and for a while I worked in a garments company in Nazimabad too. I have also lived in Patel Para, Orangi Town, Nazimabad (these are all famous places in Karachi)." Meanwhile his wife served food with a hearty smile. Javed sahab promised to visit Karachi sometime soon, "Every year I plan to visit Karachi but there is never free time from work." He started telling me a little about Chipursan. "There was Miri (Mir / a king or an aristocratic) nizaam here a few years back, just like the waderah system in Sindh (feudal system). So when they saw someone strong they would bring them here to take care of this area and the border with Afghanistan." He continued, "We came from Gulkhin village which is a little above Gulmit and settled here. I moved to Chipursan some 4 years back. My land, my fruit orchard everything is still there in Gulkhin. We can go and live there anytime." I told him that I travelled to Gulkhin last year and spent a day there. He further mentioned, "Most people here have migrated from different parts of Gilgit Baltistan, from Gulkhin, Passu, Gulmit, Hussaini and some from Wakhan corridor. Due to snowfall people don't visit from Afghanistan otherwise it is a norm for people of both ends to come and go. Many come to attend the Baba Ghundi festival there. The Kyrgyz people (also spelled Kirghiz are a Turkic ethnic group that live primarily in Kyrgyzstan) they live near the border and have migrated. They were like nomads, in March they will be here, in July and August they will go to ziarat (Baba Ghundi shrine) wherever they find grassy land for their cattle. So whenever they used to visit they would take our people forcefully with them for labour, beat them up, uneducated as they were. Our ancestors made this qilla (fort – the ruins of which we saw earlier that day). There were two large gates of the fort which would be locked by a large and heavy wooden slab so no one could enter. The fort, walled by enormous mass of stones, was more like a colony and when it all ended I remember the house that I am living in was the first construction. The people lived inside the fort for the fear of attack from outsiders before it got destroyed. God knows what happened later." Rebuilding the fort now as a tourist attraction; Rishet village being the first populated village and considered the capital center of Chipursan. Later people started settling in different parts of the valley. He continued, "There's a nala here (river) with a 7,000 – 8,000 feet long tunnel which can be reached by foot only. The locals built the tunnel after the road collapsed. Once you cross the tunnel there is a coal-mine which people can trek to and visit." Probably the same coal mine I saw on my way to the valley. "I went to Quetta also for my training and worked at the mine for 2 years as a supervisor until the project ended," he said. He has 4 brothers and all live separately in Rishet Chipursan. I found out later that we already paid a visit to three of them. "The eldest is a retired army officer and not keeping too well.

The second one has a woodcutting machine and has a shop. The third one drives a car and does cement and manure work and the last one makes homes and Javed sahab is the youngest. He was amazed to see that I preferred namkeen chai (salt tea) and was liking it. He mentioned to me how children are not in the habit of reading anymore and the lack of public libraries. He was concerned about how this generation has no interest in reading unlike the previous ones. Teachers here are not well trained and he feels children are smart and have the brains but "they need competent and well trained teachers". With that note, exchange of numbers and lots of thank you's we headed out where the jeep guy was waiting for us. Javed sahab offered free treats from his shop for my son as a sign of hospitality. Around 3:30 p.m. we were on our way to Sost. On the way you may experience unexpected cracks on the road or road blocks after rainfall. The river banks here are steep and rickety. They can be unexpectedly damaged and collapsed by floods. Fields and buildings stay at a safe distance, especially Zoodthkhoon where people and their properties might be less exposed to disasters. Though, Chipursan's precarious rough road can be cut due to landslides or broken bridges leading to a complete isolation. Gray sand, washed down from debris slopes, is collected in the river. We stopped at a waterfall near Yarzarich village. I love waterfalls and fresh water streams. No matter what people say I always fill my steel flask with fresh falling water. That is again a personal choice to drink or not to drink! Back on the grueling drive on rutted dirt roads after the rain.

*** Tip:** Make videos of the waterfalls and rivers you have visited. They keep the memory of certain places, moments alive. Besides very soothing to listen to especially if it's shot by you.

The ride back was quiet with a little chit chat, watching the sun going down leaving its traces on the mountain tops. We decided to drop off at Karimabad Hunza and stay there for a couple of days. We reached Sost in a little over an hour. Stretched our legs, used the loo and did not pay. The nice chai hotel uncle apologetically told me that, "We are charging for water. The water for the washroom has to be purchased, for not all of us have proper water lines here". I complimented him on the clean non-stinky washroom, and happily he said, "That's enough for me, please don't pay...you are our guest." I love how these people in the north always acknowledge a polite tone.

We left Sost bus stand and reached Karimabad Hunza after 2 hours. Back to the stone walls. Back to the narrow, steep cobblestone slopes between low wooden houses and orderly orchards of Karimabad after a year. Back to the terraced fields where wheat, barley, lentils, maize and other vegetables are cultivated alongside willow, fir, birch and poplar trees. Back to the roses, lilies and the zinias. Back to the valley of snow clad Rakaposhi peak that dominates Karimabad with Baltit Fort in sight the valley booming with fruit orchards such as apple, apricot, walnut, mulberry and cherry. Rakaposhi is the 12th highest peak in Pakistan and 27th highest in the world. In the local language Rakaposhi means "snow covered" or "shiny wall" it stands at an elevation of 7,788 meters (25,551 feet). You can clearly see its majestic wall of snow all the way from Hunza valley. Baltit was the capital of Hunza for over 750 years. This was later shifted to the lower part of the hills to Karimabad where buildings were erected and the town developed into a tourist site, following the development of the KKH. It is now the hub of shopping complexes dealing in handicrafts, good quality mountain equipment, dry fruit and honey, hotels, restaurants, and travel agencies.

Good to know: The Ottoman's placed carved cobblestones on streets to collect water for the thirsty birds and animals to drink water from.

Day 04 Continued – Hunza – My home away from home – 22nd June 2018

Plan: *Stay and explore Karimabad Hunza. Dinner & overnight stay (don't know until when).*

In 2016, I visited Aliabad, Hunza for the first time and I lost my heart in this valley – that moment changed my travel perspective altogether. This was my third visit to Hunza in 2 years. My son calls it home. He kept insisting, "Mama if you love the mountains so much you can homeschool me and we can stay here...forever." Part of me really want to do just that. Hunza stands out from most places I have travelled to, so far in Pakistan. It's the people that makes this place extraordinarily fascinating. The sad part is, often people who visit Hunza don't see it the way it is supposed to be seen. Majority of them believe Karimabad alone is Hunza and end up complaining and wondering, "There is not much to see, no greenery, just a market place." "What's so special?" "Why do you keep going back there?" "Karimabad is expensive now." "The food is so bland..." It's the people, the purity of the food, the homegrown juicy fruits, the landscape, the spectacular view of the sky raising peaks, the stone walls, the winding cobblestone paths, the warmth and respect that these people have when you speak to them that draws you to it time and again. Besides Hunza is a whole district which most people have not explored beyond Karimabad.

Hunza Karimabad is the only town, where you can view the five famous peaks Rakaposhi 7,788 meters, Golden peak 7,027 meters Diran 7,256mters Ultar (I) 7,388 meters, Ultar (II) 7,310 meters and Ladyfinger peak 6,000 meters, to name a few, on a clear day. Ladyfinger is the most exceptional peaks of all in the valley and remains my and Rayyan's favourite to date. The grandeur of Rakaposhi has no match and you fall in love with the mountain every morning when the sun's first rays fall on it. I have a certain emotional connection with this place. The glorious rugged mountains, the soft blossoming fruit trees, the graceful birch and poplar trees and the carpeted wheat fields against the snow covered peaks, situated at an elevation of 2,438 meters. The best time to visit Hunza is between May to October, you must witness the spring and autumn here that will melt your heart. The temperature here is normally low.

*** Tip:** When travelling towards the mountainous regions carry something warm as the temperature lowers after the sun set. This is conditional to weather changes.

Popular tourist areas here are Karimabad, Aliabad, Ganish (oldest settlement in Hunza with 800-year-old mosques) and Gulmit.   Hunza is divided into three regions:
Upper Hunza, Gojal – Central Hunza – Lower Hunza

Upper Hunza (Gojal) is a scenic valley, where three different languages are spoken, 34 % Burushaski speakers (originated from central Hunza and migrated during kingdom of Ayashoo) and 65% Wakhi speakers (originated from Wakhan corridor). The third dialect Domki is spoken by 1% mainly in Nazimabad and Shishkat villages. The upper Hunza begins from Ayeanabad village – which was sunk deep and Attabad Lake came into existence. The village had sunk completely in the naturally formed lake, after the earthquake disaster.
Upper Hunza extends to Misgar, Shimshal and Chipursan, (these are the border areas). Gulmit is a town that serves as a headquarter of Gojal, (Upper Hunza), and Sost is dry port used for commercial purposes. Upper Hunza is sub divided into four regions, as Gojal 1 – 2 – 3 and 4 respectively. Gojal 1 has the famous tourist destinations Ayeanabad (Attabad), Shishkat, Gulmit, Passu, Hussaini; Gojal 2 has Khyber, Galapan, Gircha, Nazimabad, Hussainabad, Sost and Misgar. Shimshal is in Gojal 4 and Chipursan comes under Gojal 4.

Central Hunza was the administrative region during monarchial rule of Ayashoo dynasty, a ruling family of Hunza for around 980 years and is still the main center of Hunza State. It starts from a beautiful village Murtaza Abad and ends at Attaabad. The villages in this region are most popular amongst tourists, such as Aliabad, Garelt, Ganish, Karimabad, Altit and Attabad to name a few. This is the most populous sub region of Hunza. Languages spoken here are mostly 97% Burushaski and 3% speak Domki.

Lower Hunza has boundaries with Nagar valley on the east and the south. Lower Hunza starts from a village Khizirabad and ends at Nasirabad. Nasirabad's location on KKH makes it the center village of Lower Hunza. Here you will find Shina speakers mainly migrants from nearby areas of Hunza. The Shina language is dominant here and therefore people declare it as "Shinaki". This part is culturally enriched and not much different from the culture of central Hunza.
Note: The percentages mentioned here may not be entirely accurate.

The public bus ride back to Hunza from Sost was considerably noisy, as I left behind many mountain tops. Once again we were crossing the magnificent blue topaz coloured Attabad Lake, surrounded by towering mountains, rocky cliffs and the perfectly constructed Attabad tunnels. You will often see people on motor boats, speed boats, jet skis paddling or sailing by in pairs or in groups. One can enjoy lunch, dinner or a simple snack at the lakeside cafés and restaurants dotting the shore. As you drive through you can see the remains of the village that still exists under water. Attabad tunnel is also known as Pak China Parri Tunnel and was constructed to restore the Karakoram Highway which was damaged back in 2010 due to land sliding. These five tunnels are part of a 24-kilometer long portion of the reconstructed Karakorum Highway.   Two massive bridges and seventy-eight little bridges have conjointly been made. This project was completed in a remarkable span of 3 years and 2 months as is recorded. China has now reconnected the portion of the submerged portion of the KKH in the Attabad Lake. The road is now open to all types of traffic between China and Pakistan.

The bus dropped us at Aliabad from where we had to hire a local NCP cab to go to Karimabad. It was getting dark and the sun had set, the time of the day when everything turns gloomy and sad. My trip had just started but it seemed like eternity, the 4 days spent in the mountains seemed longer than I had anticipated. As soon as we found a room in Karimabad, Rayyan insisted we go out for a walk down the winding slopes. I had to get the two most important things, water and fruit! Sadly, the apricots were still unripe but we were fortunate to devour the ripe succulent cherries. Last year in July, I got a chance to eat the juiciest apricots fresh off the trees, in Hunza, Gulmit, Gulkin and Passu. Apricots are known as the gold of Hunza Valley. The well-preserved architecture, the undeniable charm of Karimabad was buzzing with nightlife, quality restaurants and cafés along the cobblestone path where you can browse through the traditional handicraft shops and dry fruits. Hunza valley bordering China to the north-east and Pamir to the northwest is situated at an elevation of 2,438 meters. All the mountains surrounding the valley are higher than 6,000 feet.

After making my purchase of a bag full of round luscious cherries we headed straight to our favourite pizza place Pizza Pamir. Their slogan: Bringing the organic taste of mountain herbs from the Karakoram Range; serving the best Pizza in the heart of Hunza valley. My son, Rayyan has already made friends with the reputed chef Amin Xon and a couple of other permanent staff there. Like I mentioned earlier this was our third visit! Of course we ordered what this place is famous for...freshly baked Pizza (cheese pizza).

*** Tip:** The food may take a while to be ready due to two main reasons. One, altitude and two, most places prepare fresh food from scratch.

A nice clean place with the most gorgeous views of the valley and the very pleasant team that makes you feel right at home. Waiting for the pizza, Amin and I started talking about the place, my travels and general stuff as we ate the cherries. Even Amin was surprised at the enormous cherries. I knew I would go down and get some more so I shared!
He shared, "This year you will observe that a lot of restaurants and small cafés have opened up. Most of them now do not offer traditional local cuisines which is utterly sad because the demands for city-like food has increased in Karimabad. And sadly this place is becoming too commercial, more like a food-street." I am not a foodie myself but I appreciate local food the lace has to offer.

*** Tip:** Savour the local cuisines. They taste and smell differently, given the diversity of the people of Pakistan; cuisines generally differ from mountain to mountain and may be different from the mainstream Pakistani cuisine you are accustomed to. That is the purpose of travelling...living outside your comfort zone.

After finishing off the good smelling, perfectly baked pizza we made one last stop at the fruit shop to fill my cherry bag. Karimabad the heart of Hunza valley, the cultural hub was still buzzing with people as we walked up the steep stairs to our hotel room and called it a night.

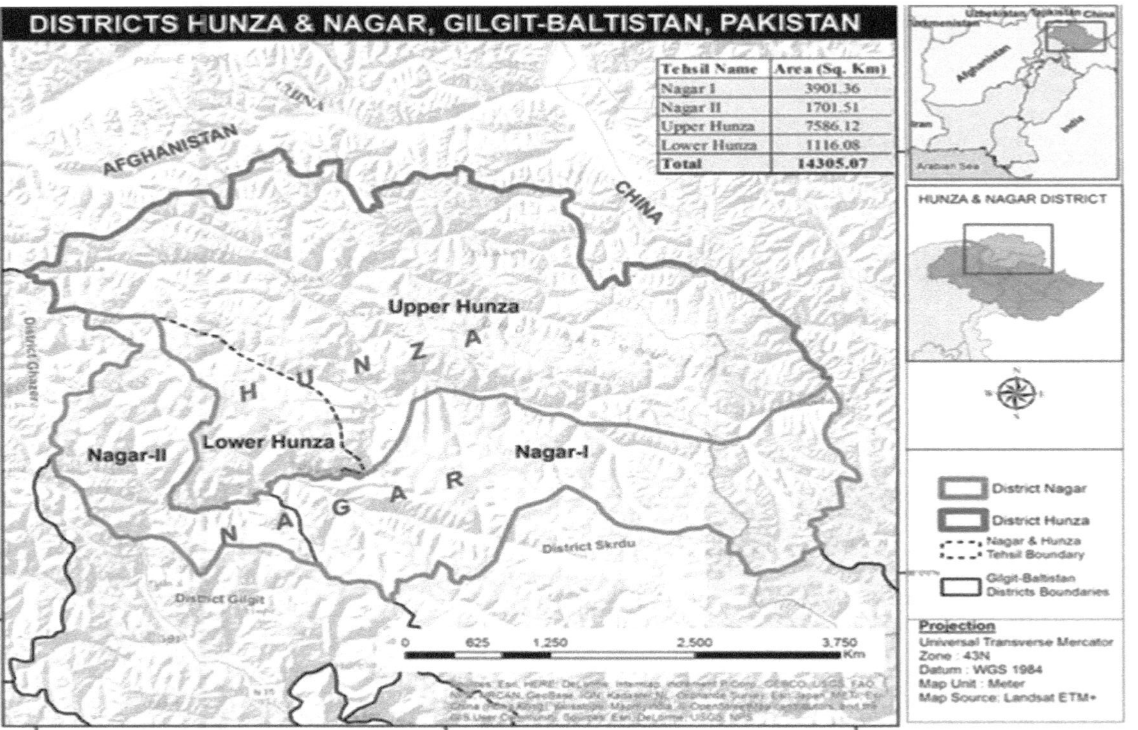

Tehsil Name	Area (Sq. Km)
Nagar I	3901.36
Nagar II	1701.51
Upper Hunza	7586.12
Lower Hunza	1116.08
Total	14305.07

AKCSP - Agha Khan Cultural Service Pakistan

Day 05 – Hunza – I can stay here forever – 23rd June 2018

Plan: *Stay and explore Karimabad Hunza. Visit the forts, shop around, meet people and try the local cuisines. Dinner & overnight stay (don't know until when).*

Imagine waking up to the mouthwatering Hunza cherries by your bedside and having them before you brush your teeth, in bed under covers! I had to click a picture and send it to my family back in Karachi. It was such a blessing in Chipursan not to have any cell phone signals and Internet connection. The need you feel to share pictures with family and friends comes automatically even if you have weak internet connection or cellular service. And that's how I felt here in Hunza.

The plan for today was to explore Karimabad on our own. When you travel to a place with a group, you follow the plan but don't get to see much on your own. In this particular part of Hunza I have always witnessed great respect and hospitality. You will find people smiling, nodding and offering you tea, making small talk, curious to know where you came from and how you find the place. My aim for the day was to interact with the locals, become more acquainted with the marketplace, learn about the culture, form relationship with people and see what a day in Karimabad is really like.

After breakfast Rayyan and I were ready for a steep hike towards the majestic 700-year-old Baltit Fort. As you walk you come across shops selling amazing antiques, local handicrafts, traditional jewelry, clothes, local woolen caps for men and embroidered caps for women; "Chogha" (in winters men wear a special long coat made of wool to keep themselves warm) and shawls, stuffed animals, organic herbs, dry fruits, local delicacies, exquisite hand knotted carpets, wooden spoons and spatulas and of course fresh off the tree fruits. As you advance forward you will come across elderly people sitting, talking or quietly observing the passerby's. A few people had gathered around an old lady who was lost in her sewing and weaving, unaware of the many silent spectators and photographers. I stopped on the way to refill my plastic bag with more cherries. We both decided to use little or no plastic bags while we were travelling. Mushtaq Ahmed the very polite owner of a shop selling both fresh and dry fruit gave us a handful of extra cherries, as a goodwill gesture and green ones too. They tasted sour but my son enjoyed them! Mushtaq smiled as he gave me a little info, "Baji, the black ones are the local Hunza ones and the red ones are Francee-cee (foreign)". Further up we met two slightly elderly men sitting under a shade, Haider Shah and Hazzara Baig. Habitually my son dashed to shake hands and say salaam and introduced himself. "Where are you from?" asked Haider Shah sahab. Rayyan was quick to answer with added information, "We are from Karachi and we come to Hunza almost every year! And this is my third trip to Hunza." Haider sahab chuckled, "So you are visiting the fort for the third time?" We both nodded. He went on, "So Rayyan sahab why don't you stay here forever!" Rayyan beamed at the offer looked at me and responded, "but all my things are back home." Haider sahab smiled and said, "It's okay, we will find a home for you then you can bring all your things here." He offered us tea and we offered him cherries. With a nod and a smile, we departed. The narrow road leading up to Baltit Fort is a beautiful example of stone masonry. The people of GB rely heavily on stonemasons to build their houses. People in this area use concrete blocks, rubble stone and ashlars masonry to build their homes and paths. A half an hour hike up to Baltit Fort figuratively and literally takes your breath away, but the panoramic view of the valley from the fort is exquisite and worth every step you take towards it. This moment I decided that this is going to be my daily routine at least twice a day, until our stay here. A good morning exercise and training for our trek ahead.

The grand Baltit fort is the cultural and historical asset of Gilgit Baltistan – a fine example of Balti architecture. Having seen seven centuries of Hunza's history, today it stands as an enduring symbol of its rich culture and eventful past. It is much grander than its predecessor Altit

Fort. Following a power struggle seven centuries ago, Baltit Fort became the royal residence of Mirs of Hunza. The British conquered Hunza in 1892. They demolished high walls surrounding the fort, exposing its structure to the valley hence diminishing its significance as a stronghold against the attacking enemy. Baltit Fort remained a royal residence until 1945.

We have visited the fort twice in last 2 years so we decided to sit under the mulberry tree on a hand constructed stone bench looking down at the valley. My son spotted a sign on a 4x4 "You can go fast but I can go anywhere" so he asked this guy cleaning it if he could click a picture with his four-wheel drive with yak horns placed on the front bumper. The guy smiled in approval. Going down we spotted some young children carrying packs of small water bottles to different shops and my son offered to help. I appreciate this kind of bonding and that is exactly what I wanted us to experience. They say the best education you will ever get is through travelling; 'nothing teaches you more than exploring the world and accumulating experiences.' An hour later we headed down to The Burger Master's Baltit Fort Chowk Karimabad and trust me these guys serve the best tea in Hunza, my kind of Karachi-tea.

Naveed, Azam and Mehmood run this small café and serve a simple breakfast with good milk tea. Pioneers of introducing burgers in Hunza they serve both fast food and local dishes, since unfortunately the demands for city-food is increasing in this area as the local tourism has taken its toll. They used to make the best Chapshuru in town but don't anymore. They also serve Chilpindok (large chapattis spread with pai – homemade yogurt, qurut – local dried cheese and butter / yak oil, stacked in piles) and you will find special mountain herbal teas Banafsha and Bozlunj other than Tumoro (wild thyme green tea).

* **Tip:** Most items on the menu may not be available or be served at all times, due to several reasons. Be considerate and keep your choices flexible.

It was mid-afternoon when I decided to visit the Altit Fort. The first time I visited Hunza I skipped Altit and chose Baltit over it. In July 2017, I was fortunate to visit both the Forts. I wanted to visit and explore the area myself. The Burger Master guys were kind enough to arrange an NCP ride at the best rate. Junaid the driver behind wheels was a nice young fellow. As we sat in the car I saw a group of women, marching altogether in a very chirpy mood. Junaid told me, "These women are protesting against power failures in Hunza. They will hold a protest outside Mir Ghazanfar Ali Khan's* residence in Karimabad. A peaceful sit-down, literally. Baji (sister), here in Hunza we value the need for empowering women and respect their say even in political matters." I really wanted to witness the dignified demonstration but couldn't wait. Junaid said this may take a tad bit longer. He further told me he has a home in Karachi at Super Highway, "I love Karachi", he stated with a smile.

* Mir Ghazanfar Ali Khan – a Pakistani politician who served as the 6th Governor of Gilgit-Baltistan. On 14 September 2018, he resigned from his post.

While talking we stopped for his chacha (uncle) who wanted a ride to Altit village. Sherbaz chacha was a nice middle-aged fellow. Junaid told him I was from Karachi, and he excitedly turned to tell me he lives and works in Karachi since last 38 years. "I live in Golimar with my family and work at Agha Khan Hospital Karachi. I continued living in Karachi even after I got married. My children are studying there and we are here for vacations. Allah na karay (God forbid) if you ever visit the AKH do pay a visit, I am the senior kitchen supervisor there and you can call me anytime. There is only one Sherbaz there." He went on saying, "May Allah protect us all from hospitals, courts and police station, you enter by your own will but leave with theirs." There was utter wisdom in his words. Curiously I asked him what he likes about Karachi. "My children are studying there but our future lies here, we have our land, home, family, relatives everything here. I just want my children to complete their studies and return home here. Hunza needs no praise, everyone has their own land and Allah has been kind to us. We have our own land in Karimabad. My home and my in-laws live in Karimabad too. There's peace here unlike insecurities in the metropolitan cities. My son can park his motorbike anywhere here, without the fear of being stolen away". I noticed that these people are so amazingly courteous that they will never speak ill about anyone. It was a pleasure meeting him, I told him as we dropped him on the way to the Fort. Junaid dropped us saying; "Baji, my relatives live here, would you like to come and have tea with us?" I smiled and politely thanked him for his generous offer. He continued, "Baji, take my number and call me when you are free. Take your time, no need to hurry. Meanwhile I will visit my relatives, relax and have tea." He smiled and left. Drive from Karimabad is roughly fifteen minutes by car. The pipelines of pure mineral water to the village from the Ultar Sar Glacier are a blessed infrastructure that allows for safe drinking water to residents and tourists all over the region of GB.

*** Tip:** Save contact information of the local drivers, hotels and shop owners. You may need to get in touch with either one of them when you travel next. But never take undue advantage of their niceness.

Altit village is one of the oldest villages in the Hunza valley. The village is known for the Altit fort, built on a steep cliff that rises 1,000 feet above the ground. This village was once the capital of the Hunza Kingdom. It's a nice walk from Ciqam Woodworks. Ciqam (meaning green or prosperous in Burushaski), engages women through skill-based trainings in carpentry, design, drafting, plumbing, construction and masonry, architectural surveys, historical restoration and documentation and hospitality. It employs almost 90 women from various backgrounds and has trained more than 150 women so far to stimulate economic empowerment in this region. Many women are serving as top managers, executives, in commercial and social entities, while a small number of women are engaged in entrepreneurial activities. In the field of sports, Samina Baig has climbed 7 highest mountains in 7 continents, while several players, including Diana Baig, are playing in the national women's team for Soccer and Cricket.

I noticed a sign board that said, Old Hunza Traditional House, constructed in 1600 AD – a 409-year-old residential house that has been renovated by AKCSP (Agha Khan Cultural Service Pakistan) and visitors are welcome to visit the momentous house. We crossed the Jamatkhana, the Altit Library and a bathing pool towards the main entrance of the fort. Taking our time since we were on our own, we walked slowly towards the shops run by women – working with wood, making jewelry, handicrafts etc. This young boy we saw playing flute was sitting in the same spot where we saw him last year, neatly dressed not-a-care-in the world playing his instrument. For a while we stood there watching him, observing people around, children playing; it seemed like a totally different world.

Rayyan and I just walked around exploring the residential area surrounding the fort. Fruit trees on both the sides, magpies flying in a jiffy, women talking across doors, nodding occasionally, a few children trying to knock a few sour green apples but flatly refused to share when asked! The sun's rays shining through and around the trees along the mud path as we walked towards a rather large green field where two young girls were busy talking. I waved and they reciprocated. The girls Karishma and Fareeda quickly joined us, introduced themselves, and started asking one question after another. "Where are you from?" "Is this your first visit?" "Are you alone?" "Do you like it here?" "Do you like the people so far?" "How many days will you stay?" "Is this your son?" "How old are you?"

I answered all their curious queries while they guided me towards the Fort. I shook hands, hugged them and with warm smiles we said goodbye.

* **Tip:** Remember - A smile and a polite tone goes a long way!

As you cross the entrance you take a moment to soak up the royalty of the enchanted Royal garden and that is just the beginning. You see rabbits hopping, sheep and goats basking under the sun, grazing the fresh grass, the rays gleaming through the thick fruit orchard – conifer and pine trees grown over an irregular plain of lush green grass fields. I just stood there by the rich quiet orchard. Altit, a charismatic village nestled in the Hunza valley skirted with sloping terraces. People welcome you with warm smiles; you come across children splashing each other in the bathing pool minutes away from the fort. Meandering through the rustic dwellings, the town will offer you gems of insight into the fort's history as you are escorted up to the towering structure, 1,000 feet above the Hunza River.

We followed the path filled with sawdust to one of the most ancient surviving structure of Gilgit Baltistan. For centuries, the fort was used by the Mirs of Hunza as royal residence. The shy young girl-guide led the way as I clicked pictures of cherry trees and thick grape vines.

* **Tip:** Do not eat the ripe fruit without permission. Most places may seem like an open option, but they usually aren't.

I wanted to explore the fort myself since I knew the history and background from last year, as our guide Karim ul Hayyat sahab was well-informed and an amazing story-teller. Twisting through Altit's mysterious narrow passageways and portals, I pointed out at the holes with wooden lids placed over them and tried playing guide for my son. "These gloomy crevices are the fort's dungeons, where prisoners were held in captivity", I proudly told him. At the top of the Shikari tower (hunter's tower) you will witness a spectacular view of the fort's panoramic vision and its ideal location. The picturesque backdrop of Gilgit Baltistan's treacherous mountain range, the stunning view where you can take dramatic pictures of glacier-tipped peaks such as Ladyfinger, Ultar Sar Peak, Rakaposhi and Shishpar Peak. Across the other bank of the river, you can spot the great Silk Road; running parallel with the blue Hunza, the ancient Karakoram highway stretches along this segment of the silk road which once served as one of the chief routes for travel between trade caravans and conquerors.

It was June and the apricots were not yet ripe therefore we did not see them drying on the square-roofed huts in the sun; as locals preserve the multi-purpose fruit for food dehydration. The orange fruit against the tan rooftops provides a soothing sight.

Rayyan and I lost our way inside as we went from one room to another, appreciating the well-preserved architecture.

A resident of Altit fort praising Agha Khan Trust told me that, "Identifying the historic value of the site, the Agha Khan Trust for Culture developed and implemented an across-the-board rehabilitation plan from 2006 – 2009. Their work involved stabilizing and restoring the fort and also providing clean water and electricity services to the village. Since then the inhabitants of the village have stabilized and many residents have returned home."

Half an hour later we were standing under the shade of grape vines with wooden benches under it, we spotted Karim ul Hayyat sahab, our guide to Altit fort last year. My son remembered him, said salaam and shook hands. Like everyone else he offered us tea and we told him we were just going to Café' Kha Basi for a snack. I asked him and another gentleman next to him to join us but they politely refused.

Located in the gardens of Altit Fort, the café' is a brief walk in the shadow of Altit. You enter a low wooden gate and walk through a lush, serene orchard and finally see the café. It is a quaint and charming simple piece of architectural grandeur, which was once the property of Prince Amin Agha Khan, Chairman of the Executive Committee of the Serena Group of Hotels, but is now part of the hotel chain itself. The café is run exclusively by women where the waitresses and the chef are all young and old local women, trained by the Serena. It has a small indoor dining space, but the best spot for a cup of tea is the veranda overlooking the adjacent valley. The food served at Kha Basi is wholesome and fresh. Although the range of food choices is quite broad, the real specialties are the local dishes that we tried earlier and I highly recommend. Dawdoo; a soup made from chicken stock, homemade noodles and chicken cubes, Burustz Berikutz; fresh mountain cottage cheese mixed with herbs, stuffed in flat roti brushed lightly with locally pressed sweet apricot kernel oil and Tumuro chai; local herbal tea made from wild thyme. We met a group of very active middle-age foreigners from UK, USA, Australia and Canada at the Café'. My son started bragging about all the trips he had taken since he was 3 years old. "My first trek was Passu glaciers when I was 5years old. Then we trekked to Fairy Meadows all the way to Nanga Parbat view point when I was 6 and this year we plan to go to Rakaposhi basecamp." Undoubtedly they seemed impressed. A little chit-chat and a group photo later we waved goodbye.

The Karighar initiative of Serena Hotel provides skills training to women in Gilgit empowering them and enhancing the quality of life of their families as well. Since its inception in October 2016 the center has provided skills training to over 500 women in GB. It also provides raw material, purchases the final product and displays it for Serena's guests. Karighar makes uniforms, bed linen, food and beverages for Serena Hotels across Pakistan.

At this point of my trip I hadn't had a decent mug of strong chai (milk tea) except at Burger Master's and I did not want to order anywhere else. Skimming through the comprehensive menu with appetizers, salads, soups, local and Pakistani dishes, desserts and beverages listed with details. I decided to have my favourite Tumoro tea and Rayyan ordered Chamus (dried apricot juice).

Clicking pictures on our way out, we met an elderly man by the main entrance pool. Everyone here smiles and strikes a conversation as soon as you greet them with a salaam. He fixed his traditional cap and agreed to take a picture with my son. In Gilgit Baltistan the men wear traditional cap. It has different names in the major local languages. In Shina and Khowar languages the cap is called Khoi, in Brushaski it is called Phartsun or Pharsen and in Wakhi it is called Sekeed. The design of cap is slightly different in Baltistan and it is called Nating in Balti. I called Junaid, who arrived soon and escorted us back to Karimabad.

* **Tip:** A sign at the edge of the pool says: 'Avoid standing in residential area'. And we must respect that.

The protest we witnessed earlier that day was still in full bloom. No cars could pass by. Women were stationed on the ground, journalists, camera men, local men had all joined in. Bakhtullah bhai from Pizza Pamir chuckled when he saw me clicking pictures of the peaceful sit-in. I told him, "I need to send this to people back home in Karachi so they know there is a civil way to voice your complaints," to which he smiled gently.

Junaid was a true gentleman he walked us back to where he picked us from. Although I insisted I will find my way back. He emphasized, "Baji, I won't let you pay me until I drop you safely." That's Hunza for you!

*** Tip:** Bear in mind, this may not happen always, due to several reasons. So don't get offended if someone refuses to do anything for you.

Bathed, rested and left for our evening walk. You will notice confident young boy scouts controlling traffic and people, as you walk down the rock-strewn path. Kaimabad at all times is beautiful, especially when it's not over-flowing with people and automobiles. It was time for some appetizing walnut cake with Hunza special green tea. In the heart of Karimabad there is the famed Café de Hunza. The Hunza Walnut Cake served here is a must-eat nutty treat. I love the dense pastry-like cake with a rich caramel walnut filling. On the way we met Sana Khan, owner of the Hunza Lodge hotel, under construction at that time. "I noticed you both yesterday also, seems like you are having a very good time here," he said. My son and I smiled in agreement. He offered, "Next time when you visit Hunza my hotel will be ready and you can stay here. Work is in full swing right now and the project will be complete soon, InshaAllah." We thanked him for his kindness and asked him if he would like to join us for a slice of cake and tea. He smiled generously and replied, "Thank you but you both enjoy the best walnut cake Karimabad has to offer. Shafqat Ali, the owner of Café de Hunza, was a dear friend who passed away last year after cardiac arrest", he concluded sadly.

Over the years my son has started enjoying travelling to places his way. He has his favourite places listed now which includes Chipursan and for obvious reasons Hunza. Being a Karachitte he feels liberated in Hunza and all these places, "where I can go for my morning walk all by myself, cross the road and play in the open fields." Also an avid reader he is fond of reading names of shops and boards. He wanted a picture taken in front of Hunza

Carpet – Old and unique carpets. He found the details on the sign rather unusual: 'Carpets made by local women using handspun wool and natural dyes'. It is merely not the peace of mind that you find here but everything is bona-fide that lies within these beautiful mountains. As soon as you enter the wooden café, there is a little shop with a collection of new and second-hand books, maps, postcards on one side and shawls, pieces of jewelry, raw gemstones and miscellaneous things on the other. Climb the narrow wooden stairs of Café de Hunza and the aroma of fresh-brewed coffee, baked cakes and brownies fills the air. Unlike the modern contemporary cafes, this place welcomes the visitors with a rich warmer ambiance. The place has fantastic views. On the first floor behind the counter you see a family working close together in utmost harmony. The kitchen is clean and everything they prepare is fresh. They have a corner on the first floor with honey, dried tumoro, homemade jams, walnut, almond and apricot oils. This family-run place is mostly packed with tourists. We instantly ordered a slice of walnut cake; the Café's specialty, a cup of steaming tumoro and their delicious Kashmiri chai (pink tea). The cake is baked using walnuts, honey and organic flowers from the mountains of Karakoram, Hindukush and Himalayan ranges. Sounds magical, doesn't it?! It tastes magical too, for those who appreciate distinctive flavours.

We knew we had to wait for our order since everything is prepared fresh and on-spot. A cup of steaming tumoro served with pure honey and the walnut cake full of walnut chunks assorted with honey glazed caramel sauce is all you need with a view to unwind a perfect evening. The rough mountain terrain, clean air and water, abundance of healthy organic foods like dried apricots, cherries and almonds, and relative isolation, up until now, are believed to have blessed the locals with admirable health and extended lives here. We sat there watching the sunset through the window across the mountains penetrating the entire region with its golden rays across the valley. The sky gleamed with effervescence surrounding the picture-perfect mountain ranges. The place is a feast for your taste-buds and mind.

Here I met a family who seemed to be enjoying Hunza as much as I did when I first stepped in this region. Fond of striking a conversation with strangers I greeted them with a rather large smile and shook hands. Instantly we started exchanging our experiences and words of praise for this marvelous part of the world. They were from Karachi and loved every minute of exploring this picturesque valley, the beguiling history, the diversity and remarkable culture, the charming people and the distinct food this valley had to offer. They seemed very curious about my trip to Chipursan and my month-long travel plans to destinations I myself wasn't sure of and the Rakaposhi basecamp trip I was to join at the end of the month. Breathlessly I told them all about my trip, stay, weather, people and the home I stayed in and answered all their curious queries. Giving them tips and do's from my earlier experiences. I don't remember the lady's name who was extremely enthusiastic and started asking about details of honey, dry fruits, handicrafts, oils, jams, herbal teas, the must-try local food and the must-see places. I did not realize that I had been talking to her for more than half an hour before we bade farewell with the promise that she will remember my name and look out for my book – Gateway to Serenity – the Karakoram Highway.

On our way back to the hotel, my son ran to say salaam to Ramazan Baig sahab. His shop Sultan Carpet Palace, which has been there since last 9 or so years, was right below the hotel we were staying in. He gave Rayyan the traditional Hunza cap with delicate embroidery on it as a gift. Not only that but they became good friends, having occasional tea and breakfast together! Around 8 O'clock we decided to go out for dinner. Determined to try something outrageously different but sticking to the local cuisine, we headed straight to Hidden Paradise. This being my favourite and safest place to enjoy the

Tried, tested and recommended by me are:
For breakfast you must try Phitti or Fitti – a crusty whole-wheat bread which is soft inside and baked in fire. Diram Phitti / Fiti – a bread made from sprouted wheat flour which gives a natural sweetness to it and is served mixed with butter, almond or apricot oil. In Gojal, wakhi people call it Pitok, in Hunza, burushaski people call it Phitti and in Gilgit people call it Chupatti.

Main local meals tried and recommend:
Mulida – made with chappatis, local cheese and apricot oil, Mulida Chhagurum – chappatis are crushed together and mixed with onion, local yogurt (pai) and apricot oil. This dish is served cold. Burustz Barikutz – local soft cheese mixed with onions, coriander and mint sandwiched between chappatis, lightly brushed with apricot oil. Burum Hanik – chappati servedwith aged butter. Yak cheese (made using yak milk) is another unique mountain produce. Some sources reveal that it is one of the most expensive kind of cheese in most parts of the world and only a small majority can afford to purchase it. We have more than 6,000 yaks in different mountain regions of Pakistan (the statistics may differ). If there is proper awareness of how more people can benefit from this animal, it would help boost our economy and facilitate the people living in the mountainous regions.
The most recognized and widely-eaten dish in the region is Chapshuro often referred to as Hunza pizza. It is made with chicken/vegetable/beef/mutton – whole wheat chappati wrapped around meat, vegetable and spices cooked and baked in oven. You may order all vegetarian one too, minus the meat. Tzamik – a creamy dish of potatoes cooked with crushed apricot kernels. Harisa – crushed wheat grains are cooked in stock to make wholesome soup and served at special occasions such as wedding and other Hunza festivals. Sharadi/Garma – one

of the many healthy dishes from GB. It is simply raw wheat dough thin pitas cooked with china cabbage. Most cuisines are high in protein and served at special occasions. Gooli is flat bread, made with wholegrain flours, rich in vitamin B-17 and is served with homemade melted butter. "Phulai" is a very unique and fiber rich traditional food of GB which is made from un-grinded wheat grains.

Soups: Qoroth xae Dowdoo is dried cheese soup. *Qoroth* is a kind of cheese here. Dawdoo Soup is made using stock, cooked with strips of chappati, Batayrin-a-Dawdoo or Haneetze Dowdo is apricot soup, Qaq-e-Moch is dried apricot and noodle soup, Tumurotze Doudo (thyme soup).

The place offers the best, most reasonable Chamus (dried apricot juice). So, if you are fond of simple, organic, healthy food this restaurant is sheer bliss and absolutely recommended. I placed an order for Chamus and Batayrin-a-Dawdoo (apricot soup), since Rayyan didn't want to eat here. "Let's have one last pizza tonight and we can have lunch here tomorrow, promise." I agreed since it was his vacation.

Unexpectedly someone from a group sitting behind us started shouting at the servers of the hotel, for not giving them enough glasses for water, tissue boxes and taking new orders. He started insulting the poor guy who stood there without uttering a word. The hostility from this middle-aged man criticizing the kebabs (marinated meat baked in a tandoor oven on long iron skewers) and the tikkas (barbecued meat), was clearly disturbing. Shouting at the manager saying, he came all the way from Lahore (a city known to have the best desi food and barbeque), to enjoy the meaty treats in Hunza was quite frankly appalling. He went on and on trying to tell him how "disappointed" he was to travel all the way from Lahore to this food! With a family of around 20 people including women, men and children no one asked him to suppress his anger over his personal choice. I remember him telling the manager, "We heard so much about Hidden Paradise and look what crap we get to eat here, poor service, bland food and no respect to people who ordered food first." That was hurtful and inappropriate. I felt bad for the hotel people who clearly seemed hurt and did not respond in the same manner, instead nodded and went back to the kitchen. I sent my son to the kitchen to tell the chef(s) that we were in no hurry to have our Chamus and Batayrin-a-Dawdoo. We sat there enjoying the night time, watching the lights flicker in the distance around the silhouette of the mountains.

The soup did not take too long and was served in a wooden bowl with a wooden spoon and looked incredibly rich and appetizing. These wooden spoons are called Khapun in Burushski language. As expected it tasted sweet with no added sugar and bits of apricots – slightly over-whelming for my taste. A pleasant night under the thick apricot tree. We watched the mountains under the sky, discussing the day as I encouraged my 7-year-old to try the soup and help me finish it, which of course he denied. I apologized to one of the member of staff serving our table that I tried my best to consume it but I couldn't. he smiled saying, "I understand".

*** Tip:** Try to compliment the chef and give your sincere, honest feedback. We all need appreciation once in a while. Be that person for the day for that individual.

Before leaving, the infuriated gentleman from Lahore called the manager and spoke politely and sort of apologized for raising his voice, which was a kind gesture. Rayyan and I looked at each other secretly smiling and appreciating.

Getting up to leave after about an hour later, this lady and her daughter on the next table politely smiled and greeted us. She was from Karachi as well and somehow sensed that this was not my first time dining at Hidden Paradise.

I affirmed her assumptions. She wanted my expert recommendation of what they should order. I was enjoying playing an expert in this magnificent part of the world, and suggested the must-try local cuisines. We left the place to eat at our favourite place in Karimabad – Pizza Pamir. On the way up we bought more cherries and fresh spring water. Pizza for dinner, cherries for dessert and that's exactly how our day ended, with one last cup of perfect namkeen chai at The Burger Masters.

Night had fallen and Hunza's view was calm and quiet, illuminated in dim lights. It was yet another beautiful Hunza night and I was grateful for every minute I was here.

Day 06 – Baltit Fort and Salahuddin Bhai – 24th June 2018

Plan: *Stay and explore Karimabad Hunza a little more. Visit the forts, shop around, meet people and try the local cuisines. Visit an amazing lady at Aliabad. Dinner & overnight stay (still unsure until when).*

As soon as I woke up I decided to hike up to the fort for an early tranquil walk and maybe find some tea on my way down. Yes, I am always looking for a decent mug of tea. I quietly left the room not wanting to wake up my little excited monster.

Gazing at the morning sky and pondering upon the journey I had taken, meandering about the trodden paths of the most glorious Hunza valley. It was almost 6:30 a.m. and I expected no one to be up. Clicking pictures, inhaling the fresh morning air, hearing the birds chirping, I walked up the cobblestone path that links the main street of Karimabad with the Baltit Fort – the enchanting fort surrounded by amazing mountain peak, that look grand under the morning sky. Puffing and panting up the steep hill with cherry, mulberry, apple and apricot trees on either side I noticed signs in Urdu that say, 'do not step on flowers' or 'do not pluck flowers', 'help us keep Hunza clean'.

*** Tip:** Show respect to places, people, things and nature. As adults it is our responsibility to be role models for our little ones, who will follow your actions more than your words.

I reached the fort to find the doors closed, as expected. But I saw a prominent figure Salahuddin bhai – the ever so friendly, humble and dignified Security Supervisor of the grand fort. He gestured me to join him and I gladly did. He has been working at the fort since last 20 years and feels he is living in "jannat (paradise) on Earth". He started talking about Hunza so affectionately, "The weather, the silence, the atmosphere, the peace and harmony, the fresh air", he paused then continued, "The fruit, the apples we eat here for free. The air we breathe. We have our land here, our homes, our family, living here peacefully and this is very important for a person. The early morning walk before breakfast is very important for a person's wellbeing. There is purity in this air," he said.

This was the first time I got the opportunity to speak to him with no interruptions and a chance to know a person who is famous for his long mustache and welcoming smile. "When foreigners visit us they say the people of Hunza are Doctors themselves and I ask them why? They say you don't use cars; you walk which is very important. Secondly, they say that we have clean water to drink. We have three different kinds of water flowing in Hunza. You must have noticed the soiled water below and that is the glacier water. Then the snow melts and flows and thirdly the natural stream water which flows directly through the taps in our homes. Our glacier water was tested in a laboratory in London and according to their report this water is very important for Hunzakutz (people of Hunza). All thanks to Allah ta'ala, the creator who created us and placed us in this part of the world where there is utmost peace and serenity, no political or religious animosity and issues, the latter being most important." I completely agreed with him. It was a pleasure hearing his views. I doubt most people ever got a chance to sit with him in peace and hear his opinions. He asked me how long my stay here was and when will I return to Karachi. Talking about Karachi he thoughtfully says, "If you are living in Karachi you never know if you will return home safely in the evening. But Alhamdulillah here, like you are here alone living in peace and tranquility (sukoon) and you will return with tranquility of mind and that is very important for a person (sukoon – he kept emphasizing this word)." After a long pause he said, "Yesterday there were some guests here and I told them that I am on duty here and requested them not to litter here and take care of the place for it is everyone's responsibility. The person in turn asked me, then where do I throw? I was surprised at his attitude and said, Oh my brother! Here is the dustbin, right in front of you, throw your trash here. Cleanliness is half our faith and people don't realize the importance of it in Islam. But the guy kicked the dustbin, right in front of me and left." We sat in silence absorbing the morning air, the birds twittering and the sun rising slowly.

I looked up at the majestic fort and asked him if it was being repaired. He responded, "On 26th October 2015 an earthquake of 7.3 magnitudes later confirmed it was 8.1 struck this area. It mostly affected areas of Khyber Pakhtunkhwa, Azad Jammu & Kashmir, Gilgit Baltistan and FATA (Federally Administered Tribal Areas). So there were a few cracks in the fort and needed maintenance. Our Agha Khan Trust for Culture who preserves and protects heritage shows no negligence when it comes to maintenance." He filled me in that Baltit is 800 and Altit is some 900 years old, making it the oldest monument in Gilgit Baltistan. He further said, "One ruler had two forts. In winters he would stay in Altit and in summers here in Baltit. Baltit had 65 rooms and Altit had 26 rooms. Altit is older and has a beautiful garden. This one belongs to the Wazir family, not us." I was really enjoying the company and the silence.

A panoramic view of the valley can be seen from the fort which makes the steep walk each time worthwhile. Sun shining across the mountain ranges and your eyes instantly turn to Rakaposhi, snow-capped, striking and beautiful. Emily Lorimer after living in Hunza for a year, in her writing calls Rakaposhi, *'by far the loveliest mountain on Earth'*. And who wouldn't agree with that. Anywhere you lay your eyes, there are rocky slopes threaded with water channels, fertile fields and snow-capped mountains. The views from the roof and the terrace of Baltit are exhilarating. I gazed at the soft white clouds covering the Ladyfinger peak and the Hunza peak.

I shared my love for fresh fruit in this valley, to which he said, "In this season you will find ripe cherries and mulberry. Soon you will find apricots. The best season for apples is September and October and we have 12 – 13 different types of apples in Hunza. Once the choice of your sweet apple tree is planted it starts giving fruit in a year's time. In 2017, I visited Punjab, Sialkot I visited a shop and saw a carton of apples, labelled as Hunza apples. The shopkeeper told me they were selling them for Rs 400 per kg; and I told him that particular kind of apple we feed to our cattle. We also cut, dry and crush them into a powder form. In this season early in the morning we mix the apple powder in cold water or milk and give it to our children. That is good for health. As you know the food is not pure anymore therefore we produce most things ourselves and consume them." I really like how he speaks, low-pitched and short pauses. He proceeded, "Last night a 100-year-old woman passed away and you know that people live longer here. As I mentioned earlier the water we drink is pure and wholesome, the air we breathe is fresh and clean, fruit orchards and we use all natural home-grown food." I told him how my son and I carry our water bottle everywhere and whenever we get a chance we fill it with fresh flowing natural water. He responded, "This glacier water has travelled all the way to London, Germany, America, France, Korea and Japan for research in laboratories and their report say they found many minerals and traces of gold and iron in it. We don't normally drink this water directly; we fill our pots and leave it for a while before drinking. This water keeps us fit." He went on, "A man from Karimabad Karachi stayed here for 2 months and he was unwell. According to him he spent a lot of money on medicines and treatment but he couldn't get better. It was until he came to Hunza, he is no longer on medication, drinks cold glacier water, eats fresh fruit and feels better already. He told his children to let him stay here for a year as his health have improved in only 2 months of hi stay here. I met him yesterday." Curiously I asked him, if non-Gilgitis can settle here? He explained, "I'll tell you something, the Islamili community is scared to let outsiders stay here permanently because we are a peace loving community and you can't be sure about other people, the outsiders. We don't want people destroying our peace and nature." And I agreed.

He pointed in the distance and said, "Our home is there. Education here is the best. We don't waste our children's time. These are our principles. Their routine is to go to school in the morning, after school they go for tuitions. Then they go for religious education. Their playtime is for an hour or so in the evening and the rest of the day it is productive." I shared my observation with him how I have noticed children are carrying stuff to the shops, helping with the traffic or picking fruit. That in contrast with the life of city children is amazing. Salahuddin bhai nodded his head and said, "If a woman is widowed her kids help her run the house."

Looking down at the valley I spotted a young fellow picking garbage and collecting empty bottles and throwing them in handmade dustbins placed all around the fort. The multitude of tourists nearly every year leave behind a lot of trash at tourist spots in the northern areas. In order to promote and encourage cleanliness and to preserve nature, the girl guides of Hunza valley fashioned handmade bins with clear bold messages: Be with Us – Let's Save Nature. Salahuddin bhai with a sad tone said, "People actually kick the baskets and overturn them. We have placed signs to keep the area clean. You must have noticed that our Hunza women wake up early and start cleaning up from the Fort chowk onwards and within half an hour the local Pakistani tourists start throwing trash." Yes, he used the word Pakistani with emphasis which is sad coming from a person who has been observing since last 20 years. One thing I noticed he did not choose to use words like, dirt – garbage – trash – litter – filth instead opted for positive words like cleanliness.

"It happened yesterday down in the marketplace there is a Rainbow hotel where a woman witnessed someone eating cherries in a car passing by and throwing seeds on the road which randomly hit someone on the face and many such incidences happen here. There are very few guests who appreciate the natural beauty and help us keep the place clean." He kept repeating, safai ka khayal rakhein (take care of cleanliness). I told him that residents of Fairy Meadows – Beyal Camp quibbled about people trashing their streams of drinking water and the meadows. "Tarbiyat (training) is very important," Salahuddin bhai remarked. "Foreigners – when they smoke they will put the stub back in the box, even the match stick goes in their pockets. You see Ultar peak up there when they climb up to the basecamp they will return with the place spotless, not even a match stick. They stand firm on their principle unlike us Pakistanis." It was nice speaking my heart out to someone who understood the agony of a local traveler. I told him in all these years I have travelled across Pakistan I have noticed two things that majority Pakistani citizens' lack – Respect and Cleanliness, which Salahuddin bhai didn't argue with. I told him the previous night's incident at Hidden Paradise, something I felt I needed to get out of my system. He listened intently but remained silent. "When we educate and train our children they will raise a better generation. As I say Tarbiyat (training) of a child is very important", he said. I sat with him for almost an hour watching the sunlight illuminating the valley, magpies flying about without a care in the world. He told me I could sit here for as long as I wished to. I started telling him, I teach at a local school and enjoy travelling with my son, especially to this part of Pakistan. He asked about my travel plans for the days to come. I told him how it was all vague and the only concrete plan was Rakaposhi base camp which was a week from now. I started talking about the travel group I was going to travel with – Climax Adventure Pakistan. "The people of our country are nice," he said thoughtfully. "The politicians of our country have ruined it; they are only busy pulling each other's leg, calling each other names, disrespecting each other… we have achieved freedom after all the pain. There should be peace…sukoon and we should work towards development. Like here we have major electricity issues. Our Mir is the current Governor, Mir Ghazanfar Ali Khan; his mansion is down the road. You must have seen towers above; amidst the trees is his mansion. People protested yesterday." I told him what I witnessed and that I took pictures of the peaceful protest unlike how it is in Karachi. "I had to send the pictures home!" To which he grinned and agreed, "People start burning and destroying property in cities. Here we have a lot of water but due to negligence of Government we are forced to live in the dark. We have Hunza river (they normally call it nala) we have water everywhere, but the Government is too laid back."

I sat there at the edge of the fort looking at the stunning scenery, fresh air and … silence! I said goodbye to Salahuddin bhai, thanking him for his precious time and promising to bring my son later that day to meet him. I took some time to breathe in the serenity in the air and descended the steps.

* **Tip:** Keep your promises!

I strolled down clicking pictures of the fruit trees, the glacier water at the foot of the fort, the poplar trees lining up the path, the cobblestone path which I love walking on, an occasional smile and a salaam to people and children passing by. The only living creatures you will find fighting would be the black crow and blue billed magpie over which branch to sit on. As you descend towards the main Karimabad market you will notice the glacial water of the Hunza River rushing dramatically and speedily at the foot of the fort. The water flowing in the channel is attractive velvety pasty white coloured caused by the minute content of fine mica particles. Suspended crushed stone, or rock flour makes glacial meltwater opaque and gritty. The crisp, glacier-chilled air blowing down from the mountains carries the sound of birdsong and the invigorating smell of rich, damp earth and fresh pine sap. Strains of stringed instruments float in the air. The irrigation channel that sometimes gushes at speed from behind the obvious gorge at the foot of Baltit Fort passes through the Karimabad town. There are plenty of water sources in this valley as Salahuddin bhai mentioned; glaciers topping the list, precipitation, river water, and the spring waters account for catering various domestic and agricultural needs. The extreme weather temperature chips in and freezes the springs and lakes thus, leaving no other option for communities except to consume contaminated, impure water of glaciers stirring a spree of epidemics and water borne diseases. The renowned longevity and good health of Hunza is primarily attributed to the glacier water and their diet of wholemeal foods.

Going down I spotted Hunza Food Pavilion – The hub of traditional food, its doors open now, which clearly suggested they served breakfast! The place run purely by women who believe in all-natural, all organic food hygienically prepared and served. They will never serve you food in newspaper or plastic. Craving and expecting a perfect mug of tea I went in the small wooden 6x6 cozy cabin with 6 seats around a table. Decorated with hand-embroidered, cross-stitch pieces they have created mostly themselves. They serve authentic local food made with best and freshest ingredients. Everything is made to order. "Normally people prefer eating eggs and omelets so what would you like to have with your tea?" Chand Bibi (co-owner) asked. I told her I needed good namkeen (salty) tea. She smiled and started chopping onions for omelet she was preparing for the two gentlemen already seated there. I picked up this fragile looking, half torn and worn out menu cum recipe book on the table and skimmed through it. "Cooking in Hunza" – Discover the secrets of a healthy and innovative mountain cuisine from Northern Pakistan; an interestingly compiled recipe book, compiled by a handful of foreigners. With a brief history and highlighting their ethnic food, a list of most used ingredients in this region followed by appetizers, soups, breads, main courses, desserts and drinks. The 'tips' and 'mountain wisdoms' are an interesting read. You can order anything from it. People here eat a lot of fruit, nuts, yogurt and use pure honey or apricots as sweeteners. They habitually season their food and tea using Himalayan pink salt.

* **Tip:** Take permission before you click anything that belongs to someone else – be it a menu!

After serving the two men, she turned to me and said I will make something special for you. And while I sat there narrating my experience so far, she prepared a runny batter. Little did I know that she was making Maltash xae Giyalin (Hunza pancakes) – a mountain crepe made from hand milled whole-meal flour that is coated with apricot, almond or walnut oil, and served with fresh butter. "These pancakes are a traditional dish prepared when a daughter visits her parents' home after her marriage. It is eaten with chai (tea). Try it for breakfast", Chand Bibi said in a soft tone. She told me she lived in Karachi some 14 years ago. She has two daughters and two sons – all born in Karachi. Out of which one daughter is engaged. "The other three are studying in Islamabad", she told me. She also showed displeasure for people visiting and clogging the roads during Eid holidays. She wants peace here and no disturbance as does everybody else in this valley. Another woman Maheeda came down to help her as her partner Lal Shehzadi (co-owner) was not well. Chand Bibi served the pancake drizzled with honey and a steaming cup of milk tea and salt. While we were chit-chatting and I was devouring my tea and the Maltash xae Giyalin, Lal Shehzadi walked in. She introduced herself and apologized for not being there. A cannula bandaged to one of her hands, she enjoys talking. A simple woman with lots of energy. Lal Shehzadi holds a Master's degree in agriculture from Japan and gotten her training from Korea as well. She has worked in food processing, and has been to Japan several times for training in natural medicines and natural pesticides arranged by Japan International Cooperation Agency (JICA). She filled me in, "I use all organic farm fresh ingredients. I cook in pure walnut or apricot oil which I make myself". Resilient, opinionated and showing displeasure for both women and men not respecting women especially in a small space or paths of Hunza. I admire how cool, calm and collected she still was, stating, "We cannot disrespect our guests or feel agitated. But I don't like the idea of men standing too close for comfort and dressed inappropriately asking for food. I firmly ask them to keep a distance or tell them to change before I can serve them. Even the women who accompany them normally do not understand our discomfort." She raised her cannula injected hand and expressed how she fell severely sick in the last week after Eid and her partner had to manage alone and someone or the other would come down to help her.

Being a Pakistani mom that I am, I saved 2 pieces of the local pancake for my son. Chand Bibi grinned and said, "I'll make a fresh one for your son, you finish this off!" She refused to pack it in paper, newspaper or plastic instead sandwiched it in between two glazed plates saying you can return it whenever. I was touched by the gesture and assured her that I will return the plates. She said, "People normally never come back to return our cutlery or crockery, in fact during the Eid chaos someone handed over fake 5,000 rupees. We are unsure if someone did it on purpose or complete ignorance".

*** Tip:** Never break anyone's trust.

Food in Hunza Valley looks and feels so simple, natural and healthy; you will find a mix of lentils with potatoes and sometimes carrots, spinach, tomatoes or whole-wheat and normally served with wild thyme tea (tumoro). The food is not fried and there is very little oil, sometimes home-pressed apricot oil brushed lightly; contrary to what we were used to with Pakistani cuisine. The oil they use commonly for cooking purposes is home pressed apricot oil, almond oil or walnut oil.

*** Tip:** Karimabad may be the perfect place to purchase pure honey and oils. Oils can be used for drinking, cooking or external use.

I climbed up the steps to my hotel room happy and fulfilled with lots of stories to share with my little one. I was glad Rayyan enjoyed the local pancakes and told him to return the plate on his way down with a thank you. Travel teaches you what classrooms don't, real-life dealing with people, expressing kindness and showing respect. Rayyan wanted to go for a walk, he felt physically liberated here! I asked him to grab a water bottle on his way back. Meanwhile I washed, cleaned and freshened up. My son returned with a big happy smile. Turned out Ramazan Baig sahab downstairs at Sultan Carpet Palace offered him breakfast and my little social butterfly agreed wholeheartedly. "On the way up I met Sitara aunty, she was washing dishes and cutting potatoes to make chips so I helped her. Now she is my friend and I told her I will bring my mama in the evening to meet you," Rayyan enlightened me on his morning walk.

In need of a fresh supply of plump crimson cherries we set out again and this time we bought them from Sunail Khan, who returns home in summers to help at his brother's shop. He lives in Gulshan-e-Iqbal in Karachi and is studying there. It's wonderful to see young individuals coming home to help and not just vacationing.

By mid-afternoon we were climbing the steep cobblestone path towards Baltit Fort to meet Salahuddin bhai as promised earlier that day. We saw young children with large blue plastic bags on a cleaning mission around Karimabad. Lost in their work, it seemed like such a norm in contrast to the metropolitan city like Karachi. On the way we met Haider Shah sahab again who smiled and nodded. I offered him cherries yet again! This time he took some.

We reached the top and Baltit was quite crowded by now. Salahuddin bhai remembered me! We greeted him and my son told him, "I see you here every year and my mama takes my picture with you every year!" I clicked another one. We did not stay long for it was a busy time of the day.

*** Tip:** Please don't strike a conversation with Salahuddin bhai while he is on duty. People up there are very considerate and will never try to shun you or break your heart. That morning I took permission from him if I could sit and speak to him, knowing his duty hadn't started.

I watched Hunza in a different light and strolled around. Rayyan stopped to shake hands with Eric from Scotland. After a brief introduction he said, "First time I visited Hunza was 25 years ago. It's a nice cool place. I have also been to Fairy Meadows and enjoyed the hike up. The drive though was scary." He asked what our travel plans were, to which I told him the only definite plan was Rakaposhi base camp. We bid farewell after clicking pictures wishing each other a joyful safe journey.

We started to walk down the steps leading to a luscious fruit orchard of the Morning Glory Restaurant, Hunza. This gorgeous restaurant at the foot of the Baltit Fort has possibly every fruit that grows in this valley – apricots, mulberry, cherries (both black and red), apples, peaches, grapes and walnut. This was the first time I was visiting the restaurant. You can see Rakaposhi and the entire valley through the magnificent cherry trees laced with delicious plump fruit. Although there were clear signs in Urdu: "Fruit picking not allowed", the restaurant guys were kind enough to offer us to pick and eat the fruit. They must've sensed our love and greedy stares. I politely thanked them for their kind gesture and told them we will follow the rules. For I felt others around us might take advantage of the exception. Besides I had to set an example for my son! French fries and tea were our lunch for the day. The scent of ripe fruits hanging from trees drifts along the summer breeze as we sat and enjoyed the rather large serving of fried potatoes.

Later that day we went down to have Chamus (dried apricot juice) at Hidden Paradise and a picture that Rayyan really wanted. Outside Silk Route Café was a hand-written sign on a whiteboard – the only of its kind in the area: 'We don't have Wi-Fi talk to each other. Pretend it's the nineties – Silk Route Café'. I had trouble explaining "nineties" to my 7-year-old.

That evening we decided to meet Hussn Bibi – a lady I had never heard of before, but I wished I did. The meeting was scheduled by Safeer, a member of Climax Adventure Pakistan. This lady seemed quite interested in why I decided to write a book, my first publication Gateway to Serenity – The Karakoram Highway (still available)! As we settled in her warm cozy kitchen, I was told that the place was hostel cum home to a dozen girls living, studying and doing household chores under one roof. A young girl served us snacks soon after I filled in a little about what I do. Talking about teaching, she knew Dilawar Baig sahab (a retired teacher) who I had met in Zoodthkhoon Chipursan. Since Safeer hadn't told me anything about her, she started narrating her story. Hussn Bibi feels privileged to be able to express herself when many people around her could not get that chance. Here is her inspirational story:

"I must have mentioned earlier I was a school teacher and now a trained teacher. I'll start from the beginning; I was very young when the first girl's school was built in Shimshal. It had a single room but that one room meant the world to me as I completed my first 8 years of education in that little room. There was no high-school and the only

option I had was to travel to Hunza to complete my Matriculation (10th grade). A distance of almost 4 and a half hours now that the roads are built and you can find 4 wheelers. At that time with no proper road from Shimshal to Hunza, one had to trek for at least 3 days to reach Passu and then from Passu you take a jeep to Hunza. Shimshal to Hunza is approximately 119 kilometers. When I came to Hunza for my Matric exams, I only had one decent looking dress to wear. I would wear it during the day and wash it at night time to wear it again the next day. I could not afford to buy books. My friend Fatima got her course books from her brother and we used to share them to prepare for our exams. After passing the exams, I started teaching at the village school, to earn money to continue studying. I completed my Intermediate (grades 11 and 12) and Bachelors without setting foot in any college or university. Many other girls were working but it was difficult to manage living in a remote village with many responsibilities apart from studies. I got married at a very young age and had to take care of all domestic chores along with my education. I used to manage cattle in the high pastures for months and it seemed like I could not pursue my dreams – my career.

In 2003, I got a chance to go to New Zealand for a year. I was the first woman in my village that got the opportunity to travel overseas at that time, a female especially. A native now a friend from New Zealand sponsored me who was actually teaching in a school as a volunteer in Shimshal at that time. There were two women, Pam Henson from New Zealand and Lynette from England. Another lady by the name of Wilma from Germany built a school in Shimshal and is in the process of building a girl's hostel in Karimabad and Aliabad, Hunza. A health center was built by a German NGO at that time also. Going abroad was a great learning experience for me and I vowed to use all that I learnt for the progress and empowerment of women. Since 2004, I have been working on this mission with the help of some local and foreign friends. My friend Pam Henson has *written two books on Shimshal; *Women of Shimshal and by the title, Shimshal. She has made a Shimshal trust there and they raise funds and provide scholarship to the deserving students of the village. It is although not a huge amount but it fulfills their basic needs. It supports 10 – 15 students per year. Every year we pan out a number of scholarships for deserving students. I am also very much into social work and my main focus is on orphan girls. I started in 2015 and I paid for 5 students' school and hostel fee. The Pakistani community in New Zealand has a group by the name of Kiwi Madad Group and they have taken the responsibility of treatment of 4 people. One of them is my cousin who was Polio affected and for two and a half years they bore all medical expenses. She was being treated at a hospital in Karachi. Three other children from our village (Shimshal) were treated at AKU (Agha Khan University) by them too. When I started my hostel in 2015, they took the responsibility of 5 orphan children and have been paying their school fee since last 3 years. There is another orphan whose medical and educational expense is sponsored by them as well. Now that student is in the final year of studies. Last year they helped us with the educational expense of around 8 girls. This year I have prepared a proposal for 12 girls so you see my primary focus is more on orphan girls. Currently I am doing it for Shimshal only. But there are villages in Gojal where there are deserving children but unfortunately I lack resources. Girls from Karimabad have approached me but again I have no resources to help all of them therefore, I try but don't promise them anything. Locally I don't get much help and I depend more on my friends in New Zealand for finances. Our Ismaili community has taken an initiative in Karachi which is a blessing. Last year I sent Safeer's first cousins Sarika and Naisa from Shimshal, one of them is in Grade 3 and the other is in 4, to study there but for them travelling long distances is challenging. And I have been thinking if we receive funds to accommodate our young students here in Hunza as we do have some good schools here. We want them to be close to family and to our culture.*

Government based institutes train their teachers continually but with my observation and experience I can conveniently state that the private school teachers are not trained professionals. Yes, they have degrees but are not professionally trained. Schools are now teacher-centered and I feel a teacher needs training on how to teach and deal with children. Most of the times the teachers are unable to identify learning disabilities in children which we are also working on. I have lived a very tough life and want to make it easier for others. Therefore, as long as I live, I shall do my best to facilitate young women so that they can pursue their dreams early on."

She served us samosas and pitok and told me one of her cousin's daughter spotted me in Karimabad and Hussn Bibi wanted to meet me as much as I wanted to meet her! So it was mutual and I am glad I met her and know her too well now. We ended up being really good friends thereafter – An amazing lady with a heart of gold.

* Women of Shimshal by Pam Henson – available on Amazon (both books published by the Shimshal Trust).

Our day ended with Pizza Pamir's perfectly seasoned pizza and of course cherries for desert. I was starting to love this combo. The guys here are delightful and unpretentious – Amin, Marafat, Wasim and Bakhtullah bhai will always be at your service in Karimabad and now at Attabad lake (their new venture at the striking new location). The first time I stayed in Hunza was at Café de Pamir in Aliabad that existed before Karim bhai decided to start up Pizza Pamir.

Early to bed, early to rise, because Rakaposhi is at its best when the first ray of light falls on it and you don't want to miss it.

Day 07 –Farewell Hunza until we meet again – 25th June 2018

Plan: *Stay and explore Gilgit on my own. Visit Kargah Nala – a place I recently read about. Dinner & overnight stay (unsure until when).*

The next morning, I noticed that the crow and the magpie, assuming they were the same pair, had made peace and were sitting together under the shade of a large tree at the bottom of our guestroom with a 'Hunza News' bike parked next to it. Rayyan had woken up early and chose to join me for a morning walk towards the Baltit Fort. "Someone has planted plants in milk cartons and used tins", he observed. We saw children going to school and mutually decided to walk and witness the assembly at F.G. Boys Model High School in Karimabad, Hunza. The assembly started with a dua from the Qura'an, followed by national anthem and ended with praises for Prophet Muhammad (peace and blessing be upon him). After the children dispersed to their classes we set off to do what we were there for – explore! Rakaposhi – standing in all its glory. The huge massif dominates the skyline for vast stretches of the Karakoram highway, first seen north of Aliabad yet still visible as far south of Gilgit. The sight of sun rising over Rakaposhi is worth waking up every day at the crack of dawn. It is an area popular with tourists and adventure-seekers, attracted by the purity and natural beauty of the region. Unfortunately, with the advent of tourism, the local tourists especially, tend to leave the area in a terrible condition. During the tourist season, popular sites become littered with wrappers, plastic bags, discarded water bottles and soda cans.

As usual we found Hunza Food Pavilion open for breakfast. My son wanted to have their Maltash xae Giyalin (Hunza pancakes) again, drizzled with loads of honey. I only wanted tea. I wanted to place an order for lunch but the lady refused to take orders and repeated, "orders are prepared fresh right before your eyes". With a smile and promise to return I left. We decided to leave Hunza the same day and head to Gilgit before evening. So, we went back, changed and packed up. We still had time to walk around Karimabad to ensure we haven't left any stone unturned. A freshly prepared Chamus was a must-have at Hidden Paradise before heading back to the hotel to collect our bags.

*** Tip:** Before leaving your hotel room or camp make sure the place looks clean, beds made, blankets folded, trash picked up and don't leave behind stinking bathrooms.

You will always notice everyone trying to help you with your luggage no matter how many or how few bags you have. One last critical check and paying the rent I handed over the keys to Ramazan Baig sahab. He offered a nephrite jade stone in raw form to my son which he hesitantly refused. In a local cab we drove to the bus station to grab the local transport to Gilgit city. With a heavy heart, I was leaving this heavenly abode, knowing I will be back soon.

Excited to be travelling in local transports through-out this trip all by myself felt like a child given unlimited access to ice cream without adult supervision. It took us almost 3 hours to reach Gilgit city; leaving behind the magnificent views and soaring peaks ready for the next adventure. Driving along the Hunza River with Rakaposhi still in sight; enjoying the company of strangers and the last bag of Hunza cherries. We crossed the historic Yadgar-e-Shuhada located in Chinar Bagh Gilgit which was re-built recently. This Yaadgar was first constructed in the early 60s in memory of the martyrs of Gilgit Scout who fought for the liberation of G.B from the Dogra occupiers in 1947. You will notice the sign 'Old Silk Road' the location of which is somewhere between Gilgit and Hunza. It is interesting to read signs at intersections Naltar – Nomal – Rupani Foundation to name a few.

Next to me were two young women smiling and one of them hesitantly initiated the conversation. Afshan introduced herself saying, "I am from Aliabad, Hunza travelling to Gilgit. I am training to be a nurse at Sehat Foundation Denyore. I have two kids a girl and a boy". Women in this part of the world appear to be very ambitious despite being married and having children. The other young girl Sadia told me, "I am doing my B.Sc. Honors from Karakoram University. Currently in my 5th semester and my exams are starting soon". She stays in a hostel close to campus. The bus ride reminded me of a school bus dropping passengers at their said locations. We dropped Sadia at Baltistan House female hostel quite close to the Karakoram International University. I wished her good luck and shook hands. Afshan, the nurse in the making asked me where I needed a drop and kept reassuring the anxious me that, "the driver will drop you at Heaven Lodge". I stayed at Heaven Lodge back in 2017 and our stay was extremely comfortable and relaxing.

*** Tip:** Make sure you book yourself a guest house or a hotel room of your choice before reaching your destination, to avoid last minute panic attacks. Do this only if you trust the place, owners and your instinct.

Heaven Lodge is located close to the River View in Gilgit. Hunza River joins the Gilgit River a mile below the town. Gilgit valley is formed by the confluence of the three rivers – the Indus, Hunza and Gilgit River. The new bridge spans the Gilgit River at Denyore, 8 kilometers below Gilgit. The KKH connects Gilgit to Chilas, Dasu, Besham, Mansehra, Abbottabad and Islamabad. Gilgit was bright and sunny, with thick fluffy clouds hovering above and the stark, steep, massive snow-capped mountains towering over the town. The driver dropped us off right at the open gates of the lodge. I invited Afshan to visit me if she could, said farewell and wished her all the best for future.

I had already reserved a room with them and had no demands in particular. The guys at the lodge are such wonderful people they had my room ready and prepared adjacent to the magnificent views of the Gilgit River and the city. Home-like environment, hospitable and courteous staff, spacious rooms with clean bathrooms, blooming and fragrant flowers all over the place with all kinds of insects in the world to observe and educate your child. I could find no better place to stay in this city. Hamid Karim sahab and some other guy, I fail to remember his name, led us to our room. "You must have received the pictures of the room and the washroom?", he emphasized the word "washroom". I thanked him and told him, "Yes, Mujahid sent me pictures earlier and the room looks great". Mujahid is one of the experienced guides of Climax Adventure who booked my room a day earlier, upon my request. Hamid sahab smiled and responded, "We have free flowing warm water 24/7!" which is exactly what I needed after a week of freezing glacial water, ice cold and literally sparkling with ground granite. Before leaving the gentleman informed me that they were trying to fix the lock earlier but couldn't. He assured me that it will be taken care of as soon as possible. I unloaded my bags and rushed to the washroom to shower.

Our bedroom was well-ventilated and had a perfectly furnished large kitchen with varieties of crockery, cutlery, baking utensils and moulds of all shapes and kinds except a stove and an oven! It was a dream-come-true for me to have an invigorating view from my kitchen window as I washed my truck art mug. I have never stayed in a kitchen-attached room before. The river on the other side of our garden was calm, the mountains daunting, the view stunning and the breeze cool. I ordered chai to go with the picture-perfect setting and our last pack of biscuits. The sun was still intense but that didn't stop us from going to the other side of the lodge. We walked by the rail near the river, smelling the gorgeous fusion of roses and flowers, paved with all kinds of plants laden with brightly coloured flowers, that blossomed most of the year. Clusters of tamarix shrubs with small pink flowers, hanging at the ends of branches giving it a feathery appearance. Poplar trees swaying and small specks of sunlight filtering through the leaves. On the other side of the lodge you will see huge apple, walnut, cherry and apricot trees laced with appetizing produce. I love how the lodge has recycled wheels and used them for plantation and decor. The first time I visited Gilgit city in 2016, I stayed at Capital Lodge which was a decent place by the main road. In my next trip to Fairy Meadows in 2017, I stayed at Heaven Lodge and a week later when I travelled with family we stayed here again. My phuppo and sister loved the gardens, the Gilgit River, the courteous staff and their almost-always working Wi-Fi facility!

Making good use of the adequate internet connection I sent a few pictures to friends and family showing off the views from "my" kitchen! Meanwhile I decided to put my teaching and the little bit of travel experience to good use in this city. So I called up this person I came across through Facebook. When and how? I don't remember clearly. Ehsam Ullah Baig – Founder and CEO of Pakistan Innovation Summit for Education (PISE), a youth based non-profit organization. He is working with peer educators on education, health, mental health, suicide and social development. Ehsam is working to shift the focus of Pakistan's public health education to include family planning and education on multiple issues reoccurring in our society. PISE is a registered NGO under the Societies Registration Act 1961; formed by a group of students in response to the community needs and providing the right of education to all.

In his words, "A lot of people ask me about my job. So the story is, I don't have an office job or anything. I am still an under-graduate student and my job actually is very simple. It is to bring smile on people's face, to make mothers happy and to give them a hope that the days ahead are going to bring peace and happiness in their lives. My job is to bring communities together, my job is to promote peace and love, my job is to make sure that every woman is a leader because she has to lead the upcoming world. My job is to make this world a better place to live. And yes I have the best job." Indeed, he does. He gets to travel and do what he knows best! He speaks passionately about his recent project – Gilgit Baltistan Fellowship Program. "Our 12-day program begins from 12th July. This fellowship is a project by PISE aiming to promote cultural and intellectual dialogues by pooling in people from different parts of Pakistan to nature's escape hub; the beautiful mountains and valleys of GB, and facilitating exchange of ideas and vision, among people of GB and other participants. Hence, contributing towards strengthening the civil society of GB, and Pakistan at large". His long-term plans include setting up an E-Rozgar centre in Gilgit Baltistan, in order to shift GB towards knowledge based economy and running a Digital GB movement. "This platform will empower youth and women to generate income by earning through digital freelancing after being trained at the e-rozgar center," he concluded.

*** Tip:** I don't have trust issues in this region, so I left my room unlocked. It is my personal choice and I would not recommend it. So follow your instinct.

Rayyan and I left the lodge for a walk to grab water, find Phitti and purchase a few essentials. On the way we saw a chirpy woman sitting outside a shop, beside a large aluminum pot of mamtu; one of Gilgit Baltistan's famous must-eat traditional food. Mamtu (dumplings) is a steam cooked dish which is filled with chopped onion, fresh herbs, chilly, garlic and meat (lamb or beef). It is steamed for several hours in a multi-layer steamer. Mamtu is served with soy sauce, vinegar, spiced red sauce or regular ketchup whichever condiment pleases your palate. I purchased water from the same shop and asked for Phitti,

which they told me wasn't available. Once again I crossed
The Gilgit College of Commerce (Since 2004). Their tag line
still eye-catching:

"Preparing Mountain Business Leaders"

*** Tip:** No matter where in the world you travel always try
the road-side dishes. The aroma will always attract you
and the experience is different from what you eat in a
restaurant. The food may taste better.

Wandering through the residential areas, high stone walls,
narrow lanes lined with water channels, all sorts of
vehicles edged their way along, hooting and honking
narrowly dodging other vehicles and pedestrians, gave
Rayyan quite a scare. You will notice men and children
walking around but rarely see women on the roads. Since
Gilgit is home to a number of diversified cultures, ethnic
groups, languages and various backgrounds belonging to
all regions of Gilgit as well as from other cities of Pakistan.
This array of cultures is because of the strategic location
of GB. Being the headquarters of the Gilgit Baltistan
almost all key offices are located in Gilgit city. Being a
multicultural city and there are a lot of different languages
spoken here such as wakhi, shina, burushaski,
khowar/chitrali and Balti. The dwellers follow old
practices and traditions while others enjoy a more modern
lifestyle which is influenced by other ethnicities, and mass
media. Majority of the inhabitants are Muslims who
belong to different communities of interpretations i.e.
Sunnis, Shias, Ismailies. A small number of Christians
also exist here. New constructions in Gilgit are made using
modern designs but majority believes it is not a good very
good idea since "it has no prevention from extreme
weather".I decided to head back to the lodge and call it a
night because we were both extremely tired and needed a
good night sleep. Missing my endless supply of delicious
fruits, I closed my eyes.

Day 08 – Kargah nala and the best trout – 26th June 2018

Plan: *Stay and explore Gilgit. Visit Kargah Nala and Denyore Bridge if possible. Dinner & overnight stay (unsure until when).*

I woke up a little after the sunrise and sat outside. This felt like my ultimate dream home, a spectacular backyard, with stunning backdrop, a gushing river, pleasant weather and pure air. An airplane flew really close to the mountains; a scene I had never witnessed before. The airport was walking distance from where we were staying.

*** Tip:** Not everything can be captured on camera. Often times set your phones and cameras aside and revel in the moments. Trust me you will remember incidences even if they aren't captured on lens.

For breakfast I requested Hamid Karim sahab if we could have Phitti and tea. He smiled, nodded and ordered. He found the best home-made Phitti for us and served it with a nice kettle full of doodh patti chai (milk tea). The people in the mountains here usually add salt in tea instead of sugar and by now I had developed a fondness for it. We literally wolfed down the crusty whole-wheat bread. Meanwhile checking how far Kargah nala is and how much will it cost.

Kargah nala is next to Shuko Gah. Shuko Gah is a stream and is located in GB and the estimate terrain elevation above sea level is 1,591 meters. Kargah valley is at a distance of 10 kilometers from Gilgit with a rock wall carved Buddha, dating back to 8th century AD. Other nearby attractions around the city are Denyore, Bagrot, Nomal, Jaglot, Oshikhandas and the Gilgit Bridge (Chinar bagh Gilgit). The bridge is constructed over the fast flowing Gilgit River, at the end of its traditional bazaar. It is the largest suspension bridge in Asia (182 meters long and 2 meters in width).

The weather changed by the time we stepped out of the dining hall. It was cloudy yet warm. Normally towns like Chilas and Gilgit are hot during the day and cold during the night time. Gilgit has a desert climate with warm summers and cold winters since it is at an altitude of 1,500 meters. During summers temperature above 30 degrees Celsius is common while winters are cold for longer periods with sub-zero temperatures. According to Climate Tracker, *the weather of GB has started changing and has become warmer every year. Summers are becoming longer and warmer than before; heavy snowfall has been recorded in April 2017, in a village Gulmit Hunza which is quite unusual; an increase in heavy rainfalls has been resulting in flooding. Glaciers are melting fast, triggering GLOFs (glacial lake outburst floods) in this region, which is another major concern for the people living in the area.* The locals are concerned about recent melting glaciers which have destroyed their economy and disrupted the social life and mobility. These are the impacts of global warming and will only increase with each passing year.

I asked Hamid sahab if he could suggest and arrange someone reasonable to take us to Kargah nala. And he did. So by mid-day we set off to explore Kargah nala, a place I recently found out about. At a distance of about 8 to 10 kilometers from Gilgit city there is a gorge in the valley of Kargah known as Kargah nala in the local shina language. The nala passes through meadows and meets Gilgit River at Baseen valley. In the primitive times this valley used to be the travelling route for the Buddhist monks to trek to Taxila. A turquoise river flows between mountains offering stunning views. If you are fond of fishing then this is the right place for you, as there are loads of trout in the river. You will notice Kargah Gulmikai written on boards but the place is commonly known as

Kargah nala. The road led us to pull road and we crossed Assembly Hall, Chinar bagh.

*** Tip:** The benefit of travelling in a rented transport is you can choose to stop wherever you please to and for how long. Travelling with a group or a public transport does not give you that advantage.

I started talking to Ghulam Sarwar sahab who was driving us to the nala. He is Hamid Karim's father, and is the owner of a large piece of land in Gilgit. You would not imagine someone like him living in the city doing that for a guest. I learned that much later and couldn't be more grateful and awed at the humbleness. He started telling me about the languages spoken in GB, "Shina is widely spoken in Gilgit, Burushaski in Hunza, Wakhi in Tajikistan, Afghanistan, Punial and even around Kargah nala". He speaks Burushaski and is from Hunza and his forefathers settled here in Gilgit since the British left. "In 1932, my paternal grandfather settled here but we are the people of Hunza", he told me. About the nala he said, "We used to consume this water in our homes but not anymore, since this place is not clean any longer. Pakistani people are not conscious or sympathetic towards the environment, littering everywhere even the waters. It is in our hands to protect and preserve our spectacular land. If you notice the weather of Gilgit in summers is more or less like Karachi. The only difference is if it gets warmer here it rains and the weather becomes pleasant. Mornings are better, afternoons are warm and you will observe that in the evenings the weather transforms, either it will be windy or it will rain". Talking about Karachi he said, "One of my daughters is doing her Bachelors in Science and working in Agha Khan Hospital in Karachi and will visit soon for vacations. My *bahu* (daughter in law) is from Clifton Karachi too; my wife and my *bahu's* mother are both sisters. One of my wife's sister is in Karachi too and we visit them once in 2 years". I had to ask him the patent question, what he feels about Karachi and its people. His response was, "Karachi used to be really good, but now it is much polluted, the sanitary conditions are very poor but the Defence area seems better". By now we had entered the nala premises and the weather had changed considerably. It was drizzling and brisk wind blowing. "People here take their domestic animals up into the greener pastures towards the end of the nala, where you trek upwards and bring them back in winters. Long ago this water course streamed till Heaven Lodge, when it was still a village. Now the place has urbanized. At that time, we enjoyed clean and clear water with plenty of trout fish but it is contaminated now and you won't find as many fish here. The clean water of the mountain is pure and strengthening and so was Kargah", he said sadly. "On the way back I will take you to the site where the famous Kargah Buddha is". As you roll up the rocky path embedded with small rocks scattered randomly, along the brilliant turquoise ravine you will notice power houses and Ghulam sahab told me he has worked in a couple of them. He pointed, "Do you see the boards Hydro Powerhouse Gulmikai Kargah and there are 7 such phases. I have worked in the power house phase 3 and 4. People living near this nala are called gujars who nurture cattle only".

The sources of water supply in Gilgit include lakes, springs, reservoirs and ground water. Glacial melt is the primary source of water supply in this region, which flows in the form of nalas and they eventually discharge into the Gilgit River. The main nalas in and around the city are Jutial, Konudas, Kargah and Denyore. The Jutial Nala provides the city with most of its irrigation and drinking water. The Hunza River flows from the north and joins the Gilgit River at the Duo Pani. The Gilgit-Hunza confluence occurs near Karakoram International University. "River flow is highest from July to September when snow melts in the mountains. Substantial rains result in landslides, heavy flooding and high turbulence in river water", he added as our vehicle came to a halt. We stepped out of the car to enjoy the foaming stream of clear turquoise water, feel the air and click pictures and that's when it started pouring. This place did not seem like an established tourist point which was quite a blessing. As you drive up further it changes to a sparkling and deeper shade of turquoise. The beauty of the nala bordered with trees, green pastures and many different kinds of intriguing birds was undeniable. My first impression of the place was this gorge can easily become a magnet for tourists, bird watchers, environmentalists and eco-innovators who are dedicated to the idea of living in harmony with nature. We stayed at the nala for almost an hour but the road deteriorates as it heads up. Zero maintenance, absolute negligence from the local Government after the recent flooding has left this area with unpaved road, large boulders and broken metallic pieces of old foot bridge. We stopped again and I really wanted to dip my feet in the water and quench my thirst.

*** Tip:** There is a thin line between being adventurous and putting your life in danger. And if a local / sign board / public notice cautions you not to take any chances DON'T. Never put your and others life in danger for a mere self-portrait or challenging yourself to the limits in the name of "adventure".

I asked Ghulam sahab if I could sit on this gigantic rock in the middle of the nala, he nodded and stood guard over both of us. I climbed up, dipping feet in the cold gushing water, puffs of spindrift blowing in my face. I sat there for quite some time, not ready to leave at all. Normally if you hire a local car service the drivers are impatient and irritated, but this elderly proprietor was quite relaxed and civil. He also offered to take pictures, filled our water bottle and started removing rocks to pave the way for the car to pass. Not taking advantage of his kindness we decided to head back. I asked him if we could find fresh trout for lunch. He said, "I will drive you to a sanctuary and get the best trout for you, which will be served to you at the lodge". Anxious and excited we drove to the sanctuary close to the nala where he spoke to some person who handed him a small bag full of fresh trout. I kept asking him how much I owe him but he simply refused to say.

Kargah nala is one of the best places for trout rearing in GB and has two renowned hatcheries that serve as the best recreational fishing spot near Gilgit city. The trees and shrubs found along the Kargah include Fraxinus, Salix, Olea, Pistacia, Juniperus, Kail, Picea, Betula, Rosa, and Daphnes oleides. Ground cover consists of Artemisia, Stipa, Haloxylon, and other grass species. Large mammals found in the area include the Astore Markhor, Musk Deer, Ibex and Snow Leopard which are listed as endangered.

From there we headed towards the Kargah rock-carved Buddha from 7th century AD. There is a rock wall carved Buddha on a cliff known to be sculpted in 7th century and excavated in 1938-1939. The local mythology about the Buddha tells of a tale recounting that an ogress named Yakhsni was devoured by a man who lived at Kargah. A monastery and three stupas were excavated at about half a kilometer from the Buddha. These prehistoric carving and stupas are only 6 kilometers from Gilgit, not accessible to visitors. The Buddhist manuscripts found here are among the oldest in the world. They are significant in Buddhist studies and in the evolution of Asian and Sanskrit literature. At present majority of the inhabitants here are Muslims belonging to different communities of interpretations i.e. Sunnis, Shias and Ismailies. A small number of Christians also reside in Gilgit. For religious practices Sunnis go to the Masjid, Shias go to Imam Bargah and Ismailies attend the Jamatkhana.

From Kargah buddha you can stroll down towards the colourful marketplace and the famed suspended bridge. The suspension bridge over the fast flowing Gilgit River is 182 meters long and said to be the largest in Asia (so far at least). If you are lucky you may witness the notable polo team of Gilgit practicing the game. Gilgit is known to have the most outstanding team of polo. The polo grounds in the city hold polo matches and other traditional festivals of the area. The festivals attract ordinary tourists and dignitaries from the world over.

On our way back to the lodge Ghulam Sarwar sahab asked if we wished to visit the market to which I expressed my longing for fruits. He needed to buy some vegetables and I wanted fresh fruit. Gilgit has a large open market which is both a commercial center and a clearance house for merchandises that come from China using the KKH route. A chaotic place with a collection of small shops next to each other with their produces exhibited in crammed racks facing the streets. The bazaar is more than just rows of shops in the alleys and lanes; you will see numerous warehouses and workshops. You may find this place often filthy, wide ditches with stinking water puddles and waste of the market; pieces of rotten vegetables, fruits, pieces of tattered newspapers, discarded cartons, broken or strewn bottles and fresh slaughtered chicken attracting flies and stray dogs. I ended up buying delicious juicy treats; cherries, apricots and fresh figs. The figs didn't taste as good as they looked.

Back at the lodge, Hamid Karim sahab told us he will serve the best trout we have ever eaten. The last time I tried this particular fish was in Naran and it definitely seemed overrated then. Much to my astonishment trout was very elegantly served garnished with freshly sliced carrots, tomatoes and bell pepper. It was slightly crunchy on the outside, gently fried and very little salt, keeping the natural flavours of the fish alive. You normally get this fish in Naran, Kaghan, Kalam, Phander valley and Skardu; heavily flavoured, dripping oil or crispy until the skin is completely charred. We were both starving and it was worth the wait. Savouring the smell of the delectable food on our platter, we decided to eat outside in our garden with the river view. It was warm but cloudy and our palate loved every bit of the trout. The only thing left in our plate was the angry looking head. Dense clouds drifted as the weather changed to imperceptibly breezy. I thanked the people for the delicious food and ordered a cup of steaming doodh patti chai (milk tea). We walked to the other side of the rail where Rayyan decided to show off his balancing skills by the narrow fence and click pictures of the exhibitionist. The tranquility and serenity here was a sharp contrast to the road on the flip-side of the lodge, with cars whizzing by.

Since we were staying here the night it was a good opportunity to do laundry. Rayyan helped me lay the clothes flat to dry on the chairs outside. I make sure I assign tasks and responsibilities to my little one even on our trips, to ensure it doesn't ever come as a burden to him. It was almost 6 p.m. and we decided to hit the road. When I travel I make sure I make the best out of the day and sightsee as much as I can. It bothers my son that we are always on the go but poor thing has no other choice.

* **Tip:** Keep at least a small pack/sachet of detergent powder or a small bar of soap in case you find a place, time and the right sunshine to wash and dry your clothing.

Today we decided to explore the other side of the lodge, where I have never walked before. Going up the road we saw boys playing football in a patch full of tall swaying trees and a little graveyard next to it. That's a common sight in the mountains, you will notice small graveyards with 2 or more graves lined up next to homes or fields. We stayed and watched them play then moved further away and I spotted a school The Oxford House – Montessori School System. An old but seemingly renovated building with the upper portion still under construction had a lot to offer for kids and adults. Claiming to train teachers professionally, providing activity-based learning center and out-of-the-book project-based learning facilities. I decided to visit it the next morning to find out more. I was looking at Gilgit from a completely different perspective and really wanted to get to know this town. Not many places are open all the time, some shopkeepers close up early, as they believe to return home early and spend quality time with their family. Most eating places will not serve food before sunset and not everything on the menu is available as some ingredients are out of stock. You will find car wash services on this side of the road lined up with thick trees, a Government hospital that looked reasonably clean from the outside, many pharmacies with a good supply of standardized medicines and dry-cleaning facilities.

*** Tip:** It is always beneficial to know of a hospital / clinic / pharmacy close to where you are staying especially if you are travelling with children or in case of any unforeseen emergency.

As the sun goes down you will see less activity on the road, lesser vehicles and people. On reaching the guesthouse I was offered to visit the Denyore Suspension Bridge while there was still some day light left. I would never miss a chance and agreed but Rayyan was quiet exhausted and preferred to stay back with his book and a pack of chips. The distance between Heaven Lodge and Denyore was 4.7 kilometers. It took us not more than 15 minutes to reach the place. Denyore Suspension Bridge is the oldest makeshift suspension bridges in this region. This bridge connects Denyore to the premises of the Karakoram University across the Hunza River. The bridge was closed for vehicles but open for pedestrians. But there was a concrete bridge constructed besides it as an alternative, which was built in 2013. This bridge constructed over a half century ago, enters a tunnel constructed by locals without any proper civil engineering equipment. I like walking on bridges; it's a daunting experience, whether it's a suspension bridge such as this or a hanging bridge like Hussaini Hanging Bridge. Last year I crossed the precarious rope bridge hanging high above the surging Hunza River, known to be the most dangerous bridge in the world with 43 meters in height and 193 meters long. Denyore Bridge on the other hand is not as rickety. It stands 510 feet-long connected to a 10-metre curve tunnel. It looked phenomenal under moonlight. The river rolling lazily, flanked by patchworks of tiny looking fields and dwellings. Surveying the grandeur, I pondered over my existence, the insignificant speck on the surface of the creation.

After being declared unsafe by the district administration this bridge is closed for vehicles and only pedestrians are allowed to pass through, so we walked all the way to the other side crossing the tunnel to a small trail of poplar trees. It was a quiet peaceful 1 hour I spent there soaking in the soft moon light and listening to the roaring river, unwinding and relaxing.

Returned back around 10 p.m. I spoke to Ehsam who told me to visit Café Dinals which was being run by two brothers, a concept not established in Gilgit yet. Hence, decided to stay another day in Gilgit before dozing off to sleep.

* **Tip:** Never try to kill a cockroach or similar kind of insect with perfume or body spray. They don't cease to exist that way. Screaming does not help either. You must call in someone to exterminate them – and fast!

Day 9 – Gilgit City – 27th June 2018

Plan: *Stay and explore a school in Gilgit, meet people, walk towards the airport; dinner & overnight stay.*

My schedule for today was to meet people, visit Dinals Café and the school I had spotted last evening, The Oxford House – Montessori School System which was a few steps away from the lodge. It was a warm cloudy day and we set off right after breakfast. Even though it was warm but it was not humid as Karachi. It was easy to walk into the Principal's office unlike the series of procedure you need to follow in most cities of Pakistan.

Although the couple running this school was originally from Lahore, I received a warm welcome and a chance to talk to them. Their children were studying abroad and after launching the school here they decided to stay here. The couple, quite young at heart, enjoy exploring nearby areas. The lady told me, "You must visit Phander and Naltar, you will simply love these places." The couple seemed very passionate and dedicated to their cause. Their 7 course package for children claimed to; enhance IQ level, vocabulary, listening and speaking, ethics, creative writing, presentation and general knowledge about the world. A lot more they claim to deliver as mentioned, independence, confidence, control & inner peace, self-esteem, rationalizing, compassion, empathy and tolerance. And I hope and pray they achieve it with excellence through their honesty, perseverance and commitment. Rayyan and I left saying goodbye to the happy couple and headed out in search of some desi-food. Being so far from home we missed home cooked Karachi veges. Fortunately, a small hotel near a pharmacy was preparing some good smelling lady's finger also called okra. The hotel also had a fresh batch of Mamtu in the large multi-layer steamer. So we bought a little of each for our lunch. From a nearby bakery we bought water and Arzoq (bread made from flour, eggs, butter and milk) that

Rayyan had grown to love. Back home, the guest house doesn't mind us bringing food from outside. I asked Hamid sahab if I could send my jacket for dry-cleaning and have it back the next day. He said that won't be a problem at all.

* **Tip:** I usually carry sachets of 3 in 1 tea and coffee for moments when I suffer agonies of instant caffeine cravings. Simply ask the kitchen people if they can provide plain hot water.

* A known fact: At higher altitudes, air pressure is lower. When atmospheric pressure is lower (at a higher altitude), it takes less energy to bring water to the boiling point. Less energy means less heat, which means water will boil at a lower temperature at a higher altitude. So, have patience.

I let my little one have coffee or tea when vacationing although he is fond of green tea and Kashmiri (pink) tea too. So after food we wandered around with our coffee mugs, looking at all the different kinds of insects' dragonflies, bees and flies, beetles, spiders, locusts and grasshoppers – getting accustomed to them and not shrieking in fear every time one landed on or near us.

* **Tip:** Don't ever transfer your fears into your children. The way we react becomes their inner-voice.

We had been noticing a home next to our guesthouse which has things hanging on its gate every day. A day before they had towels of all sizes drying out and today was a pair of blue canvas shoes on the metal rods sticking out from above the gate.

Just around 3 p.m. I got a call from Ehsam who gave me the number of one of the owners of Dinals, Wajid bhai. I called him to confirm my availability and we settled on the time he will send his driver to pick me. After I hung up we decided to rest for a while as it was still warm and cloudy that afternoon. Once inside I noticed tiny bumps all over Rayyan's body, which I hadn't noticed the previous day and wondered what it was. He wasn't scratching them but felt uncomfortable. Confused and uncertain, I decided to take him to the Government hospital close to our lodge. Upon reaching Shaheed Saif-ur-Rehman Government Hospital, I found out there was no doctor in the emergency and we were misled from one direction to another. Finally, someone on duty suggested I take him to the rear side of the hospital where normally there is a doctor and nurses. There were a bunch of ladies sitting on hospital beds in a room, and informed me that I was in the maternity ward and there was no doctor on-duty. I don't know why but I asked them if they had ever had any experience with a condition like this. One of them looked at me and perkily replied, "I only have experience in delivering a child. If you want, I can do that!" And the others including myself laughed at her spontaneous but corny joke! I thanked them and left. I went back to the on-duty gentleman who offered to take a look and then said, "It's nothing, just apply any anti-itch cream on it and avoid cleansing with soap". Sort of relieved I thanked him and left.

So internet is a blessing as well, where your phone networks don't work. I asked one of my doctor cousins' for reassurance, advice and recommendation, she told me to simply apply some Hydrocortisone. Completely relieved now!

* **Tip:** I normally travel with an Anti-Itch (Hydrocortisone) 1% Topical cream and a 'tick the wilderness' formula – an insect repellant spray. Avoid self-medication.

Upon returning I calculated how many more days left before I had to join the group for Rakaposhi basecamp trek. *So, on the 30th I have to join my Climax Adventure group at Karimabad, Hunza which means I have almost 3 days left to travelling on my own. So the next best option would be Gulmit – let's see how close it is from here.*

Hmmm…Google maps…nice idea. Ok, so if I stay in Gulmit for two days and leave early morning on the 30th I will reach Karimabad in maximum 2 hours and join the group. I can call up Gulmit Tourist Inn (where I stayed last year as well) and make reservations first then get my bus tickets. Yayyyyyy!!!

Instinctively I called up Fazl Karim sahab at Gulmit Tourist Inn – Gulmit and asked him for a room. I reminded him I had stayed at the inn last year and requested if I could get a budget-friendly room. He agreed looking at my desperation when I asked for "a single mattress or single-bed room that my son and I will manage to sleep on".

* **Tip:** It is best to save as many contact numbers on your cellphone before you start your journey, especially if you are alone. That should include emergency contacts as well.

The weather had turned slightly pleasant so we walked around the rail again, starring at the river that flowed and the road that can be seen from where we were standing. There was still time before we had to leave for the café so I decided to wash a few more clothes. Washed, cleaned, rested, showered and ready by 6 p.m. and waiting anxiously to be picked. Sajid, Wajid's brother picked us up and took us to a lovely, brightly lit café. I liked the décor which was simple yet a tad bit spunk. The small bar decorated elegantly with fancy lights, flanked by wooden stools, walls embellished with small catchphrases and showpieces with spotlights hanging above them. On Wajid bhai's insistence to order, I ordered a coffee and Rayyan wanted honey-glazed chicken wings. Both tasted really good. The culture here, I felt, is to stay at home after dark, spend time with family more than with friends. Girl boy intermingling is less as compared to other parts of the country. There is a sense of respect and trivial relations seem less. Since fast food places are not common, people are not accustomed to café cum coffee-shop culture, yet their efforts were commendable. As a tourist I expect restaurants and hotels to serve local food rather than the metropolitan cuisines. However, local tourists demand convenient food that is available in urban areas, such as club sandwiches, pizzas, French fries and burgers.

We had a good 2-hour long conversation about the area, travel points, food trends, Photoshop, menu design, café interior, school systems and Rupani Foundation – A charity organization (an NGO) which was established in 2007, by Mr. Nasruddin Rupani and Family. The Foundation's objectives are to *create economic opportunities through Skill Development and to provide services in the field of Early Childhood Development in the remote and marginalized communities of developing countries.* Their vision is to make a sustainable society for future generations and to create economic opportunities, knowledgeable leadership, and 'aristocracies of merit' for the relegated communities and populace, including women and youth. Rupani's headquarter is in Gilgit. Another project for women, the future stone masons, will start the training under the National Technical and Vocational Education and Training (TVET) program deep in the Hunza Valley. The project is being implemented by Rupani Foundation, with the support of German donor agency, GIZ. The project in stone masonry has been launched to support labour markets in the region as a component of the TVET Reform Support Program which was co-funded by the European Union, the Embassy of the Kingdom of the Netherlands and the Federal Republic of Germany. Stone work has largely been a profession for men, who are traditionally considered to be strong and more capable of using chisels, pitchers and hammers. I was imagining women clad in traditional shawls and hitting white stones with hammers and chisels. These women may very well be carving their way into history. I told Sajid that I wished to visit the foundation if it was doable the next morning. He agreed to inform me early morning if the plan would materialize. Wajid bhai packed the remaining chicken wings for us and again insisted if we would like to order anything else to go with it. I politely declined for I already felt guilty of them dropping us back to the lodge at that time. It was 8:30 p.m. when we proceeded back to the guesthouse.

I had to make a few purchases for the breakfast, and an hour later we walked to the almost closing bakeries a few steps away from Heaven Lodge. One bakery cum shop had a whole loaf of the crusty bread, which the shopkeeper claimed was "the closest to home baked Phitti".

That night I could hardly put myself to sleep for I was particularly thrilled about travelling to my second most favourite destination – Gulmit. Last year we reached Gulmit before the sunset and left early morning the following day. And that brief stay left a lasting impression on me; the stone walls, tall swaying trees, lush green pastures, the simplicity and the humbleness of people, and not to forget the history of Attabad lake.

Day 10 – Continued – Gulmit – My second home away from home – 28th June 2018
Plan: *Stay and explore Gulmit village visit Old House – Gulmit Carpet Centre, Museum and Bulbulik School that I missed last year. Meet people, walk; dinner & overnight stay until the morning of 30th June.*

The first time I journeyed on my own was in 2013 and Google helped me a lot in searching for places around Islamabad. After that I preferred travelling with small groups and I never looked up places I was journeying to. I always wanted to be surprised and learn about them on the go. This time it was different since I was completely on my own with a 7-year-old, but of course there were many kind people around for assistance and advice.

*** Tip:** Don't expect every place to have electricity, internet and warm water facilities. Make the best out of them wherever you may find them. Shower today if there is warm water. Take screenshots of maps etc. or save information you may need later.

That morning I requested Hamid Karim sahab to arrange for a transport to take us to Gulmit. He was kind enough to offer to drop us himself to the bus stand if nothing else was available. He said, "Don't worry sister the bus leaves around 1 p.m. and if nothing else is available I will drop you myself and make sure you get a comfortable place in the bus. Meanwhile have breakfast and pack up." So we did. The loaf of bread (Phitti) I bought last night with tea had become our patent breakfast choice. One last walk around the area was a must. Before leaving for a walk towards the Gilgit airport I reminded him to see if he could ask someone to collect my jacket. He had sent it to the NLI market close to where the lodge was. The distance from the Lodge to NLI market was approximately 4.2 kilometers.

NLI Market – Named after 'The Northern Light Infantry' or NLI regiment of Pakistan army, the market is where one can find Chinese goods of all kinds. With more than 700 shops, the market is situated in the heart of Gilgit city, the capital of Gilgit Baltistan, a mountainous region with a population of 1.5 million people. The traders in Gilgit would rather step across the border to get their goods than undertake the 1,900 kilometers (27-hour journey) to the port town of Karachi, Pakistan's commercial hub. The marker was built in 1992 to support families of soldiers and officers of the NLI. The infantry regiment of Pakistan army based in Gilgit, is primarily responsible for protecting the strategic northern areas that touch China, India and Afghanistan. *The infantry, a paramilitary force till 1999, has a long history traced back to the native militia and scout's infantry raised by the local rulers of the region in early 20th century and trained by the British Indian Army. It was last in the news for its role in the 1999 Kargil War with India for which it was awarded the "Presidential Colours" and turned from a paramilitary force into a regular army unit.* When the army first started building this market, businessmen from the neighbouring Khyber Pakhtunkhwa province who were already trading in Chinese goods leapt at the opportunity. They knew the importance of NLI being the hub for trade between China. Out of 300 shops constructed in the first phase, over 80% were hired by businessmen from KPK. Soon enough, the market expanded with investment from the local businessmen and currently an equal number of proprietors are local Gilgitis.

Leaving a place always depresses me and I haven't found a place yet which I am desperate to leave. Instinctively before proceeding further I take one last walk around the neighbourhood. It was partly cloudy and sunny. We just walked around the airport with no entrance or aircraft in sight. Rayyan spotted a brown locust on the ground as we walked away from the airport. Down the road to our lodge

we walked quietly when Rayyan pointed to a white Corolla and asked me to click a picture with it. It said: **I m 18!**
At the reception of Heaven Lodge, Hamid sahab asked me for my ID card so he could finalize the invoice and it occurred to me, how I never filled a form nor did he ever ask for any identification upon my arrival and just let me stay. I was all packed so I decided to call my parents before leaving. Meanwhile, I sat outside on the steps and called whoever I could, knowing my cellphone connection dies in Gulmit. By 12 p.m. Hamid sahab was ready to drop us to the bus stand himself and handed me the payment receipt as he helped put our stuff in the car. I couldn't find my wallet, not in my handbag, pockets, bag, nowhere. I went back to my room to check – nowhere. I checked at the reception too – not there either. *Oh my God! All my money, my debit card, my identification card is in it!* I panicked. Just then I remembered I may have dropped it in the verandah. Praying and hoping it is still there. And there it was my bright red wallet half an hour later after I dropped it, where I dropped it and how I dropped it. For a moment the Karachitte in me was speechless. Adrenaline spun through me and I am not exaggerating that feeling. Nothing in my wallet was missing. I went back to the car and told Hamid sahab, "It was there where I had dropped it." He smiled broadly and remarked "I knew you would find it, nothing here ever goes missing sister." I told Rayyan and being born and bred in Karachi he looked deeply at me and said, "See I told you people are so honest and kind here unlike Karachi!" We both knew that already! Last year my Phuppo (paternal aunt) left her waist bag in Karimabad twice with her passport and money and every time someone found it for her.

* **Tip:** Take care of your belongings to avoid getting yourself and others in distress.
On the way Hamid sahab told me, "I completed my studies from Islamabad. Basically I am from Hunza and now we live and work in Gilgit city." I told him that his place is

truly magnificent, our stay was extremely comfortable as always, the trout he served us was delicious and my son and I feel quite secure here. He pointed out at the Heli Chowk, near FCNA Head Quarter, Zulfiqarabad, Jutial, Gilgit City. The chopper on display that I had seen a couple of times before, and was told that it's the captured Indian Army Chetak helicopter. "Many stories are linked to this chopper," he said. "Indians claim that it crash landed in Pakistan. However, the reality is it landed during a mission in Gilgit Baltistan for a special mission in 1999 and Pakistan Army captured it. As the Indian pilots attempted to escape, they were overpowered by Major Ali Jan Orakzai and apprehended him."

"On the opposite side there is the Aga Khan Shahi Polo ground and Radio Pakistan Gilgit". He seemed to be enjoying playing guide. Our car slowed down and he asked me about the VIP culture in Karachi. I told him about the obvious road block even if it was a not-very-important minister. He pointed to a bunch of cars on my right, "That is GB's current Chief Minister Hafiz Hafeez-ur- Rehman, with a small protocol. If he blocks the road for traffic the people of Gilgit will beat him up", he laughed then continued, "No VIP culture exists here like in other cities. He has come to check the road because by June all road construction has to be complete. We have a limited time frame and normally ministers get little or no chance for corruption. And it will be his responsibility if there is any default in construction. People will question him why he did not inspect during the development. Also the debris will be cleaned up right away". We crossed Police Headquarters Gilgit, Supreme Appellate Court GB and GB Assembly. In less than an hour we reached the bus stand where the bus was to leave for Gulmit. Karim sahab helped me get the bus tickets, made sure our luggage was placed safely on top of the bus and we were comfortable in our seats and ready to go before he waved us goodbye. Sitting in the front row behind the driver's seat, I whispered under my breath, *this trip is an experience I won't regret – a journey that will stay with me forever.*

Once again back on KKH enroute to Gulmit. It is approximately 144 kilometers from Gilgit and a scenic 3-and-a-half-hour drive. A woman named Fatima was travelling towards Aliabad, Hunza to attend her friend's engagement. "I am already running late and they are all waiting for me to reach as soon as possible", she said anxiously. She is doing her MPhil from Peshawar University and teaching as a visiting faculty too. A young foreigner from England was travelling with us as well, who had "1983" tattooed on his forearm. He re-counted his journey, "I started my expedition from Lahore on a bike that I bought from there. Motorcycled from Babusar to Chillas, Chitral to Skardu and Phander, entered Gilgit and sold off my bike there. Now I am heading towards Sost to enter China and continue my journey. I have been in Pakistan since last two months now and every check-post asks me for a police card that I don't have. They insist on a police escort which I don't feel I need, nor do I want. In Chitral, I came across Army check points who also insisted I should have a soldier escorting me", he sighed.

I silently prayed the driver would stop for a break so I could purchase fruit. We briefly made a stop at Aliabad, dropped Fatima who was praying the whole way to reach her destination in time for her friend's engagement. I wished her and her friend good luck before she eagerly stepped out of the bus. I have always loved and enjoyed this route from Aliabad to Gulmit, crossing familiar places like Karimabad – Ganish – Altit (mostly boards pointing to these places) – Haldeikish Sacred rocks of Hunza, which I always wished to stop and take a closer look at. It is 39.3 kilometers away from Gulmit. That is one downside of travelling in a public transport. Although you save money but you cannot have stopovers where you desire.

* **Tip:** In all these years I have learnt if you really want something you will figure out one way or the other to make it possible. (I am talking about Haldeikish rocks not fruit!)

The driver gave us a 10-minute break to make some purchases and luckily I found a fruit shop and bought cherries – the only decent looking fruit. From Aliabad we picked two young girls, both returning home, one of them to Gulmit, the other to Khyber. They introduced themselves as Shagufta Naz and Shehnaz. Shehnaz initiated the conversation with the same curiosity as others. Where are you from? What do you do? Where are you going? Is this your first time here? And the most important of all, how do you like it here? She told me that she is studying in Islamabad and is in the final year of her bachelors and going home for vacations. She offered me to stay with her, "No one ever comes to our village." Unfortunately, I forgot the name of her village. When Rayyan pointed at Attabad, (by now he knows names of mountains, rivers and lakes), both the girls offered to take pictures and make small videos for him.

Attabad Lake – most popularly known as the landslide disaster

On January 4, 2010, in the remote Hunza Valley of Northern Pakistan a massive landslide buried the village of Attabad, destroying no less than 26 houses and killed 20 people. The landslide blocked the Hunza River and formed an extensive lake which according to the National Disaster Management Authority is more than 6.8 miles (11 kilometers) long, around 215 feet (65 meters) deep and is rising up to 1.5 feet (46 centimeters) a day. The obstruction of Hunza River caused five villages north of the barrier to be swamped with water. One village, Ayeenabad, was completely submerged. The debris obstructed nearly 1.2 miles (2 kilometers) of the once fast-flowing river and a longer stretch of the highway, a popular high-altitude route for backpackers that cuts through stunning snowcapped peaks. Major portions of another village Shishkat, was also submerged and around 40% of Gulmit was flooded too. Large portions of land in Hussaini and Ghulkin villages of Gojal were also drowned and a lake came into existence. The lake isolated 25,000

people in Gojal (upper Hunza) from the rest of the country. The villagers lost their land, homes, dispensaries, fruit orchards and agricultural products. The calamity caused damage to the educational system of Gojal. Food had to be delivered by boats and rafts, which was also used as transportation. Relief aid and major food staple items were provided by Chinese Government for almost 4 years. The turquoise lake offers an amazing experience with breathtaking scenery, where you can witness life under water that existed before the disaster struck the place – tall trees and rooftops of homes and Jamatkhana are clearly visible from various angles.
Gulmit Tourist Inn has pictures displayed on their wall at the reception area which is a reminder for all and a conversation starter. A panoramic lake with a sad history.

The driver knew where to drop us and parked the bus right in front of Gulmit Tourist Inn. Excited and tired we boarded off the bus, collected our bags and checked in at the hotel. Fazl Karim sahab wasn't there but he had arranged our accommodation in the same room I had stayed in last year. Warm water and Wi-Fi is a major concern for local tourists and so we were told. I don't mind being disconnected from the world and a chance to connect with nature instead. A humble looking abode and people with no airs, is what makes a lone female with a 7-year-old right at home. Gulmit has always enticed me with its simplicity, the glorious views of the grand Passu cathedrals and I couldn't wait to go out for a walk. Normally there is major shortage of electricity in the mountains and until the sun shines you don't really need it. I just couldn't wait to step out on the highest paved road in the world – the Karakoram Highway. Fresh crisp air, the Inn skirted with generous amounts of roses in a variety of colours, apple, apricot and cherry trees and my eternally memorable *takht* (wooden bench) under the willow tree. Vivid memories flashed back as I set my eyes on the *takht*. Back in 2017, when I stayed here with my family, the night was freezing cold; I was sitting on the *takht* by myself with my coffee and Bounty, a lantern hanging above. A family sitting around the bonfire roaring with laughter, two young women dressed in sports ensemble apparently having a serious discussion with their coach, a wakhi song playing in the distance and 2 or 3 young men dancing to the rhythm in a shop within the boundaries of the inn. I had to seize the moment and so I did. To this day the fond memories of that night are etched so deeply in my mind. We leave a little slice of our heart in every place we visit and make deeper memories and connections with the places and people we meet on the road that most people achieve in a lifetime.

Watch out when you cross the road from here and it is best that you walk along the water channel. You may be mesmerized by the magnificent Passu cones but be sure to walk close to the edge of the road. Gulmit is surrounded by towering mountains; Tupopodon on the extreme north, while Ghawush on the south. Standing tall in the east is Mount Pulpul, and rising in the west is Gulmit Tower, right above the Shutubar Glacier. Gulmit Tower is one of the several summits toward the end of the long ridge running east from Ultar, has yet to be climbed. We started our walk towards the Attabad Lake. This place generally offers serenity and tranquility which provides the real peace of mind and soul. The only sound that breaks the silence is the piercing echoes of vehicles swishing by. Walking close to the ruins we heard drums in the distance and started following the sound. The beat of the drums got closer and I spotted a campsite with a colourful boat in the background. Hesitantly I entered a small wooden gate with Rayyan towing behind. Two young guys and an elderly man were having a small jamming session, and paused to welcome us with broad smiles and offered us to sit down. I initiated the conversation by introducing myself. Jan sahab who was unable to speak was playing the drums with his hands and the other two were students of Bulbulik music school. Nawaz was singing while Basit was beating the drums with a stick before we intruded. They played a little for us and said that they practice just about every day in the evening. I didn't want to disrupt their practice and got up to leave and they politely asked us to join them at night if we are still around. I smiled at their invitation and agreed to try my best if the weather conditions permitted. I was already feeling cold as the evening loomed closer. We started walking towards the fields where we saw an aged but perfectly hale and hearty Bibi Marjaan. Her soft wrinkled hands clad in thick green and yellow gloves, cutting crops for her cow. She shook hands with us and tried telling me she could not speak or understand Urdu. I was able to use my gesture and expressions to communicate and told her that my son and I are here to visit and stay for a few days. I sought her permission to take a picture of her with my son before proceeding to leave. Wearing her traditional hand knitted cap under her white headscarf, which is quite a norm here, she maintained a gentle smile until we hugged and parted ways. On the way uphill towards Hunza Marcopolo Inn we met Shagufta harvesting vigorously. She couldn't speak Urdu very well but in fragments asked if I like her village? I admiringly looked around and told her how much I love coming and staying here, mentioning it is my second time here and I know I will be visiting every year.

I moved further and saw two women working among the potato fields, cropping grass for their cattle too. They waved and gestured me to wait for them. "Assalaamu Alaikum baji, how are you?" they smiled, greeted and shook hands. Noori Bakht and Doori Bakht introduced themselves cheerfully and I complimented them how everyone has such interesting and unusual names, to which they simultaneously laughed cheerfully. Normally people are curious to know where have you come from and where are you staying before offering a cup of tea. I told them I was exploring the place and want to visit Old House and Bulbulik. They suggested my guesthouse people should call and ask before I set out to visit them for they must be both closed at this time. It was past 5 O'clock. I wished them well and continued to walk uphill.

*** Tip:** Hug or shake hands with the locals, only if you feel comfortable, otherwise stick to your congenial smile. In most places men and women may or may not shake hands with the same or opposite gender for varied reasons.

From there we walked towards Hunza Marcopolo Inn – a place relatively distinguished for their outstanding facilities and like many lodgings in the area assure satisfaction with incredible hospitality. The place reflects the grace and elegance of the royal family of Hunza and was founded by Raja Bahadur Khan, grandson of Mir Nazeem Khan (KCIE, KCSL), the ruler of Hunza from 1892 to 1938. You will notice the historical details and the family tree mounted on the wall at the reception. Raja Hussain Khan, son of Raja Bahadur Khan is the present General Manager of Hunza Marcopolo Inn. I did not get to meet him but I got a chance to speak to him about the place. Raja Hussain Ali Khan informed me, "Marcopolo Inn was established in 1986. It was founded by Mr. Raja Bahadur Khan who back then was a tour guide with Walijs Travels. He led an expedition team to Nanga Parbat in his youth and had a great passion for preserving relics. The president of Wajlis Travels and Chairman Pakistan Tourism Corporation visited Gulmit in 1983 and suggested he should turn his old traditional Wakhi home into a display center. Thus the idea of collecting the antiques, traditional dresses, Hunza's historical musical instruments, ancient cooking utensils, weapons and other relics started. Hunza Marcopolo Inn's Cultural Museum has a unique collection of stuffed snow leopard, firearms, gems and historical guns".
Raja Hussain sahab says, "We started with 5 rooms only but now we have 30 rooms and we offer a traditional homestay and by 2019 eight yurts will be operational." A year later in a conversation he told me, "My father Raja Bahadur Khan passed away in the last week of August

(2019) at the age of 85. He was the grandson of ex-Mir of Hunza state and the owner of Marcopolo Inn and cultural museum. "He has written a book called 'The Stories of Hunza'. We are trying to finalize and proofread the book before sending it to print", he said.

The Inn is surrounded by breathtaking views of mountain peaks and glaciers. Located in the ancient village of Gulmit Hunza, it is on the ancient Silk Route. Only 150 kilometers from Gilgit, it is easily accessible from the Karakoram Highway. You enter the unbolted gates into the fragrant attractive gardens with apricot, pear, apple, cherry trees laced with fruit; an ancient walnut tree, thick mulberry trees in the backyard and flower blossoms bordering the inn. The interior reflects a traditional style of architecture. "The Inn offers thirty clean, comfortable and completely carpeted rooms, ensuite bathroom with hot and cold running water that comes from a nearby mountain spring", says Ali who we met at the reception. Enter the dining hall that renders a traditional and elegant atmosphere. "We offer our guests a series of local and continental dishes cocked by our expert chefs", Ali continues. "Delicacies include traditional pancakes served with mulberry syrup (which is a must-try must-have) as well as strawberries. Fresh local fruit is also available in spring and summer and can be picked from our garden. You may help yourself to any fruit you like", Ali offered.
Rayyan looked at me for approval before asking Ali, "Can I please have mulberry? I love it … it's my favourite fruit". Ali smiled brightly and said, "Have as much as you want and you can take some with you." And that is exactly what a 7-year-old wants! I asked Ali if we could visit the famous Cultural Museum at this time since it was past 5 o'clock. He informed that he needs to look for the keys and asked us to enjoy mulberry until he returns.
Ali steered us inside the museum and hesitantly played the guide, since he didn't know much about the history of the place. But he was good enough for the day – a kind-hearted gentleman. "The Wakhis of Gojal Valley claim to

have migrated from the Wakhan corridor. The Mir of Hunza Valley had his winter capital in Gulmit and the tomb of Salim Khan III (1790 – 1824) is founded here in the old part of the village, with old houses. This local home turned museum is 200 years old", he enlightened us. I asked if I can take pictures? "No issues, take as many as you want," he responded. That is the beauty of GB – visit any museum or fort and no one will discourage you to take pictures or touch historical remnants, but it is always good to ask or read the signs. Showing a picture of a yak he said, "The rugs and mats you see here are made purely by hand using yak hair. It needs no maintenance and lasts 100 – 1000 years. You will find them at the Old House here too. Have you ever seen a yak?" I told him yes and we had the pleasure to ride one too back in 2017, near Khunjerab border. "Many politicians, government personnel and foreign delegates have visited the old wing of our hotel," he said very modestly. What fascinated me most here were the Queen's accessories, bag about 150 years old, her silk veil (shamal) about 300 years old, preserved perfectly. "Climbing shoes", I read, "Designed not to slip. For the wealthy these were made from Ibex skin and for the poor made from sheepskin." Rayyan obviously had to do what I did, so he started reading about the ancient teapot. "The teapot of Queen Noor Jehan from India – 1600 century old." Ali was very apologetic about not being able to explain much in detail but he was good enough.

Hunza history and the diverse, unique culture of the Gojal valley are perfectly packed into this dusty Cultural Museum. With a variety of ancient artifacts and other historical objects on display such as utensils, musical instruments, stuffed snow leopard, markhor, ibex, gems and firearms, including the matchlock gun said to have injured the British commander at the Battle of Nilt in 1891, the place illustrates the cultural heritage of Upper Hunza.

Gulmit offers beautiful and spectacular short walks to Kamris, Andhra and Gulkin as well as long walks over the Gulkin glacier to Borith Lake. At Gulmit, the Hunza River can be crossed over traditional suspended bridge which leads to Shishkat, Passu and Batura glacier located at a distance of only 12 kilometers.

A fraction of people is aware of the Ondra Fort, from where one can have a panoramic view of the village. The Ondra Fort reflects the power of the Wakhi ruler Qutlug who was never defeated by the Mirs of Hunza. From the south of the Fort you can see Gulmit as far as Shishkat village and Attabad Lake and from the north the Ghulkin village. Also, from the north you can see Ghulkin glacier, Passu cones and Qaroon peak. From the west, there are amazing views of Gulmit glacier, Gulmit Tower, Shisper peak and Utlar Sar. And from the east there is a spectacular view of the Hunza River. Ondra Fort has the potential to appeal tourists if only the concerned authorities revive and restore the fort from further destruction. Not many tourists visit this place as they literally know nothing about the Ondra Fort's importance and heritage value.

From there we strolled around and accidentally found ourselves in someone's fields. It took us a while to find our way along the narrow water channel to reach the road. By 6 p.m. we were on our way back to the hotel, when I heard loud thundering echoes, "Rayyan is that an aircraft?" I asked. The words were still in my mouth when I become aware of rocks falling in the Attabad. The loud thundering sound altered Rayyan's dull moment into excitement. We watched for a while then moved on. We saw a pair of cute little baby goats with a boy Rayyan's age who shyly agreed to have his picture taken with his goats. It is in the mountains that my son grew fond of cows and goats.

* **Tip:** Traveling is the best way to learn about things that really matter. Understanding the grandeur of nature is only possible when you step out of your comfort zone, no matter how old you are.

We walked for another hour before going back to our hotel room. We realized we had skipped lunch so we ordered food early. I wanted to order something made out of potatoes but the kitchen people apologized that they are out of stock. Fazl bhai clarified that, "Last year's potatoes have lost their taste and fresh potatoes have yet to be harvested. And we do not serve to our guests that which we ourselves would not prefer eating". He continued, "Farmers bury freshly harvested potatoes in Hunza, ahead of harsh winters. Concealed under frozen earth the potatoes remain fresh and usable after several months. The ancient storage method is used widely throughout GB region". Preferring to have any form of vegetables I asked for anything that was easy and quick for the cook to make. After a dish of simply cooked vegetable noodles we decided to sit outside and have a cup of tumoro (green tea) each. It was unbelievably chilly at 16 degrees. The hotel guys had a little bonfire going and curiously Rayyan walked towards them before they asked him to join in. Meanwhile I sat under the willow tree enjoying my cup of tumoro. There were no other guests staying so all you could hear was the whizzing cars and an occasional rock fall in the Attabad. My son was having a grand time telling stories and I was too exhausted to be bothered by the two vans that had just pulled up in the Inn's parking lot with over-excited mass of people of all possible age groups. I could no longer bear the cutting wind, called Rayyan, collected the tea cups and sauntered to my room. As soon as I switched on the lamp, drew the curtains, unplugged my phone, stripped off my socks, tucked Rayyan in, I fell into a deep, peaceful slumber.

* **Tip:** Never take blessings for granted – that includes water, electricity, food and fruit. Don't leave unnecessary lights and switches tuned on. Check faucets before you leave the room or go to bed. Don't leave food or fruit to rot or for the hotel guys to clean up after you.

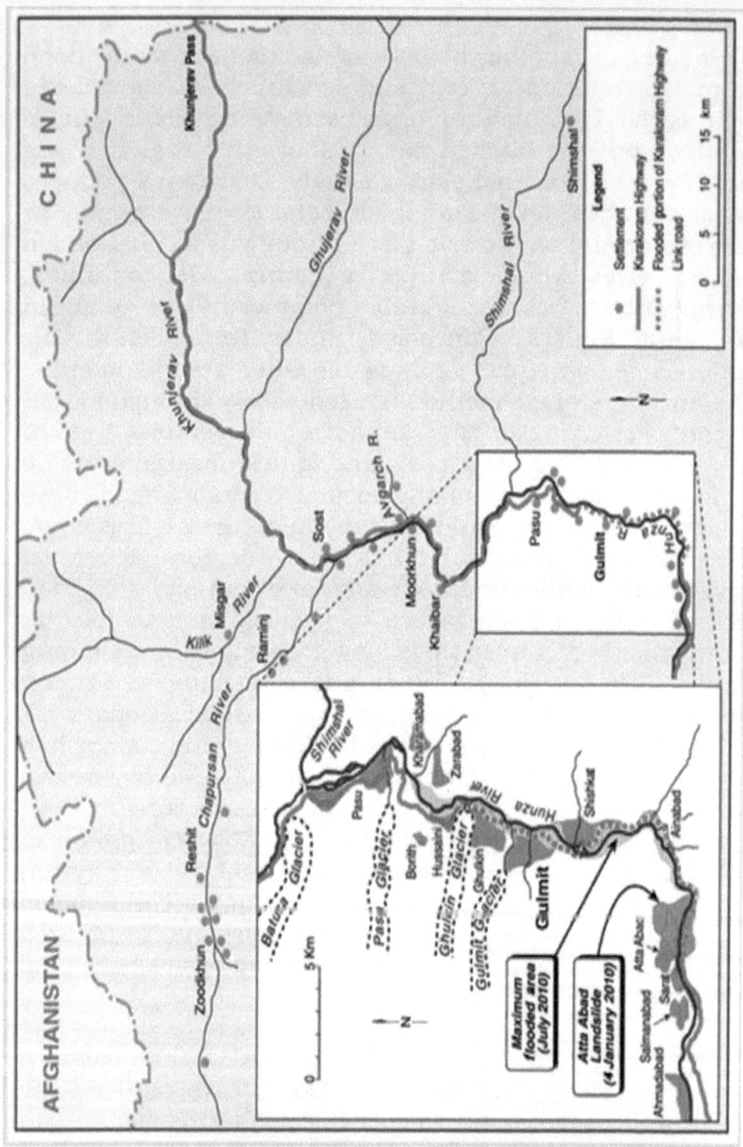

Location of Attabad disaster in Gojal Hunza, Gilgit-
Baltistan (Map by David Butz)

Day 11 – Gul – e – Gulmit – 29th June 2018

Plan: *Stay and explore Gulmit village visit Old House – Gulmit Carpet Centre, Bulbulik and Al-Amyn School, meet people, walk; dinner & overnight stay until the morning of 30th June.*

Mornings in the mountains are the best. Wake up any time after 4am to watch the colossal majesty of nature when the morning sun stretches its rays to touch everything on earth. With my son still asleep, I let myself out using a sliding wooden gate on the other side of the Inn. The gates and the main doors are rarely locked in most parts of GB. The Karachitte in me was getting accustomed to such norms with each passing year I spent in the mountains. The grandeur of Passu cones painted in the shades of lavender and pink by the rising sun, the winding KKH that twists and turns along the lake, the fresh crisp mountain air is a getaway for those who crave to relax and unwind amongst the cool serenity of the highlands.

I started walking towards the village with no one in sight except a vehicle or two swiftly driving by. On the other side of the Inn is a simple bazar with basic amenities and hotels. I walked along the lake where the water level had increased a tad after yesterday's rock fall; passed a Bank, a post office and some small shops that offer breakfast which were starting to open. I walked further into the village, a part of Gulmit that I had never discovered where the ruins of Attabad still linger. A sad place with small streams flowing with icy cold water, an occasional cow nibbling vivid purple and yellow flowers in the fluorescent green pastures, peaks glowing above, birds chirping in the morning air, tall trees with their leaves whispering in the grove to the swaying boughs. A bank of heavy clouds on the horizon obscures the rising sun. A strange silence and coolness surrounds the air. I got so carried away photographing that I found myself stuck in a maze of ruined village, rocks and barren trees, fragments of mud and stone homes. I was enjoying trampling the crisp dried leaves and started hopping on them playfully since no one was around. Just then out of nowhere a female figure wrapped in white headscarf appeared, she smiled and introduced herself, "I am Sahat Bakht, what's your name?" I told her my name, where I came from, what I was doing here and how I lost my way wandering in this part of the village early in the morning. "Are you alone or with someone? Where are you staying? Would you like to have breakfast or a cup of tea baji?" followed a series of questions that I loved answering every time I meet locals. I politely told her no for she seemed busy. I asked her if I could help her wash her dishes to which she said, 'No baji, you are our mehmaan (guest)." She declined my request to take a picture with her saying, "Our council here discourages taking pictures. My brother is part of the local council and he disapproves and I respect his opinion". And I respect hers. I shook hands and she helped me find my way out. You will notice carefully planned waterways along the homes and the fields. The open-air courtyards built around homes of stones where children and domesticated animals play and live together. Just staring at the bright courtyards makes me want to spend days here. I was falling in love with this part of Hunza once again.

* **Tip:** If you enjoy wandering around, mark the trail so you can retrace your footsteps, or wait for someone to rescue you.

The children had started pouring out of homes and were on their way to school. Most children hopped on the buses waiting for them to carry them to distant schools, I assumed. I observed here that the children are slightly reluctant to interact and not as socially interactive as most parts of Hunza, possibly due to lack of tourists roaming around in this region. I waved at a few and some gave me shy smiles with heads bowed low. Amna, a young woman was out with her cow, that was busy munching dazzling wild flowers. She smiled and introduced herself, "I am a teacher and a tailor!" I was loving the expression, "You are from Karachi?!", with a trace of wonderment and disbelief. That followed by, "Alone or with family?" "Where is your stay?" "Do you like our village?" and the obvious "It is so hot in Karachi!" I answered happily before walking back to my hotel. I spotted exclusive Biryani places here for the first time – Silk Route Biryani and Sikandar Biryani House. Sikandar Biryani place has the best chicken corn soup though. Indulge in a sizzling bowl of soup on a cool evening. Biryani is world-renowned Indian and Pakistani dish, which takes time to cook and lots of practice to master the art of a perfect dish. It is made using long-grained rice (popularly the basmati rice) flavoured with exotic spices and is layered with meat, chicken, fish or prawns mixed with thick gravy. Traditionally it is decorated with caramelized onion, mint leaves, orange food colour and saffron.

*** Tip:** Do not expect urbanism in food that these places are just learning to cook. Every place depicts its own distinctive sense of taste based on cultural identity. Preparing food from their culture is a symbol of pride for their ethnicity yet they are being forced to evolve according to tourists needs.

Muhammad Shafee sahab was standing outside the locked post office – Pakistan Post Gulmit Gojal – it's the Al-Noor market Polo ground chowk. With a broad smile he signaled me to stop and introduced himself, "I work here at the Post Office. How are you today? Where have you come from? Would you like to have some tea? Breakfast?" I courteously answered his queries and said no to the chai offer with a thank you. It is safe to say that across Pakistan offering tea is a mark of hospitality and interestingly different regions of the country have their own unique style of making chai (milk tea). Using cinnamon or cardamom makes it a divine experience. The people of GB prefer a light milky flavoured tea in contrast to the strong doodh patti preferred by the Karachittes.

On my way back to the hotel I met Jalaluddin sahab walking briskly and I soon caught up with him. After greeting and introducing myself, I seek permission to walk with him. "I was born in 1932 and that makes me 86 years' old," he smiled lightly. "Where are you from?" he asked. "Karachi." "Oh Karachi! I was in Karachi since long, probably when you weren't even born," he laughed quietly. "I was there since 1953 till 1966, for 13 years I was there. My children were there with me, studying. I did all kinds of odd jobs there, I have worked in a factory and a bank. In 1966, I came back here and went back to Karachi twice after that because my older son was working there as an in charge in a company. He returned after 23 years of service and is now in Gilgit."

Pointing to a trail of shops at the edge of the lake he said, "All these five shops belong to me, including the bank. When the Attabad disaster happened, it destroyed everything. We still haven't received our compensation, no one responds, they just make excuses. I am retired now. I was in intelligence and retired as an Inspector. It's been 20 years now. One of my son's is in Intelligence, posted in Islamabad, one is in Dubai, one is in Gilgit who returned from Karachi, two are here with me. I have five sons and two daughters, MashaAllah. My daughters are married, one is in Passu and the other is in Gulmit. Their husbands are businessmen. I was just feeding and tending my cattle and returning home. We had a home here but was completely wrecked after the 2010 tragedy. The Inn you are staying in was also half submerged in water. We had to use boats to go places. The terrain changed quickly from arable land to desert but God willing we can still grow crops like potato, peas, wheat, barley and corn. The new generation is not eager or interested in agriculture. I am Alhamdulillah still fit to take care of my land and my cattle." He continued, briefing me about

Gulmit, "The valley is comprised of 25 villages, including Ghawooshben (Ainabad), Shishkat (Nazimabad-1), Gulmit, Ghulkin, Seesoni (Hussani), Passu, Khyber, Ghalapan, Moorkhon, Jamalabad, Gircha, Sarteez, Nazimabad, Sost (Aminabad) Khudabad, Misgar, Qalandarchi, Avgarchi, Raminj, Yarz Rech, Kirmin, Reshit, Sharisafz, Kumpirdior, Zowoodkhon, Oston and Shimshal. Gulmit is Gojal's largest settlement and Tehsil headquarters. Gojal is geographically the largest Tehsil of Hunza-Nagar District in Gilgit-Baltistan spreading over an area of about 8,500 square kilometers. The valley borders with the Xinjiang-Uighur region of China and Wakhan Corridor or Little Pamir of Afghanistan."

After a long pause he said, "I am sure you feel safe here in our area, as compared to your city. It was different back then when I lived there, now it has changed completely. At that time, we could sleep on the walkway at night on our charpoy (a bedstead of woven webbing or hemp stretched on a wooden frame on four legs). Things were different back then; we could purchase a sack full of flour for Rs. 13 (current value is more or less Rs. 800). My pay back then was Rs. 50 and I would save half of it. Those were good times", he sighed. I thanked him for taking out time to talk and walk with me. He smiled and with straightforward simplicity spoke, "My home is up there in the mountains otherwise I would have invited you over for tea. Take care and enjoy your stay."

The gates of the Inn were wide open by now. My son was up and talking very comfortably to the people at the Inn. I inquired Fazl Karim bhai about, "The 2 vans that checked in last night were not there in the morning when I left for a walk. What happened?" he chortled and said, "The families were from Karachi and Sindh and did not like it here. Reason being there is no proper market here. So they left early in the morning. They were also too scared to go to the parking lot at night". Feeling a little conceited, I thought, *here we are mother and son travelling and staying at the Inn all alone*! Fazl sahab said, as if reading my mind, "You are also staying here, going out alone and walking in the village but you don't feel threatened by us. We are very peaceful and we respect people, especially our guests – that is our culture which we are very proud of". I agreed with him. I asked him if he could check if the Old House was open for us to visit and he assured me, "I will call them around 9 a.m. and let them know a guest wants to visit". Thanking him I ordered tea and returned to my room. After freshening up we had tea and Phitti that we bought from Gilgit, for breakfast. I told Rayyan about my morning walk while devouring cherries. He wanted to go out, explore and see if anyone was playing in the Polo ground and if we could have more mulberry. Outside the weather was pure bliss; cloudy with light wind bracing up adding charm to the exhilarating landscape. In the mountains you can actually feel that nature is so powerful, so mighty, so inspiring.

Today I planned to visit the Al Amyn Community School known to be the first of its kind in Pakistan to focus on preserving the linguistic heritage of the area by teaching the local Wakhi language. I wanted to meet the administrative staff and students to ascertain why this school was known to be a groundbreaking initiative. Plan two was, to visit the old winter residence of the ruling Mir of Hunza, now home to a women's carpet weaving initiative – the Old House. Gulmit has some eminent schools such as Al-Amyn school, Federal Government Boys High school, Diamond Jubilee Girls Middle school, Government Girls Higher Secondary school and Bulbulik music school. Al- Amyn Model School, an outstanding community-based organization. It has a building with a hostel facility standing next to the Health Center of Aga Khan Health Services. By the early 1990s, the government created "community schools" in Hunza, including the Al-Amyn, in the village of Gulmit, which involved the students' families to participate in lessons too. "Parents in Hunza are convinced that the best thing they can do for their children is to help them get a good education. There is a growing interest in higher education for girls," a gentleman Siddiqui we met on the way, explained, "Given the limited chances of higher education in the valley, the boys and girls of Hunza go to large cities such as Karachi, Lahore, Peshawar and Islamabad for higher education". He also emphasized that, "Parents in Hunza encourage their daughters to study and are even willing to send girls to all parts of Pakistan to obtain quality degrees. It is an approach that distinguishes Hunza from the rest of the Northern Areas," he added. And you will witness it all over Hunza; they can be seen walking along the roadside, bags on their back, water bottles hanging on their arms and books hugged closely to their chests, irrespective of weather and road conditions.

Our first stop was the same Pakistan Post I had stopped earlier and met Muhammad Shafee sahab. I wanted Rayyan to meet him and see the post office. He offered chai again and I told him I just had breakfast before stepping out again. Across the road was a small cabin where Faraghat Shah sahab was making tea and rolling parathas. He offered us "garam garam (hot) parathay" but I gently told him we just had breakfast but can stop by in the evening to have the parathas with tea. He nodded and said, "you are always welcome here sister".

We headed towards the Polo ground and met Ezzatullah Amanullah sahab, who was loading bricks in a wheelbarrow with a bunch of other men. He stopped to shake hands with Rayyan, asked his name and which grade was he in. "My son is a little older than you," he told Rayyan. He asked me where I am from and said, "Oh I work in Karachi at AKU – Agha Khan University as an Associate Librarian at the faculty of Health Sciences Library. And here I am working as a labourer to build my home," he beamed. Talking about Karachi's weather he said, "I called yesterday and found out it is unbelievably hot there with no sign of rain, but here it's pleasant. I live in Gulshan-e-Noor near DOW University Karachi. I have two children, a son and daughter. My daughter is in Agha Khan higher secondary and my son is younger, he is in Grade 7." I told him about my work and travel history, and he seemed very fascinated by Chipursan. "It is beautiful here in Gulmit, with clean water from the glaciers, you can't even imagine this life in the big city. Wait, I will give you my card and do visit me at AKU in the library." I thanked him and proceeded.

*** Tip:** Save visiting cards as you save contact numbers.

On the way towards the village we met Hameeda Sarwar, a pleasant lady. With a smile she asked where did I come from and if I liked her village? I nodded and told her how much I love visiting Gulmit every year since 2016. Our conversation was short and sweet. I wasn't bored or annoyed answering the same questions repeatedly. Walking along the water channel Rayyan was utterly amazed to see women opening shutters, saleswomen behind counters, tending domestic animals and working so hard in the fields. We visited an 'open' handicraft shop in the area where we said a quick hello to Saima, Guldana and Azra, before walking towards Hunza Marcopolo Inn to meet Ali, who like everybody else offered morning tea. This time I did not refuse and Rayyan asked him if "we could have more mulberry?" He smiled and said, "Sure. You know you can have as many as you want!" We started collecting the green, white, pink, red and black mulberry literally pouring down from the thick laden trees. The dull white and the black ones were the sweetest. By then the tea was ready. We crossed the kitchen, the dining hall and chose to sit in the well-ventilated lobby. While sipping tea Ali started telling me about the NCP cars, "If you buy cars here like Corolla GLi or Xli through NCP they will cost you much less than in most parts of Pakistan. That is why we use these big ones instead of taxi cabs. Most NCPs you will find are used as rentals or as an alternative to taxi". Talking about Karachi he told me, "My younger brother is in Karachi he is in SSG, another one younger than him is in Special Forces in Gilgit. I studied in Islamabad for 6 years and I have stayed in Karachi for a year and a half and worked at a hotel for 6 months. In 2014, I completed my B. Com (Bachelors in Commerce) then started working with Chinese people in Finance department etc. I was earning quite well so did not pursue my studies further." I started clicking photos in the lobby, where you see the family tree of 'Dynasty of Royal Family Hunza from 1550 – 2002' on the wall with history through pictures. Unlike other places in Pakistan, people in this region will let you take pictures of sites, paintings, historical relics, handicrafts, museums etc. "People camp here too, at night we have barbeque and live music too if the guests order," he said. We thanked Ali for his graciousness and walked towards the other side of the Inn, where I noticed a big hole in the ground filled with empty bottles. It was their way of disposing off trash.

The pleasure of walking in Gulmit with one of the most enchanting views of Passu cones and the visually arresting landscape is any travelers dream. Savouring the tiny details of each and every step along the way; breathing in the crisp clean air, eating the mulberry we collected. This is what I always wanted, the way travellers have always travelled. The kind of life where you don't want to see the world go by through the window of an air conditioned bus, but to get out and breathe the air and let the villages come to you one step at a time. This is exactly what I wanted to experience, approach the valley slowly, not on a highway, but along centuries old roads and truly see the villages begin to grow out of the landscape, you can truly get to know and appreciate the countryside and villages in an intimate way. They become more than just "another village with a fort and a museum". Somehow, by experiencing the world this way you become a part of it, a traveller in the landscape, and not just an observer heading from one tourist attraction to the next. Finding our trail along the rugged stone walls we began our walk towards the Old

House – Carpet Weaving centre; while crossing the extended Polo ground. Rayyan ran towards a gentleman to shake hands and started talking to Asghar sahab. By the time I walked up to them, Rayyan had already introduced himself. Like many others he too has lived and worked in Karachi. "I resided in Garden area for quite some time and have my own home in Metro-Ville Karachi. I go there often but I live here mostly now and right here is my shop," he pointed towards a row of shops. I told him we were headed to the Old House and he affirmed we were walking in the right direction. A few steps away from the Old House we met Izzat Shah sahab. It is always a pleasure to stop, greet someone and move on.

In Gojal valley, the wooden monuments of the Wakhi people are numerous especially in these two villages – Gulmit and Ghulkin and are distinguished for their spectacular wood carvings. The Old House is well known for its ornately carved door and windows. The place has now been turned into a carpet weaving centre where craftswomen make beautiful carpets, runners, mats and rugs from goat, sheep and yak wools. The place remained a summer palace for the Mirs of Hunza and is believed to be one of the oldest buildings in Gulmit and stands as a symbol of the ancient Wakhi culture. Locals estimate it maybe 350 – 400 years old. In 1998, KADO – Karakoram Area Development Organization established a Carpet Centre named as The Corgah Gulmit Carpet Centre in this building; where a number of skilled women artisans are working and supporting their families by selling the carpets to local and foreign tourists.

As you enter the building through the wooden low carved entrance you will find yourself in a raw mud house with handwritten chart papers adorning the walls, stating a brief history of the place. The building has two levels; the lower one functions as a carpet weaving center while the upper portion is used as a store house. The ceiling of the lower storey is supported by five pillars, which are decorated by intricate spiral curves. Wakhi homes have the same decorated pillars with volute capitals signifying their general culture, aesthetics and taste. The Old House is the true representation of a traditional Wakhi abode with five pillars supporting the main chamber of the house. A *ghaf* (fireplace) is positioned in the center of the room and also serves as a heating place in winters. Around this are three elevated platforms called *"razh"* which are used for sitting purposes during the day and turned into bedroom at night. The ceiling is conventionally a "lantern" style with a hole in the middle for the fireplace to let the smoke out of the chimney of the *bokhari* (stove). This sunroof above the fireplace makes for a cozy, well lit and warm room. The roof is usually flat and surrounded by four concentric wooden squares On cold days this is THE place to be. The upper storey is the hall and has three entrances. The pillars of these entrances are also heavily decorated. Currently, this hall is being used for carpentry. The roof is exclusively and purely structured using mud. The upper portion of the building is a small chamber possibly used in the summer. It has a doorway and carved wooden windows on either side. The shafts of the pillars of the portico are beautifully decorated too as well as the carvings on the door which are done to perfection. Another small opening led us into a large space which looked rather small from the outside. Four large hand-weaving carpet machines stood on all sides, while wool and carpets of all shapes, sizes and colour covered the floor. The ancient handcrafted wooden beams added antique touches to the workshop. It took me a minute to notice the three amazing women with their welcoming smiles and extended hands. It was a pleasure to finally meet these women I had heard and read so much about. "Assalaam alaikum, I am so glad to finally meet you," I said shaking hands with all three women. One woman stepped forward, "Walaikum assalaam sister, I am Aziza and welcome to our weaving center," she paused then said, "And I believe it was you who wanted to visit us yesterday?" I nodded. "Oh I believe I was a few minutes late and you had left when I arrived. I am so sorry," she said apologetically. "I didn't have my phone with me, when I returned I found out someone wanted to visit us". As we settled down, Doulat and Aziza started asking me about my journey from Karachi to Islamabad, to Chipursan to all the way to Gulmit. "Next?" she asked. "We will leave for Rakaposhi basecamp InshaAllah tomorrow and join our group in Karimabad." I told them. Aziza suggested I must visit Kamris, "It's a beautiful village and not many people visit it, except foreigners. You must have seen Altit and Baltit, Kamris gives you the same kind of feel. You can hike up or rent a car to visit the village." I liked how they both were curious and asking questions one after the other, "Ju...what do you do?" "I teach, and I have been teaching since 2006." I answered. "My younger sister lives in Gulshan-e-Noor in Karachi," Aziza told me. "She got married and lives there with her husband. She has 2 sons and a daughter. She teaches in a private Turkish school." Discussing my status as being a single parent, Aziza and Doulat were quite vocal and forthright with their opinion, "It is better for a person to be happy. Instead of disagreeing and arguing it's better to go your separate ways. Here when marriage breaks, the children stay with the father, not with the mother." Attributing television, social media and internet to be the biggest home-breakers of our times, she said, "People have started comparing their lives to what the glamourized lives portrayed on these mediums." We both agreed there should be peace in life – *sukoon* we echoed together.

Gulmit Carpet Centre (GCC) is led by Aziza Safar, Doulat Qaim and Pari Sultana. "Initially, 28 artisans were taught the art of carpet-weaving by four master trainers, three of whom were from Didar Carpet Centre in Hunza and the other one was from Afghanistan. After the session, the trainers left the city, but one of them stayed back to supervise our work for another three years. They taught us everything from how to graft patterns, put them into shape, how to make a business model, sustain it and most importantly promote it. I have been in this profession for 18 years now," Aziza, who maybe in her late 30s proudly states. "We cherish the skill we have learnt. All thanks to the professionals who taught us free of cost and we are trying to keep the legacy alive." Aziza is in charge of a team of 18 female workers (figures may vary) who make handmade carpets.

In the last many years' education has gained importance in Gilgit Baltistan especially Hunza district and many people like Aziza still believe that the great way to earn a living is through the skills you have learnt. "Not many are interested in this work. Most women in this field are from the second generation or unmarried women, or ones who want to learn a skill and earn extra money," she says. Aziza is one of five siblings and chooses to run the business and support her family. "Two of my brothers needed special care and attention and I chose to help them. One of them passed away recently, he was 25 years old and was affected by polio. The other is 32 years old. These things happen in life," she sighed. "The carpet business is doing very well. It helps me pay rent, purchase raw material and organize and hold exhibitions. I am content with what Allah has bestowed me with," she sums up her life. Talking about her community, she says, "Baji, you will observe here that the life of both men and women is virtually similar. Some men do take women for granted though but that is quite rare. Some women do it too!" She quipped. So what is your normal day like? I asked. "Like many others, I wake up early in the morning, clean my home, knead the dough, prepare breakfast, attend to our cattle, go into the fields where both men and women work. Once done I come to the Centre and make carpets." She says, "Raw material used to make the carpets is pure wool taken from our herds. A small carpet, a square of around 10 inches, takes approximately a month to make and we make almost 12 such pieces a year. If it's a big order almost three to four women are needed to work on it and we receive at least three such orders in a year. It may take around 4 – 5 months to make a single piece as well, which is conditional to size and design." There have been times when they end up making carpets as large as six feet or more. "Due to extreme weather conditions here in Gulmit, we dye the threads in summers and stock them for winters. In winters we try to sell our products across the country, take more orders, have exhibits etc. We have been to Islamabad, Lahore and China to market our pieces," her tone laced with passion. "But I have never been to Karachi. Perhaps good profitable opportunities there to showcase our work, since it is a metropolitan city", Aziza said. I felt exhilarated when she genuinely referred to Karachittes as "certainly nice people". She continued with a smile, "I like them, they are really nice and respectful when they visit."

These women are entrepreneurs but exceptionally down-to-earth and modest. They don't play the emotional feminist card, for they don't need to, they know their actual worth. They don't need anyone's acknowledgement and approval to know their worth. The unsung heroines of our nation – the women of courage.

"People think our carpets, rugs, mats are expensive, but the effort we put into it is priceless. We wish to market our products beyond China and Pakistan, on international levels hopefully," states Aziza, who sold me a piece even though I told her I have no space in my backpack and a trek to go to. She was considerate enough to choose a handmade yak *plos* (rug) which would "look great on your wall, easily foldable and can fit in your purse", she chortled as she stuffed it in my handbag! And to this date I am glad she did. When I asked if one of them could show me how they weave, Aziza said, "sure, why not." Doulat sat down with her tools and her hands moved with meticulous precision on the hand-weaving carpet loom and I couldn't help but make a small video of her, of course with permission.

* **Tip:** Remember consent is very important before you click anything.

I asked if I could take a group photograph with them and their wonderful cozy workplace, Aziza and the other girls readily agreed, saying, "We receive media coverage, our story and work is displayed on many platforms so feel free to promote us!" I love their simplicity, their unpretentious and unambiguous attitude. They will never exaggerate or beat around the bush. Women in this part of Pakistan also stitch their own traditional caps while at home. Each work of art takes roughly a month to complete. The motifs and patterns consisting of cultural symbols and vibrant colours, tell endless stories of the mountains. These are one of the best ways to preserve and promote the old traditions and civilizations of Hunza valley.

I hugged and shook hands with them promising to write about them and hoping to return again next year. "May Allah bless you and good luck," Aziza said before parting ways.

I was loving this traditional Pamiri-style hospitality and the warm abode. Closing the door behind, we were once again walking on the slightly rocky terrain with a light chill in the air. Walking back on the same path, hoping to find Bozlanj Café – the house of Wakhi / Pamirian cuisine. This café is managed by two women Malika and Shaista and the place is functional since 2016. They started the café when the need and demand for local cuisine increased by foreign and local tourists. A simple snug place fashioned out of tin and wood; a stove on one side, two monobloc chairs and a wooden rack. I greeted the dynamic Malika who was busy making samosa's along with Rasheeda and Misri Begum who was wearing her traditional cap. They initially started as an apricot oil business, for which they used kernels farmed from their own orchard. When the demand for local food increased, they started preparing homegrown food, using vegetables, wheat, cheese and apricots. What was available with them at the time was Arzoq (bread made from flour, eggs, butter and milk). "I am preparing potato filled samosas and a vegetable dish of spinach with potatoes. If you can wait..." she said. Since it was only 11:30 a.m. and I wasn't hungry I only bought Arzoq for Rayyan, who had fallen in love with this bread. I told her I will return on my way back to the Inn and meanwhile ordered a cup of bozlanj tea, that I had heard about in Chipursan. Always eager to try new teas, I wanted to have bozlanj and she was kind enough to brew one mug for me. Bozlanj are green leaves of a natural herb found in the mountains of Hunza. I hesitantly asked her if I could have the dry leaves and she gladly put some in a small bag. The ladies told me that their forthcoming plan was to extend their restaurant to serve more people at a time and offer delivery around the valley. Wandering around we found different sized graves under a huge tree and a little girl came up to us to shake hands and greet us. Asma dressed in green pullover and a floral shirt under it, was shy but friendly. She didn't really understand Urdu or so it seemed but she understood I wanted to click a picture with her. She agreed and gave me the best timid smiles. She curiously asked my name and my son's name. I hugged her (in the presence of her grandmother who was busy buying vegetables) before I moved on. Breathing in the fresh air, admiring the potato and corn fields, I met Gul-e-Bakht, a friendly soul out shopping who lived in Baadshah Chowk. She was exceptionally surprised to hear that I am visiting all the way from Karachi. She ushered me to walk with her and told me, "I have seven children, 4 sons and 3 daughters. My daughters work and run shops. Where do you work?" I told her I am a teacher by profession. "It's good to see you walking," she said. "We stay fit because we walk a lot every day. Today we have to attend an engagement ceremony. The boy works in Karachi and you should come join us." She took us home to meet her daughter Perveen and granddaughter Anisha Hoorain who were visiting her from Karachi. Anisha (nicknamed Nisha) was busy watching television. "She enjoys her vacations here than in the city", her grandmother (nani) explained. I sat in her cozy home, complementing how much I love these homes. Gul-e-Bakht smiled and asked, "Old homes?" I nodded. I also pointed at her handmade colourful bead necklace, she shrugged and said, "I don't like wearing these necklaces, my rings and necklace is very, very old. I also don't like tea, only one cup a day." I just love how straightforward the countryside people are. Her daughter served us a plate full of luscious homegrown cherries. We started talking about fresh and dried mulberry, cherries and apricots – fruits that I was purely in love with. I asked Perveen about her vacation here and she said, "I go to my in-laws' place or come back here to my mother's. I returned after a long stay at my in-laws, the door was closed and Ami (mother) wasn't home. So I came back again to check. You will find people here are very kind and generous to guests and even strangers." I nodded in agreement. During the conversation I told her about my stay at Chipursan, to which she remarked, "I have observed that the real village life can be experienced in interior Sindh – Hyderabad etc. I was working on a project and got a chance to witness the real village life, and I thought to myself that we here are quite progressive than them. We lack basic facilities here during winter season due to harsh weather conditions. But our education level is better than the villages in Sindh. A boy your son's age is normally studying in kindergarten. Girls generally don't study there unlike here where you see no difference between a son or a daughter. I met one of the Government teachers there, who was appointed as a headmistress but her husband allows her to go for an hour only and she is paid 80,000 a month! I was astonished." She started talking about her community how everyone is respectful to each other, irrespective of gender or age. "People in cities are animals," comparing the wakhi people to urban population. Between intervals she was talking in wakhi with Gul-e-Bakht, her mother. Talking about the cold weather, she said, "We have major gas issues here. We use gas cylinders which cost us 2,500 – 3000 rupees and in winters we burn wood. You must have seen it in Chipursan and here these fireplaces (angithi)" – framework of metal bars used as a partition or a grate. She offered us to take some cherry with us but I didn't want to look too greedy. "Try the local dishes here, they are full of energy," she said as we got up to leave. "I visited the Old House today," I told her while putting on my shoes. "That's our house, we have rented it out to them," she said with a broad smile. It started to drizzle and Rayyan and I sat near a stream. The milky-white water flowing, rushing between rocks, with little droplets of rain creating tiny short-lived ripples; when I spotted a large stone with wild flowers growing from the middle. Amazed at Allah's creation, Rayyan and I sat there for quite some time, admiring the delicate plantlet.

As I got up, a lady, I am forgetting her name, shook hands and just invited me to her place and offered to have breakfast. Along came her husband who started talking non-stop and took us home. He had gone to attend a wedding ceremony in the neighbourhood. Much to Rayyan's delight she served us pure cow milk and made a fresh batch of Phitti. Her husband after the introductions said, "Surrounded by the mighty Karakoram Mountains, we living here have long been rather isolated, seeing tourists but little else of global events. But now you see an improved highway and the arrival of mobile phones, computers that have let the outside world in, bringing new lifestyles and opportunities; children grow up and head off to university, fashions have changed, and technology has reshaped our tradition. Gojal has adjusted to all of this, surprising me every time, showing me just how adaptable traditions can be. Young men and women leave their lives here to study in cities, and when they come back for summer holidays, you see them dressed in new, hip styles. Shops have multiplied along the road, selling new spices, sugary snacks, junk and sodas. Biryani rice, chicken karahi is now often seen replacing the traditional turnip soup or buckwheat pancakes during celebrations", he just shook his head sadly. I agreed with what he said.

Rayyan and I thoroughly enjoyed hot-from-the-stove Phitti, milk and the light salted tea. A while later, we thanked them for their generosity and left.

The villages in Hunza District of GB are very strategically planned with Government and Private schools and Health care facilities. A barren piece of land had a Rupani Foundation board – supposedly a community center for parents. It's nice to see familiar signs.
Rayyan insisted we walk back to the Polo ground. By now some boys had returned from school and were playing. Since most of them were having their exams they got off early from school and were playing a ball game. Rayyan requested if he could play with them and they warmly welcomed him to play. According to the rules of the ball game that they called Tara Tara, whoever 'gives a catch will be out', one of them interpreted for me. So the child throwing the ball had to make sure the others were unable to catch. The girls soon joined in too. One girl Saniha stood out from the rest. She seemed like a good combination of naughty but robust and slightly in command of her girl-gang! Her friends kept chanting her name Sani...Sani. she seemed to have quite an influence on both genders. The boys playing were, Rohan looking very adorable in spectacles. Munsif in yellow sweater, Fawad Ali in grey hoody with a prominent 08 printed on it and later a boy named Shabbir joined in. The innocence and playfulness of the children was so evident. I sat there on the steps of the playground, observing people, shopkeepers, children when a woman drove by. Rarely you would see a local woman driving around and I was quite surprised when I saw one in the area. A shy little girl gestured to sit with me to watch the game. After much probing she softly revealed her name – Malaika. Dressed in yellow she quietly sat with me and periodically gazed at me. Using monosyllables and a monotone to answer my

blatant questions, she told me she enjoys "a – b – c – d" Plays? Nothing. Something? Watch TV. Where do you live? Chipursan! "My family calls me Maloo", struggling to overcome her shyness and moving closer to me. Impetuously I hugged her and she sat with me throughout the match.

* **Tip:** It may sound inappropriate, but I have been teaching small children between the ages of 3 – 6 and my motherly-instinct emerges every now and then.

We stayed there until 2 p.m. then decided to take the vegetable dish of spinach with potatoes from the Bozlanj café. Outside Rayyan got really excited because he spotted a large yellow bee with rows of black dots on abdomen – a Vespula maculifrons. Commonly known as, the eastern yellow jacket, they live in forests, meadows and forest edges, including urban and suburban environments. "Be careful, it stings," came a voice from inside the café. One click and we left.
Walking back to Gulmit Tourist Inn, loaded with food, mulberry and chai, it seemed like such a long day. Yet there was still so much left to see, learn and discover. The distinctive earthiness to this non-spicy vegetable dish was very different from what I am accustomed to. People up here are not very fond of spicy curries.

* **Tip:** Whenever and wherever you are travelling to, eat in moderation. No matter how much you enjoy the food, your digestive system may take some time to adjust to the unusually tasting food.

Finished eating, cleaned up, rested and showered, we both decided to go for a stroll again. This time I remembered to take our rain-jackets for the dense clouds had taken over once again. We hardly saw any sunlight here during the two-day stay. Drizzling as we left, Passu cones draped in clouds. Gulmit is surrounded by rolling hills and mountain peaks in the distance; marvelous and a postcard landscape. A place you need to dwell in to fall in love with. I took a bunch of pictures as we walked towards the green patches of potatoes fields against the round white stone walls. I stopped at Faraghat Shah sahab's cabin for my promised cup of tea. The weather and namkeen chai makes a great combo. Crossing the same place for apparently the third time in two days; with Attabad remains on one side and on the other side little cabins, well-tended homes, grasslands and wildflowers and of course the smiling people. A woman in the distance was flinging sand over the fields to protect them from rain. It must be ensured that dry sand is evenly distributed to avoid creating sandy zones. She waved at us and got back to her work.

We reached the ground, now swarming with energetic football players of different age groups prepping for some League next month. They were all practicing in small teams. The drizzle turned to light rain and the temperature lowered. Drenched in rain, the players paid no attention to the icy winds and their soaked T-shirts. Some players had the ability to collect, control and manipulate the ball with both feet, legs, chest & head. We both enjoyed watching them move the ball in different directions at varying speeds with the ball in full control, even the very little ones.

We spent half an hour watching the match but I could not bear the cold to stay any longer. Tired and exhausted we sauntered back to our home, for another night. Sodium lights started to illuminate the place. I wanted to have warm soup of any kind for dinner, turn-off the lights and slip under my blanket until the break of dawn. Fazl bhai insisted we must try their special daal (split chickpeas lentil) served with piping-hot puffed up naan. Naan is a kind of roti made using flour and yeast, baked in a cylindrical clay or metal oven. It took another hour or so for them to prepare the bowl of daal.

Meanwhile I made a few calls, since the internet was working. Got in-touch with Muqeem, the group leader for the trip to Rakaposhi base camp. *Ok, so I still have the morning time in Gulmit! Yayyy!! I can visit the Al-Amyn school in the village.* I cheered to myself. *So I can visit the school early morning, have breakfast and leave for Garelt Hunza. It will take around 1 and a half hours so I'll reach Garelt by midday!*

Dinner done, plan sorted, Rayyan tucked in, phone and camera charged, informed my parents who were relieved now that I was going to be with a group. *Another day in Gulmit*, with this thought I dozed off.

Day 12 – Leaving Gul – e – Gulmit – 30th June 2018

Plan: *One last morning walking in Gulmit village. Visit Bulbulik and Al- Amyn Model school, if possible. Find local transport to join Climax Adventure Pakistan in Karimabad Hunza. Overnight stay at Garelt and start trek towards Rakaposhi Basecamp the next day.*

Gul-e-Gulmit – Upper Hunza Gojal is a small village in Hunza valley. It is 2,500 meters (8,200 feet) above sea level. The town serves as a headquarter of the Gojal, also known as Upper Hunza, in Gilgit Baltistan. Gulmit is a centuries-old historic town, with mountains, peaks and glaciers, museums and schools. When Hunza used to be the princely state in 1947 Gulmit was the Summer Capital of the state during that period. The people here speak Wakhi language. It is a fertile land with irrigated fields mainly cultivating maize, wheat and potatoes besides orchards of apricots, apples, cherries, peaches and walnuts. Gojal valley is famous for its rich natural wealth, landscape, picturesque locations, noble, lofty mountains, breathtaking scenic beauty, wildlife and nature, glittering glaciers, valleys of lush green foliage and fruits, ravishing meadows, and pastures, one could gaze upon for hours on end.

Gulmit has always been my favourite place to relax, socialize, walk in the fields and into the mountain passes along the irrigation canals. There are many other villages nearby such as Gulkhin and Chaman-Gul where you can stroll around with ease and liberty. Additionally, you can explore Gulmit to Borith Lake which is at a distance of 13.6 kilometers – a picturesque walk along the irrigation canal that goes across and reaches Gulkhin Glacier which is around 11.4 kilometers. The glacier can be a little rough for most trekkers but you will not regret taking a trip. A small road separates the main highway and mounts over a ridge to Borith Lake, which is another popular tourist destination and is 3.3 kilometers from Hussaini village and 2 kilometers to the north of Gulkhin. It will take an average backpacker roughly 40 minutes to reach Borith

Lake which is one of the most exquisite green-blue natural saltwater bodies this country has. The saline water is home to many croaking frogs, ram-chaukors, ducks and birds. The lake shimmers in the bright midday sunlight, surrounded by dry, rock-strewn mountains. *Khundha* mulberry syrup eaten with *Qisstaa* (bread) and homemade melted butter that I had in Gulkhin is so far the best thing I have feasted on. White, pink, dark red or black-ish mulberries are used to make this syrup. First the mulberries are squeezed through a cloth and juiced. This juice cooks for hours on low flame. It gets this dark colour once the natural sugar starts to caramelize. A time and lots of wood consuming process therefore very rare to find.

Borith Lake – an epitome of nature's beauty

Situated at an altitude of 2,600 meters (8,500feet) above sea level the lake is a stunning sanctuary for migrating birds and waterfowls. The water is not exactly brine (saltwater), but leaves a white crust on your skin once it is dry. It has an unusual taste similar to sulfur or high in alkaline. Some say the locals often call it a soda lake. Naturally there aren't any fish because they are unable to survive in this water. It was once a popular bird hunting place for the Mir of Hunza during winters. A small house was built for the Mir on a hill surrounding the lake just over the edge. Today this house is known as the Borith Lake Hotel & Resort. The lake has now reduced in size and has become salty over the years due to a reduction in the underground seepage that feeds it. This is the result of receding glaciers and an impact of climatic changes.

Visit this place to unravel from your everyday tough routine for a pleasant stay at the most comfortable hotel with the utmost openhearted people at Borith Lake Hotel & Resort. I have been to this Lake twice but had no plans this year. I wonder now why was it not on my list, along with Glacier Breeze – another famous spot that I missed this year. Glacier Breeze – House of Apricot cake, where you will always find the humblest and politest Ahmed Ali Khan sahab, the man behind the idea of putting simple home-grown apricots in a simple home-baked sponge cake. Baked and served fresh along with a French-pressed cup of coffee or tumoro. The aroma of the famous apricot cake fills the air which makes the almost 120 steps worth climbing. The superb location has the glacier stream rushing besides it with a 360-degree panoramic view of the Passu Cathedrals.

Borith hotel was undergoing some new construction around it when we last visited it in 2017. They have a nice collection of travel books from which I bought like a dozen Gilbert Kolonko books: 'Let's Go to My Favourite Travel Country — Let's Go to Pakistan'. Known to have written it while he stayed here at the hotel. One must have lunch or tea at the picturesque lake with views of Ultar Peak (6,735 meters). You are always welcome to take a dip in the lake or go boating.

* **Tip:** Seek permission before you head off swimming in the lake or decide to boat ride.

Mr. Tawakal Khan runs the place with his two sons. You will often meet Zahid; Tawakal sahab's younger son at the reception, receiving guests with a bright smile and an upbeat attitude. He supports local tourism widely, speaks highly of this spectacular place and enjoys hosting people from Pakistan and overseas and often escorts them on day trips. Zahid is always delighted to give wakhi lessons over a cup of his famous namkeen chai (salt milk tea). Over the years he has taught me a few: *Tashakur bisyor* which means 'lots of thanks' (in Persian) – *Zaqyor* is used for little brother and *Lopyor* for big brother – this can be used for both brother and sister. Lopyor in general is used for 'the elder one'. *Shobosh* in wakhi is also used for saying 'thank you'. *Chiz holi* is 'how are you?' Dandelion is called *krill* in wakhi meaning 'sharp leaves'. Dandelion, grown in abundance in GB is called *ishkinaji* in Gilgit and *pasandu* in Balti. Dandelion is a versatile flower and every part of it is useful; root, leaves, flower and can be used for food, medicine and dye for colouring. They have one of the longest flowering seasons of any plant. Back to the vocabulary lessons – *Pul* in wakhi means 'money'. Fluent in Wakhi and Pashto he can speak Burushaski and Shina too. *Awkana ror jana, rishta waya,'* yeah bro you are right' in Pashto language. "I am also learning Turkish," he says. "So far I have learnt *Ashkeem* 'my life' – *Ashkeem sanistiyoram* 'my life I need you' and *Bendi sanistiyoram* 'I need you too". The person who taught him certainly thought these phrases might be very significant! The last foreign word I learnt from him was *Harigato*, 'thank you' in Japanese language.

A longer walk to Passu Gar Glacier is another attraction, crossing both Ghulkin Glacier and Borith Lake. Passu Glacier is spread over 115 square kilometers Continue walking on the southern side of Borith Lake past the settlement of Borith bala and the now almost uninhabited settlement of Shahabad. The shortage of continuous water supply led to the desertification of this village several years back. On reaching Passu Gar you will find spectacular views of icy glaciers along its length. The walk takes about 4–5 hours from Ghulkin to Passu. From the glacier, a path leads down to the Karakorum Highway. Passu Gar Glacier flows from the mountain tops and melts into a lake above the Passu Village, while Borith Lake receives melted water from the Gulkhin Glacier. Passu is one of the bases and onset point for trekkers heading towards the different valleys. You can hike up to Passu from Gulmit which is 19.7 kilometers. Another popular option that tourists choose is from Gulmit to Hussaini which is 11.6 kilometers. This measure of distance may vary given the route you choose to travel or commence your hike from. On this trip I learnt that the oldest home that exists in Gulmit is more than six centuries old. Also I found out about the next famous bridge in the area – the Passu Suspension Bridge, locally known as "Passu Dutt" that connects Passu village and Khuramabad across the Khunjerab river. The 444 step wooden bridge supported by metal ropes is also one of the famous tourist spot in Gojal Hunza, as is the Hussaini Suspension Bridge.

We packed up early in the morning, had a quick fried egg and Phitti breakfast. After making the payment, we left our bags on the concrete outside the Inn's shop and went for a stroll. Fazl Karim sahab had asked a few boys at the Inn to look out for the public transport to escort us back to Karimabad. I turned down the opportunity to visit Al-Amyn school, for I wasn't sure how long the wait would be. It was a little over 2-hours.

*** Tip:** Do not expect public transport (bus – van – jeep) to arrive on time and every day.

While wandering we spotted a scarecrow lookalike near the Attabad; fashioned out of a cardboard, taped together with black adhesive tape with a triangular golden crown for head. I waved at Muhammad Shafee sahab who was again standing outside the post office. We decided to explore the other side of the Inn where we walked pass the close woodwork place, tea hotels, small grocery, butcher and barber shops, electronic and hardware shops, an auto-parts shop and a few lodges. Here Rayyan met a gathering of local men outside Shah Chiragh Hotel, one of them wished him saying, "God bless you little one!" We proceeded further and met Amin Khan sahab, who stopped for a brief moment to greet and asked if we were able to sightsee around Gulmit. We also met Tawakal Khan sahab from Borith Lake Hotel and Resort. A man with a huge smile on his face whenever and wherever you meet him. He stopped to communicate, using his wakhi and hand gestures and modestly responded that he is unable to communicate otherwise. A picture with him was a must.

*** Tip:** Do not expect people to recognize you instantly if you met them before as well. They meet plenty of tourists from all over the world to remember one particular individual.

With no transport in sight we went back to inquire. "Seems like you will have to take a rental if you really want to reach Karimabad today", one of the boys suggested and I agreed. By 10:45 a.m. an NCP marked car pulled up and agreed to drop us at Garelt Hunza, a distance of 43.6 kilometers. Ghulam Hussain sahab said, "I am originally from Nagar. I have been to Karachi once in 2005, but did not really like it," he said apologetically. A not-so-talkative and not-very-curious gentleman, he asked where exactly I needed a drop. "From Gulmit to Garelt it takes approximately 1 and a half hours. When we reach there we will coordinate with your group," he said. Taking advantage of a hired car all for us, I requested if he could stop at Attabad lake and the sacred rocks. Ghulam sahab had no issues and was in no hurry. Attabad lake is at its best early in the morning, with a quick stop and a few clicks later I thanked him for stopping. As soon as we crossed the last Attabad tunnel our eager eyes were in search of Ladyfinger peak – which has been our favourite mountain peak to this date since we first saw it in 2016. Rayyan and I both screamed with joy when we spotted it; clouds lift, revealing the stunning Ladyfinger peak only for a few minutes before the clouds covered it again. Unlike other peaks the Ladyfinger peak hardly had any snow on its apex due to the sharp pinnacle.

Ladyfinger Peak lesser known as Bubulimuting, is a "distinctive rock spire" in the Batura Muztagh, the westernmost sub-range of the KKH. It lies on the southwest ridge of the Ultar Sar massif. The entire massif rises above the Hunza Valley to the southeast. Bublimotin is conspicuous among other snow peaks, due to its relatively sharp, rock spire with no snow on its apex. That combined with its height above the valley, makes it quite remarkable; therefore, given the distinctive name. It provides a 6,000 meters (19,685 feet) with a high-altitude rock.

Meanwhile, my phone reception was better once we had crossed Attabad lake and I was eager to coordinate with Muqeem Baig (CEO Climax Adventure Pakistan) who was to lead us to Rakaposhi Basecamp the following day. He explained to Ghulam sahab where he needed to drop us – Garelt, which I had never heard of, but passed by many times. I wanted to make the best out of the opportunity to have a private car and make stopovers at places I missed. Remember I mentioned earlier 'In all these years I have learnt if you really want something you will figure out one way or the other to make it possible'. I have always been curious about the Haldeikish – Sacred Rocks of Hunza. So the next short stop was Haldeikish Sacred Rocks of Hunza.

Haldeikish Sacred Rocks of Hunza in the Karakoram region

Haldeikish Sacred Rocks of Hunza is 4.3 kilometers away from Garelt. The 30 feet high and 200 yards long rocks are on top of a hill which is at the left bank of Hunza river. It is easily accessible from the Karakoram Highway. The isolated rock which is further divided into two portions – Upper and Lower, with carvings, inscriptions and images from Pre-Historic era.

The upper portion of the rock consist of inscriptions which are carved in Sogdian, Kharoshi, Brahmi languages. The names of the Emperors of the Kushana Empire appear in these inscriptions as well as names of other Emperors and Empires. The name of the Trukha King Ramadusa is also mentioned in the writings which are carved in Brahmi language. The lower portion is engraved by the images of Ibexes which are shown in different states such as being hunted. The carvings also contain horned-human idols playing with the ibexes. The carvings of the Ibexes amongst all represents the cultural importance to Buddhists as well as to the region in primeval era. One of the figurines is that of an ancient Chinese King while some carvings illustrate a Tibetan-fashioned Stupa.

In the past there used to be many Buddhist shelter caves which later collapsed over time. Altogether there are six rocks with inscriptions and drawings; 4 clustered together, one to the south of the Heldeikish site and one rock is in the upstream. Number of inscriptions is in six languages known to be: Kharoshti, Brahmi, Soghdian, Bactrian, Chinese and Tibetan. Most inscriptions are said to be found on the eastern face of Rock – I. it has a portrait of a Kushan king in a central Asian dress with the name Gondophernes written on it in Kharoshi language. On Rock – II, located on the southern side, at the ground level in the middle has the petroglyphs (prehistoric rock carving). Written in Brahmi language on the large boulder is the Buddhist name which means 'protected by Buddha'. This rock also contains inscriptions in Guptan script. Rock – III and II also have some inscriptions; while Rock – IV has the illustrations with an exception of engravings. Rock III has Sogdian and Guptan scripts which tells the story of Harisena, a Guptan General. He defeated the local Hunza ruler around 5th century AD and introduced Buddhist law in this area. Along with the graffiti and rock carvings on Rock – V and VI, there are also found some inscriptions and writings. These hundreds and thousands of names, titles, drawings, engravings and rock-carvings emphasize the significant role of Hunza valley from linguistic to cultural exchange en route the primitive Silk Route.

The Sacred Rocks of Hunza are a Cultural Heritage Site of Pakistan, a tourist attraction, is quite well-preserved, nevertheless some carvings carrying inscriptions are effected due to aging and tourist negligence. Commissioner of Northern Areas of Pakistan and Director of Archaeology are responsible for the preservation of the site, both acting under the Government of Pakistan. Due to recent flooding in Hunza River and a flow of local and foreign tourism the site faces extreme danger in future.

Haldeikish Sumak a local carpet inspired from the ancient carvings on the sacred rock of Hunza is on display at a resort in Gulmit – a replica of the carvings on the rock that dates back to the 1st millennium AD. More than 100 such antique carpets are on display at Moksha Resort Gulmit.

* **Tip:** Even if you have hired anyone or using tourist services never expect a human being to be compelled to satisfy or meet all your demands. Remember a polite tone goes a long way.

We passed Ganish – oldest settlements of Hunza and a recipient of UNESCO's Asia-Pacific Awards of Cultural Heritage Conservation. Another place I really wanted to visit but not today. The driver very patiently followed Muqeem's directions to the place of stay in Garelt. The group I was to join for the Rakaposhi basecamp was already settled in the coaster, ready to leave for Karimabad. The plan was to visit Baltit Fort, Karimabad market and have lunch there. I asked Muqeem if it was okay for me to join them later in the day, which he agreed and left with the group.

I got dropped off at Karimabad once again! Third time in this part of Hunza in less than 2 weeks sure was a treat for me. As expected we sauntered around the buzzing market place. I wanted to see if I could meet Amir Khan sahab from North Gems & Handicrafts and he was there right behind the counter of one of the most stunning looking handicraft shop – the only one of its kind in the vicinity with racks of books tucked away on one end of the shop. A humble, calm and very well opinionated gentleman who bluntly told me, "Literate? Highly literacy rate here? Sincerely I will only accept the compliment when someone here has a book to their credit". He is very forthright when speaking about Hunza, its culture, heritage, cuisine, young generation's altering ways of eating and donning attire that doesn't compliment their history. He also told me, "Next time you visit Hunza, try and spend some time in Nasirabad. It's not very far just a 50 minute drive (26.1 kilometers) from here. Take the Karakoram Highway, along the Hunza river from Karimabad to Aliabad to Haiderabad to Murtazabad to Nasirabad. It's a small town and known to be one of the ancient villages of GB. Lower Hunza starts from a village Khizirabad and ends at Nasirabad. Its location on KKH makes it as a center village of Lower Hunza. You will find Shina speakers there, mainly migrants from nearby areas of Hunza, and many families belong to families of center Hunza. The shina language is dominated language that's why people declare it as "Shinaki". It is very culturally enriched and not very different from the culture of central Hunza".

He is very passionate about books and respects people who read and write. Even though my first travel journal was still in print he agreed to place his order and confidentially stated, "I'll make sure people buy it and read it and realize your efforts." I wanted Rayyan to remember this man of resilience, took a couple of pictures with him and promised to contact him once my book was out.

A few steps away from Hidden Paradise hotel, Rayyan and I both had this sudden Chamus craving. In we went and ordered a glass each. I wanted my son to try Tzamik Potatoes in their menu that I had last year and thoroughly enjoyed the grainy textured meal. It's a creamy dish made using crushed apricot kernels cooked with cut-up potatoes. Slightly overpowering dense base that can fill your belly with half a wooden bowl, it is served in. Apparently they were phasing out the whole wooden crockery and cutlery theme this restaurant once had, which was sad to know. I enjoyed eating local food in the handmade bowls and spoons fashioned out of apricot, cherry, apple, pear and mulberry trees.

*** Tip:** Express what you value as a local tourist, whether its food and flavours, the handcrafts or the tableware that you are served in. Everyone enjoys a good compliment any day.

By mid-afternoon we were still walking in Karimabad on the distinctly bumpy, round stones, perhaps originally designed for horses and their hooves, to get a good grip. The history, the magnetism and nostalgia the cobblestone streets have, is truly a way of winning over any self-proclaimed modernist. That's when Muqeem spotted us and ushered to join the rest of the group at Hunza Food Pavilion enjoying the fresh cooked food by Lal Shehzadi. I refused to eat another morsel after the hearty serving of Tzamik Potatoes. We sat outside while Rayyan ran off to meet Ramazan Baig sahab relaxing outside Sultan Carpet Palace, who met him with equal enthusiasm.

A quick introduction of all group members between offering and munching food, talking and enjoying the sunny weather in a small cabin. I sat on the bench outside and began talking to Fatimah about my travel journey that started some thirteen days back. We seemed to be getting along quite well and that is what I love about travelling with strangers in a group. Everyone has a story to tell. Each individual has a "why they decided to sign up for this particular trip" story. I joined because Muqeem (the trekking enthusiast) decided my son and I should opt for Rakaposhi basecamp. According to the itinerary it was time for us to visit Attabad lake for a boat ride. Been there done that before so I wanted to stay back. So did Fatimah. I really wanted to get to know this mysterious but very friendly looking woman. The rest of them bundled up in the coaster and left while we started walking down the path aimlessly. We made a few photography stops, your gaze just falls in the direction of the sunny, snowy Rakaposhi, standing out from its neighboring mountains with a stunning vertical rise of nearly 20,000 feet. We made our first stop at Didar Karim sahab's shop Mountaineering Equipment where you can buy, rent or sell all sorts of good quality mountaineering equipment. We both needed a lightweight durable trekking pole. This place has everything under one roof, adventure clothing, outdoor camping equipment, camping backpacks, hiking tents, climbing shoes, camping sleeping bags, trekking poles, climbing gear including ice-axes, crampons, harnesses, snow-grippers, ropes; down jackets, windbreakers, rain gear and a lot more. You will never be cheated so don't worry about the quality and cost.

* **Tip:** Even if you feel the need to bargain, beware of your tone and the volume of your voice. Your tone determines whether you will make your relationship or break it. Any undesirable loudness in your voice could put off the nicest of people.

It took us almost half an hour to decide upon a down jacket and trekking poles. Longing for a good cup of tea we moved towards Café de Hunza, a few steps away. I ordered tumoro for myself, a Kashmiri tea and chocolate brownie for Rayyan and black coffee for my new-found friend, who ordered a full sized walnut cake to go. An hour later we were back on the street; a shade more experienced, a tad more at ease here than ever before and more appreciative of this mountain paradise. Across the road I wanted to stop and visit Hunza Wood Art which was closed last week I was here. It was fortunately open. This place exhibits an amazing craftsmanship by Ismail Jatoori; a display of all kinds of spoons made with mulberry, apricot, cherry, birch, walnut, pear trees, proudly hanging in all shapes, sizes and designs. Each has its own distinct smell, texture and colour. Everything was handcrafted in this little shop which has a small workshop attached to it. Photographing, admiring, and making a good purchase we left the shop. It felt nice chit chatting, going into one shop or another, looking at handicrafts, dried delicious treats and that's when my eyes fell on my most-loved plump luscious fruit. I made a large purchase of ripe cherries and decided to rest and enjoy them. Pizza Pamir was the chosen spot. We met Amin again, who come what may, will always welcome you with the warmest welcoming smile. He laughed as he dug into my bag of cherries and asked if we wanted to have tea but we refused. Rayyan wanted to order a cheese pizza which he did. Casual conversation, devouring delicious cherries, with the huge massif dominating the skyline – The Mighty Rakaposhi. Due to its prominent position in the valley many have considered scaling the peak but relatively few have attempted the summit. For this reason, the mountain maintains a certain mystery for many.

Rakaposhi Peak – the 27th highest peak in the world & 12th highest in Pakistan is in the Karakoram mountain range in Pakistan. It is sometimes referred to as Rakaposhi-Haramosh Mountains. Situated in the Bagrot valley Gilgit and Nagar district, it is roughly 100 kilometers north of the city of Gilgit. Rakaposhi means "snow covered". The fact that you can see its exceptional rise of its snow-covered peaks all the way from the Karakoram Highway route that goes through Nagar Valley. You can even see its majestic wall of snow all the way from Hunza Valley. In Burushaski language it means "Shining Wall" (Gasherbrum-I also means "Shining Wall" in the local Balti language). The peak is also known as Dumani which means Mother of Mist. The northern part is in knot of four great mountain ranges, Himalayas, Karakorum, Hindu-Kush and the Pamirs, with densest concentration of high peaks on earth, including the second highest peak in the world, K-2 (8611metres). Sadly, with the passage of time the natural diversity of these breathtaking areas is threatened by anthropogenic activities mainly because of local tourists. The first major glimpse that you can enjoy is from an area called Zero point which is right on the KKH. It is here that you get a magnificent view of the peak, with glacier fed streams running down. If you have the time, you could also trek up to the glacier visible from the road side. Locals suggest it will take around 2 hours to go up there (a further 3,000 – 4,000 feet up). Technically it is difficult and dangerous due to extreme avalanche risk. This mountain is extremely broad measuring almost 20 kilometers from East to West. It is the only peak on Earth that drops directly, uninterrupted, for almost 6,000 meters from the summit to the base.

After six failed expeditions the peak was first climbed by "British-Pakistani Forces Himalayan Expedition" in 1958. This British expedition was aided by the help of all available high-altitude porters of Hunza valley. The climbing was hampered by continuous snowfall, avalanches and blizzards. Despite the severe conditions Banks and Patey, two of the seven climbers in the expedition made an attempt for the summit. That was almost thirty-six days after setting up base camp. They reached the summit five hours later without oxygen. They did not stay longer and descended quickly back to their tent and returned to base camp three days later. It was not until 1979, that the mountain was scaled again.

Amin is a friendly young man, who rarely gets a chance to sit and talk at his workplace. Since the ovens weren't lit up yet there were no customers. I asked him if he has ever been to Karachi? "I visited in 2010 or 2011, and I realized the worth of the place I live in; free flow of clean water, the uncontaminated environment, fresh fruit and I realized how people from the South cherish these beauties," he says. There are plenty of water sources in the valley; glaciers topping the list, precipitation, river water, and the spring waters account for catering various domestic and agricultural needs. "I don't consider life in city as a quality life, everyone is stuck in a rat race. Ultimate goal for them is to earn money to buy a house and a luxurious car. Life is here... in the mountains close to nature, where people care about one another. But things are changing here. You will notice that a lot of guesthouses and hotels have opened especially in Aliabad. After the emergence of so many tour groups, self-driven cars and self-guided people and the quality of the road has turned this part of Pakistan a major tourist destination," says Amin. Discussing flow of tourism in Pakistan, he shares his views, "The roads were not as carpeted as they are now and the political conditions in the country have improved.

These roads were properly constructed in 2010, and before that it would take us 24 – 28 hours to reach here which now takes some 16 hours. Now there is easy access and social media has played an important role but people do not appreciate and end up complaining. When they visit these places they should expect natural beauty not the luxurious life they have left behind." Fatimah and I both agreed and I added, "If they cannot come out of their comfort zones they shouldn't travel." We started talking about other attractive places in Pakistan and I declared I wanted to visit Shimshal valley next year. "Don't just go to Shimshal, go to Shimshal Pass if you have the stamina and the determination. Now they have paved trekking routes built by the locals and if you are not scared of heights you must go. One wrong step and you are gone. But there have been no causalities yet because either us Shimshalis go or people who are used to such tough treks. Besides the local Shimshal people are there to escort tourists along the way. Our old generations have fought with a lot of things, earlier when there were no roads, no ropes, no protections people were still living there and moving around. They paved these roads themselves with no available modern technology. They placed every step themselves using yak horns in the process. Did you know that yak horns are so strong you can dig holes with them? People have made various documentaries but never covered the real stories behind the now repaired roads. Those people were real scientists and masterminds. Imagine living up in the mountain and do what your intellect tells you. They even fashioned the water channels using wood and natural material. They didn't Google or YouTube those ideas." He continued, "I'll tell you about Shimshal, the Mir used to punish people by sending them to Shimshal knowing how tough the terrain was. People stayed there knowing nothing about the outside world. Back then the Mir did not allow people to leave Gilgit, so people used their own strength and abilities to survive the harsh conditions. Sadly, that generation is gone and no one knows about them or what they did. Now if you visit

Shimshal you will meet people like myself who haven't done much as compared to the ones who were intelligent – the unsung heroes of our times. Rajab Shah the outstanding mountaineer from Shimshal, who knows about him? No one," he sighed.

Rajab Shah, the high-altitude mountaineer cum porter was the first Pakistani to summit all five 8,000 meter peaks in the country – K2, Nanga Parbat, Gasherbrum I (twice), Gasherbrum II and Broad Peak, without using supplemental oxygen during most of his climbs. This was all back in the 80's when he started his career in 1987, and accompanied a team of French travelers in 1988. He was awarded Pride of Performance Award for mountaineering by the President of Pakistan. He has accomplished much more than what people actually know. The amazing feat of all five summits within nine years as a high altitude porter is a big deal to achieve. Carrying loads up to 20 kilograms or clearing the way for expeditions, he has literally earned his way to the top list of extraordinary people of Shimshal. Unfortunately, he didn't get a chance to summit any of the 6,000 or 7,000ers before working with an army expedition on Nanga Parbat, the 8,126 meters (26,660 feet) high which is the 9th highest mountain in the world and the 2nd highest in Pakistan. To give back to his community through his skill, he voluntarily chose to train the next generation instead of chasing fame and fortune. He donated all his hard-earned equipment before he got some help setting up a mountaineering school in Shimshal. This school has produced the celebrated mountaineers of our times, including Meherban Shah, Mirza Ali, Samina Baig, Qudrat Ali and Shaheen Baig. He passed away in April 2016, but continued his mission to promote, guide and teach the skills. Unfortunately, like many others, he also felt that there was no value (qadar) for mountaineering in our country. Immensely saddened when he spoke about this, saying, "I served the country for 20 years on the mountains but now I am old and at home with no regular income or pension. If God forbid I fall sick, there won't be anyone to inquire about me. There is no value in this country and that makes me a little sad," the dignified gentleman spoke a few months before he passed away at the age of 63.

"None of the outstanding people of Shimshal have gotten any recognition by the Government or the people of Pakistan," Amin said. "The uneducated ones at that time did not know how to publicize their victories and share their proud moments with the rest of the world. People have been part of rescue missions on Nanga Parbat, K2 and other peaks but they don't do it for mere recognition, I feel they just never got the respect and acknowledgement they deserved. Many have lost their lives in the process too." He continued, "The real heroes are the porters that accompany people who wish to summit peaks. For them there is no name, no fame and no income which they truly deserve. Have you watched the movie by the name of Summit? The part where the guy goes back to rescue is the guy from Shimshal, it was humanity that led him to return. Unfortunately, the poor chap slipped and lost his life. What did he get in return? Nothing. His young kids lost their loving father and sole bread-earner. Almost all porters that accompany trekkers are from Shimshal – the extraordinaire high-altitude porters." After a short pause Amin said, "I am not fond of climbing, I cannot bear the cold up there. At Shimshal Pass the weather conditions around October makes you feel the same as K2 does and I am not exaggerating. Last I went in 2014, our yaks graze on the green pastures so we have to stay there for 3 days or so before bringing them down. Yak is a very submissive animal, you call them and they follow. So it was my turn and I was up for some adventure too. The first day passed by but the second day it rained and snowed so the grass was covered in snow. Thus, we decided to take them to the other far-off side. When it was time to return, we lost our way and night fell. Now it is a big responsibility to put them all back in a safe place since everyone's yak is there, altogether they must be 24 in number. It was like a blizzard and we couldn't find our way out, it felt like a near-death experience," he smiled at his tragedy. It is here that you learn life-long lessons. Lessons that no classroom or school will teach you. A shepherd herding his cattle has the leadership skills in its true sense.

* **Tip:** Everyone who is born and brought up in the mountains is not acclimatized with severe weather conditions therefore do not express shock and disbelief when you hear them saying, 'I feel cold' or 'I can't bear winters'!

After an hour we collected the pizza, thanked Amin for all his stories and left. Walking down the road we stopped to enjoy the two-minute drum beat of a *baraat* (wedding procession). A nice refresher it was. Walking further down from Pizza Pamir, we crossed Hidden Paradise, Café de Hunza, Hunza Serena Inn, Sweet Tooth Hunza and stopped outside Karakuram Caravan Information Center. The place stands out for its crowd-pleasing yak motorbikes. Dressed in real yak skin, horns, rough tail Rayyan wanted to ride it. You can rent these and patrol around Karimabad. It was 7:30 p.m. and the sun had set down. We decided to sit near the edge of Serena Inn from where you can view **Ganish** village – now a well preserved heritage site. Said to be one of the earliest settlements on the ancient Silk Route, it is 3.1 kilometers from Karimabad. 1000-year-old historic Ganish means gold in Durushaski. A site of various ancient watch towers, traditional mosques, religious centers and a reservoir. History says this settlement was inhabited by 10th century caravans; Shish Kin, a Chinese visitor whose ancestors belonged to this region. Nominated twice and Recipient of two UNESCO Asia-Pacific Awards for Cultural Heritage Conservation in 2002 and 2009. I was wondering why I never went down to explore the place, though I knew very well it existed and why has Muqeem never added it in his itineraries. Not a very known and popular tourist spot,

Ganish is home to 4 mosques that are 300-to-400 years old.

The sub-villages of Ganish include Garelt, Chaboikushal, Shukunoshal, Gamun Ganish, Buldas and Chillganish.

Chaboikushal village is located right in the heart of Hunza Valley with about 25 houses or families. Chaboikushal was derived from Chaboi, the grandfather of Sheril.

Chillganish has 25 families living there. Chillganish is one of the most ancient villages of Ganish with a rich history. The word chill means water and Ganiskuz means residents of Ganish.

Garelt has a population of about 135 families (the statistics may vary).

I decided to put that in my bucket list for 2019, including Shimshal, Chitral, Phander and many others.

The group returned around 8 p.m. and between bathroom trips, shopping for jackets, trekking sticks, chocolates, fruits, dry fruits and kilao* we gathered to have dinner at a hotel in Karimabad. It was around 11 p.m. when we reached Garelt our hotel and were informed that we need to wake up early. Wisdom is to leave for any trek before the day breaks or as soon as the day breaks to avoid the blazing rays.

* Kilao is an organic product produced in Ghizer district of Gilgit-Baltistan and Chitral. Kuju village in south of Chitral is also known for the production of Kilao. Rich in taste and rough in texture, it is made by using pure organic products including grape juice, walnut/apricot kernel. Two major variations of Kilao are: apricot and walnut kernel.

My prior research had been:
Minapin to Hapakun 3- 4 hours, 5.8 kilometers, 792 meters' ascent
Hapakun to Tagaphari 2- 3 hours, 3 kilometers, 457 meters' ascent

Askoreshung 3 hours, 5.8 kilometers, 1319 meters' ascent, 1319 meters' descent
Diran Base Camp 7- 8 hours, 12 kilometers, 389 meters' ascent, 389 meters' descent
Kacheli Lake 3 hours, 8 kilometers, 300 meters' ascent, 300 meters' descent
Tagaphari to Minapin 3- 3½ hours, 8.8 kilometers, 1249 meters' descent
Retracing your steps down towards the valley to Minapin via Hapakun.
Tagaphari to Minapin 4- 4½ hours, 8.4 kilometers, 389 meters' ascent, 1638 meters' descent

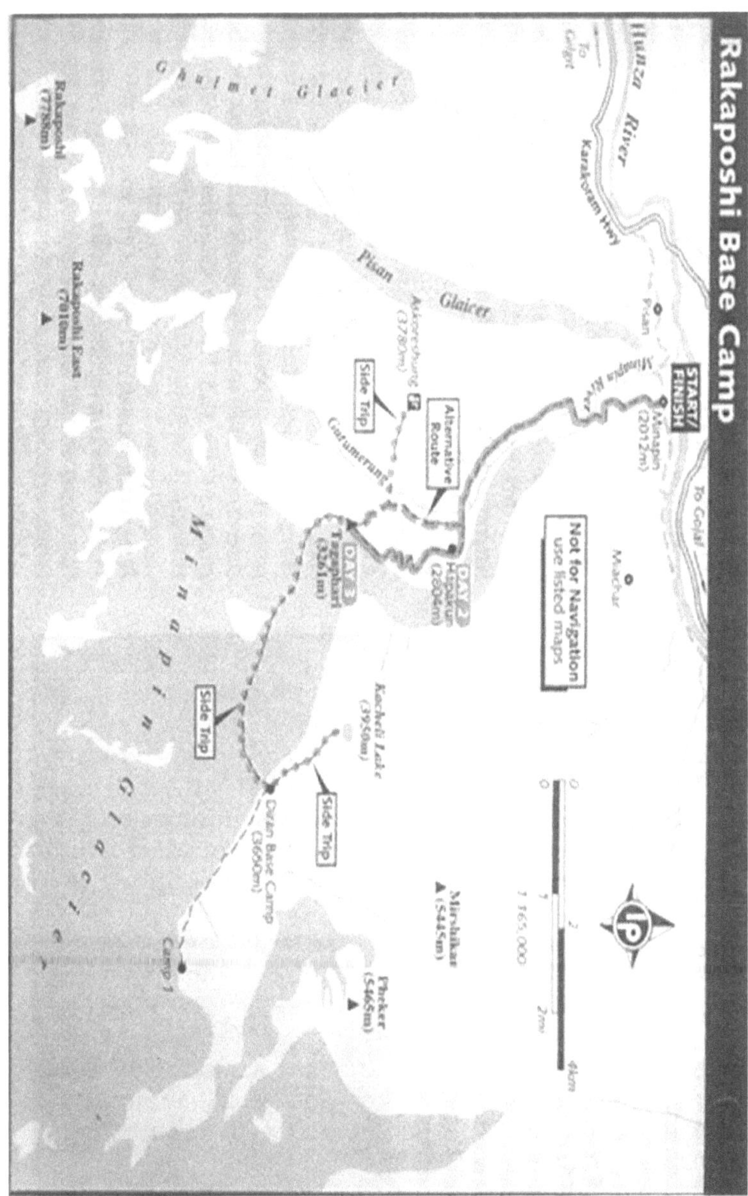

Rakaposhi Base Camp
Hunza River
To Gilgit
Ghulmet Glacier
Pisan Glacier
Pisan
Minapin River
Rakaposhi (7788m)
Rakaposhi East (7010m)
Askorchung (3780m)
Side Trip
(outumerang)
Alternative Route
START/ FINISH
Minapin (2012m)
Machar
To Gilgit
Not for Navigation use listed maps
DAY 2 Hapakun (2804m)
DAY 3 Tagaphari (3551m)
Minapin Glacier
Side Trip
Kacheli Lake (3950m)
Side Trip
Duran Base Camp (3650m)
Camp 1
Mirshikar (5445m)
Phoker (5465m)
1:165,000
0   1   2   3   4km

Day 13 – And the trek begins – Minapin to Hapakun – 1ˢᵗ July 2018

Plan: *Breakfast and Drive to Minapin (45 minutes), start trekking from Minapin to Hapakun (4 – 5 hours' trek – 5.8kilometres, 792metres ascent). If not tired can continue to basecamp directly which is another 3-4 hours hike further.*

*** Tip:** When in the mountains try not to miss the incredible sunrises and the sunsets as it paints the mountains in gorgeous shades of orange, red, and gold.

I woke up around 7 a.m. and went outside to check if anyone else was up. Outside the sky was clear and Rakaposhi was standing tall in all its glory. You will often find this 7,800-meter-high peak cloudless. It is, undoubtedly the most iconic mountains from the Karakoram range which can be visible from the Karakoram Highway.

I loved my silent early morning walk. Soon all the other group members started waking up, half drowsy half excited. As always, I was liking my group already. A bunch of nice people. I tried waking up a tired Rayyan. Yesterday was a long tiresome day for him. Between finding the right washroom with warm water to take a bath, sunscreen lotions, what to wear, what not to wear, discussions over will it be hot and sunny, where are my sunglasses, oh I need to buy a pair, and a warm cap, I am hungry we all got ready to leave for breakfast. Getting to know each other better over a cup of Lavazza that Fatimah brought with her, we added a touch of Hunza – some salt. Soon after we decided to head outside to the market place to get a pair of sunglasses because I left mine in a public bus somewhere, a warm cap and I most certainly had to buy cherries. I was mocked (all in good humour) for purchasing and carrying cherries but they all solemnly agreed that they were heavenly.

Back on the road and as luck would have it, it was a clear sunny day. Yeah I am being sarcastic! Whenever I have planned trekking trips the sunshine follows with all its strength. As much as I like exploring on my own, travelling with a group of strangers that turn into good friends, is always an experience that shouldn't be missed. My son enjoys socializing and mingling with people and has grown quite fond of 'Muqeem bhai' over the last three trips. This was my 4th trip with Climax Adventure and each time we have had a decent group of people from Islamabad, Karachi and Lahore. Eugenia from Argentina was the only foreigner travelling with us and it was her first visit to Pakistan.

From Garelt to Minapin it is 29.1 kilometers and you will cross Aliabad, Haiderabad, Murtazabad, Nasirabad, Pissan along the Hunza River. The magnificent Rakaposhi, Diran peak and Golden peak are located in Nagar valley however, Hunza valley is both locally and internationally a more famous tourist destination. Nagar has been neglected by tourists although it has exceptional views; Golden Peak, glinting with snow, framed by slopes of green cultivated fields, poplar trees, fruit orchards and blossoms.

Passing through small towns and villages on the flank of the mountain, reveling in the unconditional high snowy peaks, with lush green valleys below, endless fruit orchards, and people whose hospitality is unmatched. Driving along the highway taking in the spectacular view that at times become extremely dangerous at various points, as the paved international highway has been cut through the highest and the mightiest mountains of the world, The Himalayas and The Karakoram. Yes, I feel absolutely blessed to be able to travel safely in Pakistan. The Karachitte in me has mellowed down with all these trips up north. I have learnt to trust my instincts and be grateful for my blessings. I feel glad to unearth my passion in life which many fail to accomplish. Nature is the best teacher. It always humbles you and makes you ponder upon your creator and your existence.

I had never read about a trek before attempting or signing up for it. Rayyan and I first trekked in 2016, to Passu Glacier, which was not only strenuous but painful too. My body hadn't expected hardships that I suddenly hurled on it and neither was I mentally prepared to hike that much that long. That was the first time I realized how many other things I was capable of doing if only I tried. And I told my son the same thing. We travelled to Fairy Meadows in 2017, but because I was recovering from a foot injury (broke 2 bones) so I covered half on foot and half on the horse to reach Fairy Meadows. Though Rayyan did the two-day trek when he was only 6 years. Beyal camp was easier. *Going to Hapakun takes around 4 to 5 hours depending upon your fitness, speed and stamina. The trail is "beginner level trek" and very easy to follow, except for the last few kilometers which are slightly rough and confusing*, is what I read and was made to believe. But that wasn't the case. It was definitely not a beginner level trek. Some are of the opinion that it is a moderate level trek, which makes sense to me!

The trek located in Nagar Valley is also known as Minapin trek. It can easily be accessed through the Karakoram Highway. A popular opinion is that this is one of the easiest treks leading to 7,000 meters Karakoram peaks with fascinating views of Rakaposhi and Diran peak. The Minapin Glacier (also known as Barpu Boulter glacier), sweeps down from the 16 kilometers long fluted ridge that connects Rakaposhi and Diran respectively. The trek leads up from the village of Minapin along the Minapin River, above the confluence of Hunza and Minapin Rivers. The most scenic approach to Rakaposhi basecamp is from Minapin to Tagaphari and Kacheli. This route takes you through thick forests, fruit orchards, wild flowers, pastures, green valleys and matchless tranquility.

We reached Minapin, a small, sung and cozy village which is the starting point for both Rakaposhi and Diran basecamps. According to the plan our first stop and campsite was Hapakun, which we kept mispronouncing (Hakapun). The campsite is sandwiched between Minapin and the Rakaposhi basecamp and is the perfect place to spend the first night, rest and continue the next day if you are not too adventurous. From here you can proceed to Diran glacier, a vast sea of ice, composed of ice blocks of nearly 20 meters. Minapin has a few budget hotels, where we dropped our unwanted luggage. We were asked to keep what was necessary for the next 3 days and we hired porters collectively. Normally the porters in the mountains have donkeys or horses to carry stuff with them. But you will also find extremely strong and spirited porters ready to pick heavy luggage. I always feel the work these guys do is not paid for nor respected accordingly. Hotel Osho Thang and Hills n Huts are the best budget hotel in this region with relatively economical restaurants and rooms. The people are friendly and can communicate both in Urdu and English. If you visit the place in spring, you will see the gardens full of blossoming cherry trees. We were asked to keep a daypack to carry on-the-go valuables, such as water bottle, camera gear, sunscreen and an extra warm clothing.

*** Tip:** Be prepared with: durable shoes – weather and waterproof jackets – snacks – water – trekking poles and sun protection.

Rakaposhi base camp is one of the most epic camping spots, after Fairy Meadows I have ever camped at. At 3,500 meters, Rakaposhi basecamp stands for any trekkers / hikers to climb and witness the majestic mountain up close and personal. If you climb any of the surrounding hills, some being steep, you will witness an amazing 360-degree view of the entire area. With no inhabitants or other campers along the trek; cows and donkeys silently grazing, the wild plantation strewn all over, a long stream making its way across the grassland, flowing from the glaciers, the place will keep you busy the entire day. However, you are likely to find colourful flags and shepherds to lead the way, but it's best to have company on treks for various reasons. Best time to trek is in summers from May to October when the trails are snow-free. Adventurers have attempted in winters as well.

* **Tip:** Respect people, norms and cultural values.

Minapin village, like most parts of GB is very hospitable and traditional but slightly conservative. Villagers would prefer visitors to dress more moderately and traditionally as opposed to western clothing. Women are normally escorted by men in the village and on trek. The Burushaski name 'Minapin' is derived from compacted (pin) mud (resembling mina, the dry meal of pressed nuts, such as walnut, or apricots after their oil is extracted) that the glacier once deposited in the village.

We started our trek with loading up our required luggage and leaving the rest behind. It was 11 a.m. and the sun's rays were descending very aggressively, so we weren't sure if we should keep warm clothing or not.

* **Tip:** For any trek this may be the best remedy. Fill your water bottle with plain or fresh, clean spring water and place a handful of dried apricots and shake it rigorously. Refill as many times as needed. This will keep you well hydrated.

When you are travelling in a group you tend to look out for each other like a family. It is a beautiful feeling. Lots of sunblock and covering up against the sunbeams we started off, strolling on the dirt lane, waiting for everyone to join in. A few minutes' walk along the village canal, turn right and follow the path along the canal for another 15 minutes or less towards the Minapin River. When passing through village you will notice curious gazes peering at you, local children playing, men and women stretching their backs into the sunshine amid work, and domestic animals grazing fields.

The entire hike will take approximately 7 hours without breaks, moderate speed, if you begin early in the morning. From Minapin, head south along the village road until you come across a bridge to a well-constructed hydro-plant. The trail turned towards the gorge and we crossed the wooden footbridge about 2,103 meters above the gushing water to the river's bank and we stopped for the much needed photography. Thereon, follow a gravel path up the rocky mountain. The paths zigzag up the side of a mountain and then the trail becomes leveled as you walk through thick forest. Walnut trees shade the path that provide a home for nesting birds. The trail rises and twists for another half an hour or so, before it eases off and you enter an aromatic juniper and rose bush forest.

Juniper (*yarz*, in wakhi) is an evergreen shrub found on the mountains. The tree grows to a height of 6-25 feet and has stiff, pointed needles that grow around 1 centimeters long. The female bears' cones that produce small round bluish-black berries, which take three years to fully mature. Juniper belongs to the pine family. It has diuretic, antiseptic, stomachic, antimicrobial, anti-inflammatory, and anti-rheumatic properties. The tree's therapeutic properties stem from a volatile oil found in the berries. This oil contains terpenes, flavonoid glycosides, tannins, sugar, tar, and resin. (Encyclopedia.com)

For me trekking is not about how fast I can reach my destination, but to enjoy the beauty as I walk, take pictures, splash and drink water from a stream or a waterfall, record sounds, smell the trees in the forest make videos to watch later and fathom the symmetry in nature. So, if you are that kind of person it may take you slightly longer to reach your destination. You may climb up rocks to take a short cut if you are adventurous and athletic. Trekking / Hiking is meant to be an enjoyable activity and ought to be done at a more relaxed pace.

In all these years of traveling I have sort of divided the trekkers into 3 categories; the *leaders* aka *mad-dashers* who want to outdo everyone, conceivably in a good way, *slow and steady scramblers* who may be slow but more consistent and *I'll hike my own hike*, hiking a trail in the manner that they enjoy. I fall in between the latter 2 categories and end up walking with the second and the third group of people. There may sometimes be another category of people who may exhibit a strong emotion of agony at every step.

*** Remember:** If you are just embarking on your journey: take pleasure from it. Savour every minute. Remember your real goal, the thing that brought you out of your comfort zone in the first place, and fight hard for it. If you make it all the way to the end, then you'll have done a beautiful thing. Just remember: the end can be anywhere, and you get to choose it, so choose wisely!

Wherever we found some shade or water we would sit down and rest, enjoy cherries or our trail mix. I kept hearing comments like, *"You look like you are selling cherries on the way!"*, *"can't believe you are actually carrying them with you"* and that followed by *"they are so refreshing on a hot day"*, *"I am telling you they will keep you hydrated"*, *"the Hunza ones are the best in taste"* and *"why didn't you get more of these?"* This is the best time to bond with fellow trekkers and listen to life and travel stories and who they left behind. When you turn and look at the village it is a ravishing sight from up above. You can feel a certain spiritual serenity and enjoy the pleasures of meaningful time among the magnificent rural landscapes. Luscious green pasturage with Golden Peak in the backdrop.

Hunza – Nagar the lakeside paradise was previously known as Brushal. Hunza and Nagar used to be separate princely states parted by the River Hunza which marked the border between the two states. These states were notorious for looting traders and caravans that entered from China. The British wanted to expand their trade to Russia from here, but the states refused to. In 1891, Nagar was invaded by the British Army led by Colonel Durand. British surrounded Nagar's Nalt Fort, and eventually took control of it six months later. Soon the power was vested from the British to the Maharaja of Kashmir. Owing to the distance, locals continued to live freely. Dongs, the capital of Nagar, was in Nagar Khas where royal courts and palaces of marble still exist. The place remained the capital until the last royal of Maghlot Dynasty, Mir Shaukat Ali Khan, was in power. He ruled the place for over 1200 years till the state was suspended by Zulfiqar Ali Bhutto in 1974. Popular languages spoken in this area are Burushaski and Shina. Many recall the era when Shimshal was part of the independent principality of Hunza, ruled and taxed by the Mir until Bhutto declared an end to the remaining princely states in Pakistan, including Hunza.

Hooper is the most beautiful place in Nagar Khas. This less explored land of snow-clad mountains with absolute power of glaciers to carve out new landscapes makes it intricately gorgeous too. Once you leave Hunza and cross the river bridge after Ganish, a road turning right leads you to Hooper valley, dotted with fruit trees including cherries, apples, and apricots. I visited Hooper for the first time in 2017.

A road from the Nagar Khas bazar leads to the last village Hispar, and another towards Hooper, which houses glaciers and the famous Rush lake. You will find no human settlement beyond Hooper yet.

You will rarely see local people with their cattle or tourists on the Rakaposhi trek and today was an exception. A horde of students casually walking by, wearing normal shoes, beating a large drum, carrying a bulky music box and not panting like us, stopped for a trivial conversation. They were out for a fieldtrip and planned to reach the basecamp and return home before sunset. Easy for them to say and do, we mutually thought.

By 3 p.m. the sun shine had eased upon us. Keep your fruits, water bottles and trail mixes close to you while enjoying the wild flowers, plants growing in the streams that you come across as you trek, huge rocks on the side and thick roots paving your way. We spotted a stunning brown and white horse which belonged to an old man dressed simply, wearing a Hunza cap, praying on the concrete facing the rivulet under thick wild trees. This looked so peaceful.

We continued along the broad, less-shaded trail, rising gradually for another one and a half hours to the huts at Bang-i-das, along a clear stream that drops over a cascade at the head of this pleasant, lush green valley. Bang-i-das is a summer settlement along the irrigation channel and stranded huts. The trail follows the stream to the base of the waterfall, where it splits. To the right you will cross the stream over a footbridge and towards the smaller left cleft, climb for another 15 to 20 minutes to the grassy meadow of Hapakun at 2,804 meters fenced by mature fir trees. The Burushaski name Hapakun is given to a place *Kun*, within a day's walk of a main village, which is defined as *Hapa* meaning 'close enough to carry a child'. Camping is free in the open meadow. Diran and Rakaposhi remain hidden at this point. If you are fortunate, you may find Ibex in the steep cliffs above the Minapin Glacier. A small silted stream flows near the herdsmen huts at Hapakun. The landscape begins to unroll and reveals the overflowing gems of colossal beauty.

The benefits of signing up with a trusted group is that everything from travelling to accommodation to food is taken care of.
The base camp is merely 4 or 5 kilometers from Hapakun but the trail is so steep that it might take you around 3 to 4 hours to reach it. Therefore, advisable to start your trek

early, as the sun's rays are quite lethal up in the mountains. It was close to 4 p.m. and we had reached a point where we all wanted to simply remove our shoes and socks, dip our feet in cold gushing torrent flowing from under a wooden bridge that led us to a vast area of grass plain. This resting place serves you lassi (churned curd which is a sweet or savoury drink made from yogurt or buttermilk base with water), tumoro and instant noodles.

* **Tip:** Please bear in mind that this is a far-flung place so don't expect things to be available at all times.

When we reached Muqeem asked us if we needed green tea, tumoro of course. We all chorused a Yes! It is always the best option at high altitude, then tea or coffee prepared with milk. The men present there prepared tumoro and instant noodles for us – another fairly quick option. The noodles were served in the same steel mugs as the tea. Air pressure is lower at higher altitudes. Less energy means less heat, which means water will boil at a lower temperature at a higher altitude. It is here that the Walnut cake, purchased yesterday from Café de Hunza came to the rescue. Thanks to Muqeem who agreed to carry the as-heavy-as-a-brick cake. We literally crushed the whole cake into small chunks and the ones who seemed disappointed by the renowned cake a night before were now chowing it down appreciatively. Rayyan had found an adorable looking black baby goat and started following and playing with it along the stream. It seemed like Rayyan had discovered something new and was having a jolly good time in his own little world. I like how nature teaches us subconsciously and that happens with children as well. They learn to be sensitive, compassionate and empathetic. *I should consider homeschooling my child,* the thought occurred but I brushed it off instantaneously.

While we all relaxed; lying on the grass, drinking tumoro, eating, enjoying the water flow and clicking pictures laughing at how horrific we all looked in a matter of few hours. We also started looking for a place for our bathroom needs in nature.

*** Tip:** If you intend to use an open place for your 'nature's call' please make sure that you cover your excrement(s). You will always find soil / mud / leaves to cover the area. Do not leave paper or tissues behind.

The students from Nagar who were returning home from their field-trip sat down with us and agreed to perform a little dance for us. The girls shyly stated that they don't dance in public. Two young boys danced a traditional dance to the beat of live drums, which was quite energizing. "Let's get back on our feet", Muqeem announced cheerfully, after giving us an almost 2-hour break. Wistfully, passively and reluctantly we all got up and someone announced with utter conviction, "See that red flag? The trek for today ends there". *That doesn't look too far,* we mouthed looking at each other. No one in our group was a pro, yes some were better than others but we audibly and inaudibly were supporting one another. The climb from here was dusty and steep. We trekked through the forest for about an hour. After the ascent up the hill over endless complains you arrive at the Hapakun campsite! A sigh of relief!

*** Tip:** Many short breaks are better than one long one, while trekking

Sprawled on the grass once again with all our luggage that had reached before we did. You will see one rather large-sized white camp here which is used as a kitchen and the coziest place to spend the night. The young gentlemen that accompanied Muqeem on our trek started setting up our camps and soon we were all told to keep our baggage in and relax until dinner was served.
We all gathered outside to feel the night falling in. By now the temperature had dropped but none of us knew how

low it was. As I stand in the valley shaking with cold, I see a falling star, following one another in quick succession. then another one and another. With a frisson of excitement, I closed my eyes; away from the world, in the wilderness, under the clear star-filled sky, no connection with the outside world, just a bunch of us and the occasional braying of the donkeys. Overwhelmed by the awareness of how little of the world I have experienced. In the wilderness, close-calls to death are a thrilling experience too. These ditched lands are not only filled with beauty and serenity, but also with fear and anxiety.

"Dinner time!", a voice thundered breaking my string of thoughts. We scurried into the kitchen camp rubbing our frozen palms. This was the warmest place and we all wanted to sleep there that night.

* **Tip:** Food takes time to cook. Most ingredients are unavailable so be pleased with what is served and how it is served. Thank the people for their efforts.

The daal (lentil) and rice was cooked simply and we all devoured it with genuine gratitude. The young boys insisted we have a bonfire although not promised in our itinerary but arrangements were made. While no one wanted to leave the cozy kitchen but we were all tempted to go out and enjoy the bonfire. So when you are in the mountains expect a little traditional dance around the bonfire. Some of us decided to retire to our camps, the others decided to sit around the fire and tell stories. They started off with funny ones and ended on spine-tingling horror tales. Somewhere between donkeys braying and walking past our camps and cross-camp talking, we all dozed off in a peaceful slumber tucked in our warm sleeping bags, except Eugenia who had setup her camera gear to click the night sky. This was the first time on this trip that I was sharing camp with someone other than my son.

Day 14 – And the trek continues – Hapakun to Rakaposhi basecamp – 2nd July 2018

Plan: *Breakfast and continue trekking to Rakaposhi basecamp (3-4 hours). Arrive at basecamp, free time to enjoy the views around, lunch break. Hike up to viewpoint (1 hour). Enjoy the views of Muztagh mountains in the evening, Minapin glacier and hike back to the campsite for dinner and overnight camping. Minapin glacier which lies at the foot of Rakaposhi Peak (7,788m) and in the shadows of Diran Peak (7,266 m).*

I normally wake up early when I am traveling, in order to not miss anything. So I peeped out to see if anyone else was outside their camps. It was half past 5 and I could see no one. It was a chilly morning, with a clear sky. Towards the extreme end of our campsite was a small pond next to what looked like a temporary tent, made out of plastic, cloth and the top covered with leaves. And I remembered it was our temporary bathroom. Last night when I used it I couldn't really tell what it looked like in sheer darkness and flash lights. Slowly people started coming out of their camps, hugging their jackets, wraps and tooth brushes. I was appreciating the creativity of these mountain people. A plastic bottle very neatly wedged in a mud hole in the ground, attached to a strait with water pouring in from the narrow end of the bottle like a tap; extremely chilled teeth chattering glacier water. Ideally you will find a water source around the spot where homes or tents are pitched. Water is one thing which is not always readily available out in the mountains and forests. Even though you are walking on snow or can view glacial mountain peaks all around you, while on a trek or otherwise; your bottle of water becomes the most prized possession for survival. It is true 'we always learn to value things in their absence'.

Comfort is a paradox. We are trained to choose the 'easy' option. In life we naturally and impetuously make decisions that minimize stress and avert risks. Our 'comfort zone' provides us with regular happiness and low anxiety and it's nurturing nature is perfectly suited to our human condition. However, too much comfort can become uncomfortable for some of us. Living in these conditions tests your boundaries and capabilities. When you travel to the underdeveloped wilderness for long you end up being grateful for many blessings you have been taking for granted; such as moving from one place to another, hot water, taking a bath, sleeping in comfort and normal temperatures and even caffeine. My appreciation for life's small things grew exponentially on this trip. Since it was the longest trip I have ever taken. This trip raised my bar for daily gratitude. Spending lengthy amounts of time with limited resources and even less companionship reset my expectations. I enjoyed and counted every blessing a little bit more when I eventually rejoined civilization.

Unfortunately, it was quite a cloudless, sunny day for the trek but we all mutually agreed to have breakfast out in the sun. The warmth of the sun felt really good on our backs on a cold morning. The weather in the mountain is never consistent. Eggs, paratha and dry roti was served with hot water and tea. The people in the mountains are not only hardworking but will always serve you with a smile.

* **Tip:** Avoid oily, buttery, heavy-on-the-stomach food and milk tea. Bread, biscuits, boiled eggs, dry roti, plain omelet, tumoro, black coffee or black tea are good options. Remember, eggs will not be hard-boiled.

Packed, camp checked, bathroom trips, filling our water bottles with melted glacier water which was our only option, greasing our faces with sunblock, stretching our leg muscles, daypacks and trekking poles ready we started marching across the field. It was a little over 8:30 a.m. when we all gathered to start our trek.

Walking slowly at first enthralled by the mountains surrounding the valley, clear blue sky, vast green meadows and the dense forests in the morning light. These ventures to high altitude terrains, moving away from the dust and pollution of city life, sometimes to take a break from repetitive and boring life and mostly to have some exclusive time with nature is what we humans really need. I have always been fascinated by the beauty of mountains – inhaling the fresh mountain air while hiking in the woods, walking through fragrant orchards, lazing around and feeling the warmth of the sun. I used to underestimate myself thinking I can never scale such heights till I was pushed to do it. Since my first trip on the KKH with Climax Adventure, Muqeem has made sure (perhaps unintentionally) my trips involve trekking of some sort. "Oh just go ahead and sign up for Fairy Meadows," he said when my cast had just open last December. This time he didn't even bother to ask and just put me in this trip, saying "you and your son will have a good time." And so were we! I guess he really wants to secretly train my son to become a mountain climber. This being my fourth trip to the northern parts of Pakistan I slowly began to see things differently beyond the hardships and discomforts that nature bestowed upon me. I started to closely observe, feel and see the beauty of things around me. It's only possible when we are exposed to impassable rough terrains, cut off from civilization and see local communities with bare minimum necessities to live on, yet seldom or never complaining and living in harmony and complete submission with nature. The wounds, the injuries, the pains and the discomfort you embrace during your journey will make you and your children happier and stronger. Never underestimate yourself or your kids.

* **Tip:** Start with smaller goals, if it's your first time. See how far you can go, improve your abilities, preferences and your itinerary.

Be a little more sensitive, talk to the locals, understand their lives, their problems, their desires, their blessings, their stories, their strengths... Mountain life is tedious, difficult and monotonous. They live in wooden or stone houses with basic facilities and in areas that are always prone to natural calamities; bearing incredulous cold weather, miles of walk to fetch clean water or timber from the forests. Kids with cracked red cheeks due to harsh weather conditions often walk for hours to attend school yet you will always find the locals hospitable, welcoming and offer whatever little they have with a genuine smile when met enroute. Sometimes they will selflessly lend a helping hand or just pass a smile, say good luck or a little prayer and move on. If you can manage to break free of your cluttered city life every once in a while and travel; I assure you, you will come across people who are kind, caring, and who bond with strangers with no high expectations in return.

I had once read "The adventure is not in arriving; it is in the 'On the way' experience". And that is exactly what the *slow and steady scramblers* and *I'll hike my own hike*, ones do. Crossing the canal, the trail appears not parallel but perpendicular to the canal, it rises for a couple minutes across rock-strewn open ground beyond Hapakun's largest hut and then climbs instantly up the dusty twists and bends through the fir forest for a little over 15 minutes. The trail eases off and outlines the rocky slope for roughly half an hour to a lush green patch where wildflowers and birds thrive. Sweeping gently through the meadow, the trail enters scattered juniper stands and switchbacks to the winding ridge crest where Diran, Rakaposhi and their interconnecting ice wall finally comes into view. It was 11 a.m. and we were awestruck when we saw the frozen icy layers. You see the scenery change as you move closer to the destination and it will surely make you fall in love with the place and every ache worth it!

The trail thins and crisscrosses a rocky cliff above the spectacularly broken Minapin Glacier to Tagaphari (3,261 meters). Once a muddy 'taga' lake 'phari', as its

Burushaski name indicates, it's now a leveled pasture where donkeys, goats, cows and oxen graze. A shepherds' hut is next to the gravelly hillside, with plenty of lush camp sites along the snaky meandering stream. From here on it is all a steep climb that zigzags through the alpine forest for at least an hour and a half until you are out of the forest, and are completely exposed. By now you will get used to rocks and pebbles rolling under your feet but this path seemed less rocky and dusty. You will find striking raw pieces of rocks, cairns (mounds of small stones), an array of wildflowers and most commonly see willow, poplar, fir, oleander thickets that occur along the watercourses in the Karakoram range. Juniper is found on high slopes as well as shrubs of various species of genus Artemisia. Thick roots radiating from the base of a large birch tree and a few prickly wild pale pink rose (dog rose) plants with fresh rosehips hanging, just below the petals. I have been using dried rosehips in my green tea since last 2 years, for no apparent reason. I enjoy using all sorts of herbs that I get from all around GB to make a good earthy smelling cup of tea.

Dried rosehips are used for its medicinal properties. The fresh ones are full of vitamin C therefore, often used to prevent and treat colds, flu, and vitamin C deficiencies. However, much of the vitamin C is destroyed during the process of drying, packaging and storage. It is also used for tea, jam, soups, pies and stews. The flowers can be made into a syrup or can be eaten in salads. It can also be candied or preserved in vinegar and honey. People often take rosehip powder or the dried ones to try and boost their immune system, treat or prevent colds. It has also been linked to, lowering blood sugar levels, help treat diabetes, lowering cholesterol, reverse obesity, arthritis and osteoporosis. Many go to the extent of saying it prevents cancer too.

* **Tip:** Research before you use any product in its raw or synthetic form. You may be allergic to certain herbs,

rosebushes or flowers. Never take one person's recommendation. There may be severe risks involved, as every individual's body reacts differently.

You will start to see Rakaposhi soaring in the background as you come out of the forest. A small seasonal spring lies at the base of the rocky slope towards the head of this valley. The parallel moraine above the valley is a fun place to watch avalanches crashing down from the ridge between Rakaposhi and Diran, and to catch the sunset on Diran peak. Rakaposhi itself is mostly hidden from view behind the obvious snow dome of Rakaposhi East which is 7,010 meters. The visibility of glacier with 30 kilometers deep crevasses to a basecamp from where you see endless peaks of the Karakoram range. For hardcore adventure seekers, this trek is a must-do! The trail eases off and contours the rocky slope for another 30 minutes to a lush green bowl. It is here that you can view Diran Peak, Rakaposhi and their interconnecting ice wall that finally comes into full view. You will get the chills when you see yourself surrounded by the rocky glaciers – Nothing, absolutely nothing apart from glaciers composed of high ice blocks... Silence...

I was standing there all by myself in that sublime silence, interrupted only by the sound of the breaking glaciers. The massive thunderous sound commands attention nonetheless. A puff of wind welcomes you with others encouraging you to climb a few more steps to be completely mesmerized by the exotic Minapin glacier. Watching the glacier at such close proximity was breathtaking. The rough and uneven clutters of icy, razorback humps, ridges and deep crevasses. All of a sudden the weather and the winds had transformed; from warm and sunny to piercingly icy blows in our face. It was a good thing we packed our jackets. We all sat there admiring the marvelous creation of nature and in that moment I remembered, "the climb is tough but the view from the top is worth it," worth every second! Come to think of it, that quote may have multiple meanings to it. We stayed at this point for half an hour before proceeding. After a short rest we followed a path which appeared to be a steep inner frontage of the glacier moraine – unconsolidated glacial detritus of soil and rock became visible. A thrilling shiver overtook me. For the first time ever I felt scared and I was worried about my 7-year-old. All of a sudden I remembered, Michael Koblmuller (1974-1999) who died in the avalanche accident on July 26th 1999, at Diran peak. Michael died at the age of 24 during the ascent in an avalanche. Some narratives say, his friend pushed him deliberately to his death. Diran is 7,266 meters (23,839 feet) – a pyramid shaped mountain lies to the east of Rakaposhi. It is considered as the third most dangerous mountains in Pakistan after K2 and Nanga Parbat. Its snow faces are often laden with avalanche prone snow slopes and so far has caused many events resulting in dozens of deaths. Muqeem while encouraging me to progress carefully, advised me not to transfer any irrational fears in the little one. "Let him run, let him find his own path. Kids are smart and fearless. Being in the mountains will make him confident and bold".

The last part of the hike is kind of strenuous but as you get closer to the peak and the white glacial seracs you will be motivated to advance further. The estimate terrain elevation is 3,640 meters above sea-level. After reaching Tagaphari you can climb the ridge to have nice view of valley and the mountains. The beauty and peace of the place is something you can never imagine and the ultimate place for nature lovers and photographers. The deserted landscapes above and the lush green valley below make it the most astonishing trek. We just plopped on the grass, it was like reaching home. You will notice signs of camping sites and CKNP instructions. CKNP is Central Karakoram National Park GB and have a list of guidelines to obey which include, do not litter, do not hunt or disturb wild animals and birds and avoid burning wild plants for fire. Dragging our feet up to the raw mud house with chunks of stones. Facing the mud house is a large kitchen tent along the shallow glacial meltwater channel, like a snake gliding a sandy path. The insides of the mud house were constructed with unbaked earth. A humble looking primitive dwelling. These mud houses are naturally insulated, thus, will be cool in summers and warm in winters. They are not only eco-friendly, sustainable and affordable but extremely strong if constructed properly. People claim they are resistant to tremors and earthquakes.

Hungry, tired and irked by the long hike, some of us decided not to talk, just lay down silently or sleep. Upon arrival nice and warm tumoro was served. By 2:30 p.m. the most delicious daal (lentil) chawal (rice) with fresh glacier water was served. Sitting down in a mud house, on an extended lunch mat with steel dishes, plates, cups and spoons. Each one of us sincerely complimented the chefs. A little rest and few self-clicks later we set out to explore the place. To the left of the mud house, a few wobbly steps leading to a stone house with wooden doors. Inside was a very strange looking squat bathroom arranged at floor level, with two holes for bowl, opposite each other with ceramic lids on them. So a few girls in our group decided to fashion our own squat bowl, using bricks and stones. We also found a shovel and while we were figuring out a comfortable way to squat, we heard rustling sounds from the stone house next to our makeshift lavatory. Realizing this was a makeshift kitchen area we changed our minds and decided to use the bizarre looking bowls with lids.

* **Tip:** The only option available at this point is glacier meltwater or to bring your own water for survival, which means carrying gallons of water.

Muqeem announced, "Whoever wants to go down to the glacier should come now while there is still daylight." We all scooted with our warm coverings as it was getting chilly by the hour. Rayyan wanted to stay with the group in the mud house saying, "I am already freezing and too tired to walk." So half the group decided to trek up to the little hill down to the Minapin glacier. On our way out we met with an almost newlywed couple. The young girl was from Germany and the guy hailed from Lahore settled and working in Germany. She was loving Pakistan to the core. "I had no plans of visiting Pakistan this year. I was travelling to India to attend my husband's cousin's wedding. Fortunately, I had no trouble getting the visa but my husband did. So he came to Lahore, while I attended the wedding in India and returned to Lahore. Then we decided to travel up north and here we are, completely oblivious to where we were headed to. With no proper preparation we just started our hike and now going back tomorrow morning." We bid farewell for the day, as they were also camping close to our campsite. It was 4:30 p.m., leg muscles sore, tired but we did not want to miss a chance to see the massive glacier. Fatimah, Kiran and myself decided to stay up on the crest of the hill, for we didn't want to over-exhaust ourselves for the descent the next day. The climb up offers sweeping panoramic views of Rakaposhi and Diran and exceptional views into the extensive crevassed mass of lustrous ice of the Minapin Glacier. This trek is the standard route to the base camps of both the peaks. In the quiet of the evening we could hear the frequent roars of the glaciers cracking. When these glaciers melt in the summers, rivers form that run down into the Hunza River. People who went down could be seen from above, crossing the icy glacier, streams emerging from small grottos and filling water from the running water. We sat there until the sun went down illuminating Diran – the golden hour, not to be missed. We returned back around 7 p.m., after the sun had set.

Experiencing a new place should be inspiring, not exhausting. Savouring slow travel and absorbing and appreciating your surroundings is ultimately more valuable than hurriedly ticking it off your bucket list. If you have time and energy you can spend the third day trekking to Diran base camp, a 7,200 meters high peak. Its base camp is right across the glacier and to reach it you will have to walk over it, occasionally jumping over a 30 meters' deep crevasse which is quite an adventure. These crevasses make the crossing really dangerous. One must be particularly careful, because one wrong step may turn fatal. Falling and remaining forgotten in one of those holes can be lethal. It is not recommended to go alone, unless you have plenty of experience in crossing glaciers. This trek is normally done from mid-May to September. For Diran Base Camp one has to cross the Kacheli Glacier that takes 2 – 3 hours on the moraine to go. It is optional to go and return in one day which takes 6 – 7 hours. Another option is to spend the night there and return to Tagaphari in the morning or to stay in Tagaphari and explore around Rakaposhi Base Camp. The rapid shrinking, thinning and diminishing glaciers, due to the rising temperatures and sudden rainfalls caused by global warming pose a real threat to the millions who depend on these rivers for everyday sustenance.

Diran is located between Rakaposhi and Haramosh massif of the mighty Karakoram Range. Significant and an attractive peak in the Nagar valley, due to its treacherous storms and avalanches. In 1964, another Austrian Expedition tried to get on the summit from Northwest face but couldn't proceed due to bad weather. Technically it is known to be difficult because of ice walls and hidden crevasses and its soft snow fields. It was climbed by Austrian Expedition in 1968, also who found hidden crevasses and high snow domes on the Northwest ridge very tough.

I was the first one to climb down because I couldn't take the biting wind anymore. I found Rayyan soaking wet with no jacket; his double-layered trousers, shoes, T-shirt everything was drenched. I was horrified and his only concern was where to keep his treasure of stones he had gathered all the while I was away. I was infuriated and panicky. Quickly changed him between his justifications, "I was trying to jump across the water channel and fell more than once." He thought I was reacting too much and was not the least bit interested in his precious pieces of rocks. My concerns at this point, *he will catch a fever or get really sick, how in the world will I ever dry his clothes and shoes...and carry it all back...I don't even have an extra pair of warm clothing....* Changed and napped while I spread his clothes by the edge of our camp and looked around for a place to dry the dripping wet shoes. Not boasting at all, but the team of Climax Adventure will go out of the way and offer help. Muqeem handed over Rayyan's shoes to someone in the kitchen who placed them near fire in the little makeshift shed and assured me they will be as dry as a bone by next morning. Relieved! The boys in our group started playing Snakes and Ladders using headlamps, as these and the handheld emergency lights were the only source of light available except the hazy moonlight. That night canned tuna and mixed vegetables (carrots, potatoes and peas) were served with dry flat roti. "When I felt hungry in the evening, some uncle gave me carrots and offered me to sit in the kitchen," Rayyan informed me. "I am telling you mama these people are very kind," he whispered.

* **Tip:** When travelling, let your children experience and learn things on their own. However, sometimes our honourable endeavours blur that thin line between freedom and spoiling a child. Dictate them less on vacations. Give them what they need and use that to teach them general consciousness and responsibility.

As the sunset turned the sky to shades of indigo, we could hear the greetings of the donkeys and the cows in the distance instead of expected nocturnal creatures of the forest. The world filled with peace and tranquility when good friends gather together for a mountain vacation dream that's tailor-made for nature lovers. "Early to bed, early to rise," implied Muqeem. "We have to reach Gilgit by evening, before it gets dark, so get some rest because we have a long way to go. The descent will take approximately 4 – 5 hours including rest at Hapakun. So we must leave by 8 a.m." Slowly we all got up to use the washroom, change and got into our sleeping bags. No stories and no bonfire tonight!

Day 15 – Back to civilization – Rakaposhi basecamp to Hapakun to Minapin– 3rd July 2018

Plan: *Breakfast and trek to Minapin glacier, enjoy the hike on the glacier, photography and return back to campsite, packing and hike back to Minapin for dinner and overnight stay.*

Slight change of plan, since half of us already went to the glacier, the remaining half didn't want to. Therefore, it was decided we will return to Minapin / Nagar and drive back to Gilgit for the night stay.

I peered out at 6 a.m. to find no one in sight. Carefully not to disturb Rayyan or Eugenia I put on my down jacket, shoes and climbed out. It was a cold morning. Walking around the water stream I bent down to wash my face. Barely had I wet my hands I decided against it. Another girl from our group Khadija, woke up and refused to even try dipping her finger in the icy cold water. The men in the kitchen were already up and had started preparing breakfast, making me wonder if they slept properly or not. One of them was kind enough to bring a large round kettle of tepid water for us to wash our faces and brush our teeth. The few early risers got a chance to use this facility. Semi-boiled eggs, omelets, jam and roti was served soon after everyone woke up and gathered in the tent next to the kitchen. Rayyan's shoes and clothes were dry now, but he woke up tired and grumpy.

After having black coffee with salt and no milk we took turns to use the washroom. Early morning the view from the loo was stunningly gorgeous. With no covering on top you could view Rakaposhi under the sun in all its glory, standing tall and firm. An awe-inspiring view of nature displaying its rich colors. Backpack packed, camps down and folded, everything loaded, we were all geared up to leave. Asif another member was kind enough to share his perfume since I had packed everything. Unquestionably I had to click a picture of his Emporio Armani 'Because It's You Fragrance', for memory's-sake. The couple we had met yesterday was also leaving. We said our goodbyes and exchanged email addresses and promised to stay in touch. Lots of pictures later we all started off strolling down. Eugenia was offering some kind of leaves enclosed in her zip lock bag. "These are coca leaves," as she shoved a few coca leaves in her mouth. It helps you during your hike", she said. She showed how to use them, "Insert a few leaves into the corner of your mouth. Ideally, you want it lodged between your cheek and molars. Leave it there for a few hours, gently chew often. Throughout the day, expect your mouth to go slightly numb or you might feel a bitter flavour. Doesn't sound fun, I know", she tittered. "But the boost of energy can be well worth it and may save your life in a survival situation. After a while, you might even start to enjoy the taste." So we all tried it, I did not feel numbness or bitterness as I had anticipated.

The leaf is considered a source of energy, since it relieves hunger and thirst, and provides a boost of energy. It is recommended to chew coca leaves or have coca tea while trekking in order to avoid the various symptoms of altitude sickness.

Note: Never tried, read or researched about coca leaves. Hence, I personally would not endorse the use of this product. I repeat, before you use any product in its raw or synthetic form find out. You may be allergic to certain eatables. Every individual's body reacts differently. Since I am always keen to try unusual and exotic looking eatables, I took some. In fact, we all took some and nothing out of the ordinary happened.

Our hike began. Somehow it feels relaxing when you are descending. Probably because your body and mind knows the tough part is over. Technically, ascending is easier than descending. As you climb down you unexpectedly happen to transfer all your weight on your knees and legs. When ascending avoid overextension at the knees and ankles. The toughest part is to regulate pace and breathing. Maintain a steady stride throughout the day. Find a rhythm between your breathing and your steps. This is more important on long gradual climbs than on an easy terrain, because it is fairly easier to go faster than your lungs allow. A good rule of thumb is *you should be walking at a conversation pace - you should be able to keep talking as you walk and not run out of breath.* What I have learned over the years is:

- Shorten your steps
- Use zigzag trails or traverse slope sideways
- Use your hands when climbing rocks or high step ups; or sit down and use your hands for balance on high step downs
- Use trekking poles (at least one)
- Take rest steps - with each forward step, straighten your knees to temporarily shift stress from the muscles to the joints

While descending, avoid leaning backwards and keep your center of gravity low allowing you to land on your toes instead of your heels on steeper terrains. "Repetitively landing directly on your heels can cause high impact forces on your ankles and knees. Shorten your pace and try landing on your toes", Muqeem told us. I have also learnt the skill of employing the standard heel-to-toe technique on shallow land. Keep your knees slightly bent on impact to keep the stress on the muscles. Pay attention to foot placement as well. One must maintain a steady pace that helps avoid slips and reduces the potential for injury. Take short, controlled steps, especially on pieces if stones, rocks and sand.

According to Mujahid, "It is better to walk slowly and take fewer breaks than to walk fast with a lot of breaks. Minimize the overuse of muscles in particular areas. Keep your muscles flexible and avoid injuries by stretching before starting, during breaks and at the end of the day.

Stay in control and maintain your strength, especially on stones, sand and other loose terrains".

*A study suggests that the body and brain go from a stage of activity to a stage of fatigue every 90 minutes. Walk 60 – 90 minutes, and take a 15 – 20-minute break.

* **Tip:** Learn to listen to the experts.

Rayyan was now on his own, practically running down the meandering mountains along the slope covered with evergreen shrubs and trees. The majestic mountain ranges of the Karakoram, the grandeur, the enormity of the setting cannot be overstated. Under the bright blue sky stood Rakaposhi and the glacier's creeping down the mountain has brought so much debris from subsequent rockslides and avalanches that grey and charcoal swirls can be visible with the white backdrop of the gleaming glacier. Surreal. Time stood still as we gazed at the panoramic view for the last time. No sooner were we being followed by a puzzled drooling black goat with a chocolate brown patch, who, between our shrieks and fears, managed to find its way out. It was sad leaving a place studded with glaciers, snow-crested mountains, lush green forests, waterfalls, abundant wildflowers and the vibrant village. The basecamp is a testament to the splendour and beauty of Nagar.

By 11 a.m. we all had gathered at Bang-i-das, dropped everything and sat under the trees, the branches extended above us felt like wearing SPF 10 sunscreen. Freshening up our lipsticks, sharing biscuits, finishing off the remaining walnut cake and teasing each other for their tantrums and outbursts during the trek. I liked this place, stretching on the green patch, along the stream edged with green pines and drinking tumoro with no one but us – happy to have achieved what we all were apprehensive about the first day. After a good 45-minute break and over a dozen group pictures we all started getting up, leaving behind the Minapin glacier, Rakaposhi, Diran, the meadows, the irrigation channels and the stranded shepherd huts. The sun intensified by midafternoon and so was our muscular strength and patience.

On the way down I noticed quite a few more streams than there had been... either we had taken a different route or the abrasive movement produced glacial silts. Rayyan was busy adding to his rock collection and was mostly on his own. Trudging downhill, the last two hours felt like an eternity but we knew we could get through it somehow. Looking at the captivating beauty of the mountains that appear grey – brown from a distance but depict all sorts of mesmerizing colours when you move closer. A perfect natural blend of red, yellow, brown and rustic orange. With the passage of time, the movement and collision of tectonic plates give rise to new mountains and new colours. This is due to the sediments that change when exposed to environmental conditions such as wind, snow and water. The red in the mountains is because of the weathering of the iron-sulfide minerals within its rocks. It is darker where its broken surfaces are fresh, but stained red where it has been coarsened by air and water depression.

The last 2 hours were arduous and tiresome. Exasperated we dragged ourselves down until we reached the wooden footbridge along the Minapin village, standing across the hydro plant. This time not stopping by the gushing river bank but resting under the shade of a large rock. Around the village there are extensive cultivated fields and orchards, containing apples, cherries and apricots. You will see bright orange coloured apricots drying on large rocks, bottles and juice cartons in plastic crates in narrow icy irrigation channels, wood work with large machinery. This time I noticed Central Karakoram National Park which none of us were least curious about. Back on the familiar trail with a series of boards displaying "Welcome to Nagar Valley" with pictures and descriptions of legends of Pakistan – the road that was the end of our walk – the road that leads us back to the hotel. We literally ran when we read Hills n Huts – 100 meters – 1-minute drive; unsure if this was the place we were supposed to rest but it made our legs carry us faster. As soon as we entered the extensive hall we collapsed on the teal carpet, each one of us at different time intervals – too exhausted to speak or think.

It was roughly 2 p.m. when we reached the hotel in time for lunch. Nagar to Gilgit is 105 kilometers and the drive takes 2 hours and 15 minutes. Heaven Lodge Gilgit was 98.4 kilometers and in 2 hours' time we would check in. We wolfed down the food, drinks and kehwa as soon as it was served. We collected our things, cleaned up the place, thanked the nice people, loaded up and drove off to our next destination – Gilgit. The drive was silent between naps.

We checked in at Heaven Lodge Gilgit close to 6 p.m., still bright and sunny. It seemed like the oxygen in our lungs had returned, for everyone was glued to their cellphones. It is worrisome for people back home when someone is gone for 3 straight days without any updates. Showered, changed and reclining in the chairs out in the blossoming garden everyone started making phone calls, returning messages and basically updating their status to their near and dear ones. Sunburnt, drained and silent we all basked in the evening sun, talking about how it was all worth it. The feeling of accomplishment was greater than the muscle aches. Each one of us felt their persistence at any level paid off. Each one of us learnt a little more about ourselves; our strengths, our weaknesses, our resilience, our shortcomings and all in a chivalrous manner.
That night we had dinner in a fairly warmer setting. After a couple of days spent hiking and zipping our way through the mountains, there's no better way to relax than to eat good food, mouthwatering fruit and a steaming cup of doodh patti with people who now became good friends.

Sharing good memories of the days spent along with lots of laughter and cherries. Some young members of the group decided to retire, while a few of us went out for a ride to the departmental store and to withdraw cash from an ATM. Hamid Karim sahab from Heaven Lodge was kind enough to drive us. Once returned we all said good night and headed straight to our rooms to catch a good night sleep.

* **Tip:** Whenever, wherever you get the opportunity to withdraw cash, avail it.

Day 16 – Off to Naran – Once a virtual Paradise – 4th July 2018

Plan: *Breakfast and drive back to Naran for dinner, explore and overnight stay.*

Naran has always been one of the many popular tourist destinations for its admirable uniqueness and natural beauty. This wasn't the first time I was travelling to Naran, therefore, familiar with the landscape, developed roads and over crowded market place. It is located in Kaghan Valley near Mansehra District, situated at an altitude of 2,409 meters it's a scenic part of Khyber Pakhtunkhwa. Naran is quite an entertainer for local tourists in particular. People often travel here for food and shopping then to experience the hanging bridges over the lakes, the narrow ways on the mountains, boating in the lake and the glaciers that often or never melt.

Jheel Saif ul Muluk or Saif ul Muluk Lake was named after a Persian prince Saif ul Muluk. History has it that it was formed 300,000 years ago when the melting glaciers settled in the arms of mountains of Himalayan Region. Since then the lake has maintained its character as one of the most scenic beauties in this region. It is 50 feet deep and home to various species of vascular plants. Having a fairytale legend to its existence, this lake has mythical roots as told by a Sufi poet. This being my third trip to Naran, I had never been to the famous lake and was exceptionally euphoric to visit it the next day. Gilgit to Naran is 234 kilometers which is 4 hours and 48 minutes to be precise.

We all gathered in the garden next to the kitchen laden with fruit trees of all kinds, green apples hanging low in bunches, cherries and green walnuts. Showered, changed, packed and ready for breakfast. the spread before us seemed like a feast – boiled eggs, omelets, fried eggs, roti, paratha, bread, butter, jam, milk tea and separate hot water and milk for coffee.

Although we were all packed and ready to leave after breakfast, but one of our group members wasn't well. So we all waited until his condition was stable enough to travel the long distance from Gilgit to Naran and take a public transport to Lahore. From Naran to Lahore its 623 kilometers – a good 10 hours on the road! All huddled up in the verandah, and in no hurry to leave, we waited patiently until Asif said he was ready to hit the road. Knowing the trip is coming to an end, it was sort of emotional. After every journey, memories remain. Moments that cannot be relived but etched in mind as the fondest of all memories.

Our coaster halted at Nanga Parbat viewpoint. Nanga Parbat – a Kashmiri originated name meaning "naked mountain", anchors the western Himalayan Range and is the 9th highest in the world. It is not just a single peak but a series of ridges culminating in an ice crest at 8,126 meters in the great Himalayan range, which stretches up to 2,400 kilometers to the east, running through six nations and ending in Tibet. Popularly known as "Killer Mountain", it earned this title because it is notoriously difficult climb and many lost their lives during the attempt. The shroud of sky rocketing peaks, the puffy clouds concealed the captivating charm and splendour of Nanga Parbat. So we did the next best thing – bought cherries!

^ **Tip:** The best of the best tasting fruit ends here so this may be your last chosen place to make a purchase.

Back on the road, driving along the Indus river on the Karakoram Highway. We stopped midway at a hotel to stretch our legs, use the restroom and eat. Outside we saw perfectly lined up fruit in rectangular baskets. An array of colours – colourful plums and bright yellow apricots and mangoes. It is here that we had the best Kashmiri tea (pink tea). It is also known as *Noon chai* among the Kashmiris, because of the salt which is locally called '*noon*'. The pink colour in the tea is because of a reaction that occurs between the chlorophyll of its green tea leaves and a pinch of baking soda that is added to it.

Noon chai is traditionally made from a kind of green tea leaves (unlike the regular tea leaves), milk, salt, baking soda and usually prepared in a brass kettle known as *samovar,* which is often engraved or embossed with calligraphic motifs. A samovar consists of a "fire-container" running as a central cavity, in which live coals are placed that keep the tea perpetually hot. Around the fire-container, there is a space for water to boil and the tea leaves and other ingredients are mixed with the water. A pinch of baking soda gives it a pronounced pink colour. The chai is milky and creamy and is usually garnished with a sprinkling of chopped almonds and pistachios. Kashmiri kahwa on the other hand is different, flavoured with cardamom and infused with cloves, cinnamon and saffron. Someone told me once that in Kashmir, where the temperature drops below zero degree they often add cream and butter along with powdered dry fruits in the tea.

The route we took was Gilgit – Jaglot – Bunji – Babusar – Gittidas – Besal – Jalkhad – Batakundi – Domel – Naran. Somewhere along the road the Indus river interchanges to Kunhar river. With 3 hours of endless drive we entered the Naran bazar. It was 6:30 p.m. The hotel we checked in for the night was – Lahore Hotel – Main bazar Naran, a decent place in a very chaotic market place with its kitchen right at the entrance. We all decided to freshen up and head out to explore the market until dinner time.

*** Tip:** Don't get too over-whelmed and tempted to procure everything you set your eyes on. Make wise decisions, whether its food, warm or cold drinks, clothes, handicrafts, dry fruits, herbs, travel accessories etc. Be wise!

Regrettably Naran is the most convenient and reachable holiday place much like Muree and Nathiagali, offering a range of hotels, restaurants and budget stays. Babusar Pass, which is the final point of Naran – Kaghan Valley, has unbelievably beautiful panoramic views of the surrounding mountains and valleys and perhaps the most fortunate short cut in the entire country. It gives access to Gilgit Baltistan through a journey of just a few hours in beautiful and green Upper Naran Valley as compared to a day long journey on the most rugged, difficult and God forsaken patch of Karakorum Highway between Besham and Chilas. The bitter truth is that these touristy places are neglected by the authorities. Ever since volumes of holiday planners have entered these easy-access places, a maze of crude concrete constructions such as multi storey hotels, semi-clean and filthy hotels and restaurants and makeshift shops have come into existence. Due to this a bypass had to be built to ensure the smooth flow of traffic over the years. Between the two roads many unattractive, nature-damaging campsites have emerged too, utilizing the subsidized Chinese or Turkish tents and camps, which never reached the earthquake victims in the past. The place many years ago was surrounded by dense forests over the mountain slopes and green banks of River Kunhar.

* **Tip:** Avoid telling people not to litter. Avoid telling them to pick up the trash they threw right before your eyes. No matter how sweet, genuine and sincere you sound you will offend the other person. Be it an adult or a child. But do give it a shot, it might work!

So before and after dinner we mutually planned to march and thoroughly explore the Naran bazar. In 2016, we were staying in Batakundi, some 14 kilometers from Naran, but most of us decided to stay back and play cards and charades. In 2017, we explored very little. But this time we wanted to see what the hype is all about. Rayyan wanted to go back to the hotel, watch some football match with the youngsters in our group before going to bed. Permission granted – because he was on a vacation – because it was our last night with the group – because I wanted him to bond with them.

* **Tip:** As a parent you should know when and where to say yes or no. Choose wisely!

Apart from the normal desi, Chinese, barbecue and grilled trout fish you will find a variety of cuisines in the heart of this bazar. All sorts of thirst-quenchers, hot brewing tea, coffee, Kashmiri and green teas and varieties of munchies and dry fruits are found here besides clothes, local handicrafts, dry fruits and shoes. As you walk on the filthy, choked road you will notice flashy glittering illuminated signs; an explosion of advetisments and some interesting things around the market; a man fashioning a *paan** (betel leaf) his storage box set well on his bicycle; using around 10 – 12 different assortments including a piece of chocolate, which is not a norm; a whole lemon above a pressure cooker, flying in the air as the steam whistles; a man-cum-walking shop with around 20 men's waistcoats on him; an assortment of herbal medicines and cures all available and many foreign eatery brands and labels you will see on roadside carts. A little after midnight we got so exhausted we decided to have tea and get some rest, because Naran didn't seem to be resting at all. Most of us were excited, but not everyone planned to visit Saif ul Muluk early in the morning before leaving for Islamabad.
The trip isn't over yet! With that thought I dozed off.

* Paan is prepared using betel leaf with areca nut, slaked lime, red paste (made from Acacia catechu - khair tree) and is widely consumed throughout Southeast Asia, East Asia and the Indian subcontinent. It is chewed for its stimulant and psychotropic effects. After chewing it is either spat out or swallowed.

Day 17 – Saif ul Muluk and the Majestic Malka / Malika Parbat Mountain – 5th July 2018

Plan: *Early morning visit Saif ul Muluk which is 45 minutes' drive. Breakfast and drive back to Islamabad.*

Saif ul Muluk – the land of fairies has a mythical tale attributed to it. The lake is located at the northern end of the Kaghan Valley, near the town of Naran in the Saif ul Muluk National Park. The lake is apparently a major source of the Kunhar river. At an elevation of 3,224 metres (10,578 feet) above sea level, the lake is said to be the highest lakes in Pakistan. The scintillating natural beauty, the pleasant environment and the associated tale and history, attracts masses of tourists each year from all around the world, especially during the summers. It is additionally famous for the uncommon brown trout fish which attracts foodies especially from Punjab. Shaped like a bowl, rich in eco-diversity, holds many species of blue-green algae, a variety of plants and contains multiple glaciers.

The weather is extremely pleasant through out the year. Boating facilities, like many other lakes in Pakistan also fascinates tourists. Surprisingly many locals and foreigners have tried to measure the depth of the lake but it is still unknown. Some researches show that the depth of Saif ul Muluk is around 34 metres (113 feet) and covers the surface area of 2.75 kilometres. The famous myth associated with the lake must be enjoyed while you are standing right in front of enchanted landscape with Malika Parbat standing tall behind the veil of clouds.

Malika means "Queen" and Parbat means "Mountain", stands at an elevation of 5,290 metres (17,360 feet). It is considered to be the highest peak in the Kaghan Valley of Khyber Pakhtunkhwa. It is around 6 kilometres south of Saif ul Muluk. This peak is accessible from Naran - Lake Saif ul Muluk side and from Batakundi - Dadar Chitta glacier. So far twelve climbers have reached the top of its North Peak till date, for the mountain is considered to be the most technical peak above 5,000 metres. Some popular specifics are, that the ridge-line that contains the Malika Parbat peaks has 4 prominent summits. Malika Parbat (South) is the main peak and also the highest in the entire Kaghan valley. This peak was climbed by Pakistani climber Rashid Butt and Omer Bin Abdul Aziz in 1998, however, Rashid Butt fell to his death while climbing down the mountain. This mountain was earlier climbed by the Europeans, Malika Parbat Fore Summit and Malika Parbat (North) climbed by two expeditions in 2012 summer season, but there is a controversy going on between the two claimanants. All its summits are technical in nature, therefore, not many attempt to summit or even trek.

I had never been on this road and I was told that this jeep trek to Saif ul Muluk was once a drive through dense forest, over fragile wooden bridges that were positioned over running streams of clean flowing water. Now the same pretty picture has turned into an unpleasant jarring, coarse road for nearly half the distance and the rest of the ride is through rugged slopes devoid of very little greenery. Beautiful surroundings of the lake have been entirely ruined with make shift market, hotels and endless litter. Its natural beauty is fast deteriorating and before long the place would become an environmental hazard. Although the lake before sunrise is a sight extraordinaire, with its greenish-blue clear and freezing water. The captivating lake is completely frozen during winters due to heavy snowfall and the perfect time to visit it starts from June until September. At night the temperature drops to three degrees centigrade and during day time it is about 15 – 20 degrees. People often plan and camp by the bank of the lake under the gleaming night sky. For sightseeing around the lake, there are caves that you can find at walking distance. If you are fit enough you can also trek to the sky touching Ansoo Lake – the tear shaped lake, that requires an hour to trek to after the two hours of horse ride from Saif ul Muluk. We all stood there in silence, watching what nature has bestowed us with and how unlucky are we to ruin it with our own hands. Once the most desirable places to visit with its lush green pastures capped by snowy peaks, and bucolic setting is in shambles and needs our attention. Only we can try and save this beauty – the beauty that has been described in many different ways by the travelers. But the truth is when you visit it you will have no words to explain this art of nature, minus the waste around the mesmerizing lake, with cattle grazing on the otherside.

We left the place after clicking several pictures and listening to the story from a local, the story that you only enjoy in the native language the way the old man narrates, with gestures and describing the visuals, pointing in all directions. It was still cloudy and foggy until we left for Naran. Our plan for the day was to pack up, have breakfast and leave for Islamabad – earlier the better, to avoid any heavy traffic. Most of the group members wanted to have halwa purri. But the four of us including Muqeem, Eugenia, Fatimah and myself preferred to have a lighter breakfast of omelet and dry paratha and a little bit of halwa. So for the first time the group sat at different tables.

Puri / Poori is a soft dough, deep-fried bread made from unleavened whole-wheat flour, water, salt, and unimaginable amount of oil. It is shaped into a thin, flat disk, and once deep-fried it puffs up. It originated in the Indian subcontinent, eaten normally for breakfast or as a snack. Halwa purri is usually served with a savory curry of chickpeas and potato, packed with flavour and spices. Now a traditional Pakistani and Indian breakfast featuring semolina pudding or halwa Halwa is typically made with a mixture of fried semolina and sugar syrup, which is then combined with nuts (optional) such as pistachios and almonds and cardamom was a pleasant smell. Most commonly it is enhanced with yellow or orange food colouring to look a little vibrant.

By 10:00 a.m. we had hit the road. The sky was overcast with thick gray clouds and weather was a pleasant mix of light wind and drizzle. The 6 hour 20 minutes ride back to Islamabad was filled with laughter, immitations, naps and some quite moments. It is near Abbotabad I remembered I had to make reservations at a guest house for the night.

* **Tip:** "Make sure you book yourself a guest house or a hotel room of your choice before reaching your destination, to avoid last minute panic attacks". Yeah, at this point I clearly ceased to remember the advice.

As luck would have it I found the perfect place to stay the night – Apex Guesthouse in F/6 – 3 Islamabad. Perfect because it was on the main road, within my budget and strategic location.
We stopped on the way somewhere, to have our last lunch, and by sunset we were on Kashmir Highway, from where my journey had begun 17 days ago. *Another week left*, I tried cheering myself.
My 4th trip with Climax Adventure was coming to an end and trust me, like always I am a satisfied, happy customer. Whether it is Muqeem, Mujahid or any other member of their team, the experience is seamless, organized, respectful and loads of fun. The trip ended with promises of meeting soon and planning another trip together in the years to come.

I spent another one week in Islamabad where I moved from one guesthouse to another. From Apex in F/6 – 3 to Amyl Garden in F/6 – 2 to Grand Inn guesthouse in F/6 – 1. And that's where I stayed until my flight back to Karachi on the 13th of July 2018. Abbasi sahab at Grand Inn was extremely hospitable, kind and a generous soul who made sure our stay was as comfortable as home. Rayyan and I had plans of visiting and staying in Nathiagali for a night or two but that didn't pan out as we had expected. So the next best plan was, to go around Islamabad on foot. You often don't see women quite aimlessly walking on the roads but that's perhaps the most economical way of going around the capital city.

Normally we like sitting by the roadside and enjoy a nice icecream or fresh juice on hot days. A few places I like going back to are; Saeed Book Bank, Mr. Books and a few old book places for literary pleasures. At Kohsar market there are two wonderful places to visit The London Book Co. and Table Talk and the best place to eat is right next to it, Tuscany Courtyard.

We did take a day trip to Khewra Salt Mine, which my son really wanted to visit and generously agreed to pay for it with his Eidi money. Khewra Salt Mine is 160 kilometres from Islamabad. Pakistan's largest and the world's 2nd largest salt mine, which is located in Khewra, north of Pind Dadan Khan, an administrative subdivision of Jhelum District, Punjab Region, Pakistan. The mine is located in the Salt Range, Potowar pleateau. It is famous for its production of pink salt, and has turned into a major tourist attraction, inviting up to 250,000 visitors a year. To date Khewra salt mine remains the largest source of salt in the country, producing more than 350,000 tons per annum and estimates of the reserves of salt in the mine vary from 82 million tons to 600 million tons. We also bought the best tasting lychees and apples on our way back.

Day 25 – Back Home – 13th July 2018

Karachi – Back home.
With a heavy heart and many stories to tell, I packed my bags. I couldn't sleep that night. I sat by the window watching the pitter patter on the long concrete porch. It rained the entire night. Originally I had booked my tickets for the 11th but I wasn't ready to head home yet, so I extended. I scrolled through my photographs, videos, sounds and notes I had made. Sitting in the darkness I looked back at all the journeys I had taken so far, and wondered how travelling has shaped and moulded me in a way that's difficult to articulate. Once your expeditions are over, you realise how much your reality differs from others. Travel does make you grateful and appreciative of all that you have. It's hard to describe the feeling that's left with you once your journey is over. The traces it leaves can either be bitter, or sweet; depending on how you view the experience. The approach you take when encountering new places can either make or break your time spent.
For me, Gilgit Baltistan will always be a fond, enduring memory of people, places, sights, tastes and smells. It's a land of eternal optimism and natural wonder, and I fall in love with it a 1000 times over.

Karachi – my home – my reality. Located on the Arabian Sea, documented to be one of the largest and most populous cosmopolitan city in Pakistan and the capital of Sindh province. It was once known as the "City of Lights" due to its vibrant nightlife. Karachi nights are still particularly pleasant with an active night scene. For some it may be chaotic, straggling, under-resourced and poorly managed but it's a poor man's abode, enriched with courteous, generous people.

Basic Sentences for Communication

English	Wakhi	Burushaski	Shina
Hello. How r u?	Saloom Alikum. Chez hol e?	Asalam Allikum. Bay hal bila?	Assalam Alikum. Jak haal han?
I am fine, thank you	wuzam baf, shobosh	ja shuwa ba, shukrya	sum han, ju
What is your name?	te nug e chez?	unn hik basan bila?	tai nom jak han?
Where are you from?	tu ath kumran?	hun amlom ba?	tu kono hanu?
What language do you speak?	kum zik ash khan?	aamit bash achan?	thai zaban k hin?
I like it here / I like the place	yam jay e mar khush	kuty dish ja hairum be	mas anu dish pasand tamus
I love your village	te dyor e mar khush	una khn jar ayrum be	thai gaw bat lao pasand han

English	Wakhi	Burushaski	Shina
Do you have food?	shapik e tay aa?	sheyasr basan be ya	jak kokat hana?
I want tea or green tea	choi e taya	chai bila	chai hana
How much money? How much do I pay?	xumar rpyaa vita?	baurm rupia manimi?	kachak rupai bili?
I think I'm lost	mar sduith kumram neshatk	jay amlu awala wa	ma kon natanus
It was nice meeting u	gafch khushi vita daton muloqot vita	ma ka mila manasa bhot shuryar manimi	lao khushi bili tu bsath dok bigas
Thank you	shukrya/ mehrbani	juu	juu
See you	muloqoth ap vost voz	mulaqat maymi	nay dok bon

Counting 1 – 10 in wakhi language:

1	2	3	4	5
yew	bui	trui	xubur	panz
6	**7**	**8**	**9**	**10**
shadh	yub	hath	naho	das
20	*50*	*100*	*500*	*1000*
esth	bu vesth das	yi saad	pan saad	yi hozor

2000	*5000*
bu hozor	panz hozor

Courtesy- Mujahid Ali (Climax Adventure Pakistan)

Recipes

I – Hunza Bread (also known as diet bread)

Hunza Diet Bread is a delicious, dense, chewy bread that's very nutritious and is almost impervious to spoilage. The following recipe makes a huge batch of approximately 60 (sixty) 2 inch squares, high in protein, vitamins and minerals. Keeps weeks at room temperature, even longer in the fridge and indefinitely in the freezer.

Ingredients:
4 cups of plain water
3.5 to 4 pounds of natural buckwheat or millet flour
1.5 cups of canola oil or any vegetable oil
1.5 cups of natural unrefined sugar
16 ounces of honey
16 ounces of molasses
4 ounces of powdered soya milk (half cup)
1 teaspoon sea salt
1 teaspoon cinnamon
1 teaspoon ground nutmeg
2 teaspoons baking powder

How to prepare:
Optional: You may add dried apricots, raisins, chopped walnuts, almonds, sliced dehydrated dates to the above ingredients, if needed.

Step 1: Mix the ingredients well, knead it in a dough. Meanwhile grease and lightly sprinkle flour in the cooking pan(s). Ideally use baking trays which may be about 1 inch high.
Step 2: Pour batter in the pan half an inch over the base. Bake at about 300 degrees Fahrenheit (150 C.) for 1 hour.
Step 3: Once you turn off the heat, dry the bread in the oven for 2 hours at a very low heat at 90 degrees Fahrenheit (50 C). set it to cool off then tip out and cut into small squares.

Step 4: Store it wrapped in cloth in a container. You may need to repeat the baking depending on the size of your baking pan, and oven, until all the mixture has been used.

II – Chamus - Sun-dried organic apricot juice known as Chamus in Hunza

Ingredients:
200 grams of dried apricots / fresh ones
1 litre of water / or less depending on your preference of thickness
Sugar or Honey to taste - if you need to sweeten the juice
How to prepare:
Step 1: Soak the dried apricots in hot water for about an hour. You can use fresh apricots or a mix of fresh and dried ones.
Step 2: Traditionally the juice is kneaded using hands for hours until the apricots become soft. Mix completely with water.
Alternative solution: Simply mix the soaked apricots with water in a blender and blend through.
Step 3: Strain the apricot juice and garnish with chopped apricot kernels

Apricots - the gold of Hunza Valley
Apricot orchards are more common in Hunza and Nagar valleys, the legendary fruit of the valley. Often a family's economic stability is measured by the number of trees they have under cultivation. The juicy yellow fruit is the major diet in summers and dried and stored throughout the winters. The pits are cracked to obtain the kernel that is crushed to obtain the oil for cooking and for lamps. The oil contains substance that are said to protect against heart diseases, circulation issues and cancer, which may or may not be true. The hard shell is kept for fire fuel. The kernel and oil could be eaten from the variety of apricots with a sweet kernel, but the bitter kernel variety has oil containing poisonous prussic acid. Besides apricots, the Hunzakuts also grow apples, pears, peaches, mulberries,

black and red cherries, and grapes. Mulberries, which resemble blackberries in size and shape, are a favourite fruit. When fully ripe, their flavor is sweet-sour but somewhat bland. The variety grown in Hunza is most likely a golden colour – Witnessed this as we drove past the apricot laden roads, streets, hotels from Hussainabad to Aliabad to Karimabad and also caught sight of apple and cherry trees. Hunzakuts take pride in growing their own plantations. Apart from their cherished gold trees (apricots) they cultivate other fruits and vegetables, some even go to the extent of growing mountain herbs in their gardens. In spring, apricot trees are examined for pests and diseases, as the use of artificial fertilizers and pesticides is inconceivable here. Therefore, infected or damaged parts are either removed or treated with a mixture of charcoal dust and glacier water.

III – Tumoro – Wild Thyme Hunza green tea

Ingredients:
1 cup plain water
2 teaspoons of dried thyme leaves
Sugar or honey to taste - if you need to sweeten your tea
People here normally prefer it with no added sweetness

How to prepare:
Step 1: Boil water in a pan.
Step 2: Add 2 teaspoons on dried leaves and turn off your burner.
Step 3: Let it simmer for 2-4 minutes before you strain and pour.
(Recipe by Café de Hunza)

IV – Balingi Chai – Not as popular as Tumoro

Ingredients:

2 cups plain water
8 walnuts, shelled
4 teaspoons black tea
Milk if desired

How to prepare:
Follow the same procedure above

V – Kashmiri Kahwa Tea
(recipe serves 2 people)

Ingredients:
1 teaspoon Kashmiri Green Tea (special tea – Google to find the closest place available)
3 cups water
10-12 strands saffron
1/2 inch stick cinnamon
1 clove
1 cardamom – crushed
1/2 teaspoon dried rose petals
2 teaspoon almonds (splinters)
1 teaspoon honey to taste - if you need to sweeten your tea

How to prepare:
Step 1: Heat water in a pan.
Step 2: Add saffron, cinnamon, cloves, dried rose petals and cardamom in water and let it simmer for 3-4 minutes.
Step 3: Switch off the heat and add green tea in the water. Let the tea steep for a minute.
Step 4: Strain the kahwa in 2 cups. Add splinters of almond and a few strands of saffron. Add honey if required.

Please Note: If Kashmiri green tea is not available, you can use any green tea to make kahwa. The results won't be the same.

VI – Kashmiri Pink Tea (Noon chai)

(recipe serves 2 people)

Ingredients:
1 cup water
1.5 tablespoon kashmiri tea leaves (for a more authentic taste and aroma)
4.5 green cardamom – crushed
1.5-inch cinnamon
Pinch of 0.25 teaspoon salt
0.5/2 teaspoon baking soda
1/2 cup cold water
1 cup milk for strong flavoured tea or 2-3 cups milk for light
A quarter cup cream (optional)
grounded almonds and pistachios (optional)
Sugar or honey to taste

Please Note: in some regions, jasmine flowers – star anise – cloves are also added.

How to prepare:
Step 1: Heat water in a pan / wide based skillet
Step 2: Add Kashmiri tea leaves, salt, cardamom and cinnamon. Bring it to a boil. Step 3: Add baking soda.
Step 4: Cook until you get a deep red colour and water is reduced to half. This will take 20 – 30 minutes.
Step 5: Add ice cold water in boiling hot tea. Mix well for a minute.
(The kehwa is ready. Strain, cool and refrigerate for 3 – 4 days).
Step 6: When preparing tea add milk, sugar / honey / salt and powdered dry fruits.
Step 7: Let it cook for another 2 – 3 minutes and serve. Garnish with nuts, if needed.

VII – Dandelion Root Tea

A caffeine-free herbal drink the dandelion root tea is prepared from the fresh or dried roasted roots of the plant.

Considered to be a good source of vitamin A, B, C, and D as well as minerals such as magnesium, zinc, potassium, calcium, manganese, and iron, its consumption can provide a host of health benefits. Most people also batter and fry the flowers to serve as fritters.

(recipe serves 4 people)

Ingredients:
4 cups plain water
2 tablespoons of the chopped roots (raw or dried roots can be used)
Sugar or honey to taste - if you need to sweeten your tea

How to prepare: (fresh dandelion root tea)
Step 1: Boil the water in a saucepan and add the chopped roots.
Step 2: Let it simmer for about a minute or two and remove it from heat.
Step 3: Allow the mixture to steep for 40 minutes, then strain the mixture and sweeten it with honey or sugar.
How to prepare: (roasted dandelion root tea)
Step 1: Dry and roast the raw chopped root on medium heat in a pan or a baking oven for 2 hours.
Step 2: Add 2 tablespoons of the root to the water and boil for 5-10 minutes.
Step 3: Allow it to steep for 10 minutes to obtain a richer flavor, then strain the mixture.
Step 4: Add sugar or honey to enhance the taste.

VIII – Dandelion Honey (using flowers)
Dandelion honey isn't honey made by bees, but it is really dandelion syrup made with the flowers and sugar. It is a good substitute for honey, with a surprisingly similar flavor, although the consistency is thinner than most honey, but has a very similar appearance in color.

Ingredients:

4 cups dandelion petals
4 cups water
3 lemon slices
1/2 vanilla essence / vanilla bean (split in half)
2 1/2 cups granulated sugar

How to prepare:
Step 1: Pick dandelion flowers during the daylight while in full bloom. Soak the flowers in cold water for five minutes to allow any insects to exit. Remove the petals, and discard the center of the flower and the stem.
Step 2: Place the petals in a heavy saucepan along with the water, lemon slices, and a few drops of vanilla essence or vanilla bean.
Step 3: Bring it to a boil, reduce the heat, and simmer it for 30 minutes. Remove the pan from the heat and let steep for 6 hours.
Step 4: Strain the dandelion tea through a cheesecloth and discard the solids.
Step 5: Place the dandelion tea in a heavy saucepan and bring it to a low boil. Gradually add sugar to the boiling liquid while stirring until the sugar is dissolved.
Step 6: Lower the heat and let it simmer uncovered until it reaches the desired syrupy thickness. This may take up to 4 hours or a little more. Store in a cool, dry place or refrigerate.

Epilogue

Travel changes people in so many ways. One of the things I'm most thankful for is how much I've experienced and discovered and how much I have matured as a person – all thanks to the countless adventures, people I have met along the way, stories I have heard and the cultural diversity and respect I have witnessed. Only when you begin to explore the most exotic natural wonders of the world, you will begin to realize the colossal majesty of nature.

Traveling, for me, puts things into perspective. It allows me to realize that there are far bigger matters to deal with than my tiny problems. So what if the Wi-Fi is slow or not there at all or no hot water when my hair is a mess or if my favourite place is inaccessible. Traveling allows you to see that the world is not always about you, your problems, your worries, your likes and your desires. It allows you to see how other people live and what they have to deal with every passing day. Travel continually exposes you to people and contexts much different than your own. Listening to, understanding and connecting with the feelings, thoughts, and stories of others help strengthen your empathy muscles. Indeed, travel helps us press the edges of our perceived limitations, so that we may re-imagine them and continue to reach beyond.

Traveling to the exquisite Northern areas of Pakistan has humbled me and has broadened my perspective in so many ways. Traveling to places like Gilgit Baltistan, journeying across the Karakoram Highway with the world-famous mountain peaks in view and walking around the impoverished but very well refined areas; has given me a sense of gratefulness for the modern day comforts that I am able to enjoy without batting an eye. These expeditions have also given me a sense of inspiration to travel to more less and unexplored destinations in future.

Pakistan – From the ancient Mughal city of Lahore to the soaring snow covered peaks of the Karakoram mountain range; Pakistan is a diverse nation defined not just by its natural beauty and architectural splendor, but by its friendly inhabitants, exotic wildlife, rich culture and delicious culinary traditions. The North-West Frontier Province and Gilgit-Baltistan region are home to some of the world's most famous mountain ranges and summits, including the Himalayas, Karakoram and Hindu Kush. From jaw-dropping landscape to bustling cities, Pakistan's each vibrant city has its own distinctive flavour – Islamabad being the most beautiful capital city; cultural capital Lahore known for its stunning history and lavish Mughal architectural structures; and Karachi the former capital and the economic powerhouse of the country.

As a travel writer, I try my hardest to describe places and destinations for my esteemed readers, however, there are just some things and experiences that are too enchanting to put down in words or click pictures of. To me, one of the most beautiful things about travel is the fact that every day is different. There are no set routines, no fixed rules, little or no expectations. You can do what you want, whenever you want and however you want. I have been traveling together with my little one who has turned 9 as I write, and one of the things we love, appreciate and cherish the most is the freedom that travel and this lifestyle has given us. Travel breaks down routines, monotony and brings back adventure, excitement, and exploration to one's life and endless stories to tell for many, many years to come.
In the coming months I plan to journey across all districts of Gilgit Baltistan, explore parts of Khyber Pakhtunkhwa (KPK), Chitral, Kumrat, Kashmir and Peshawar.

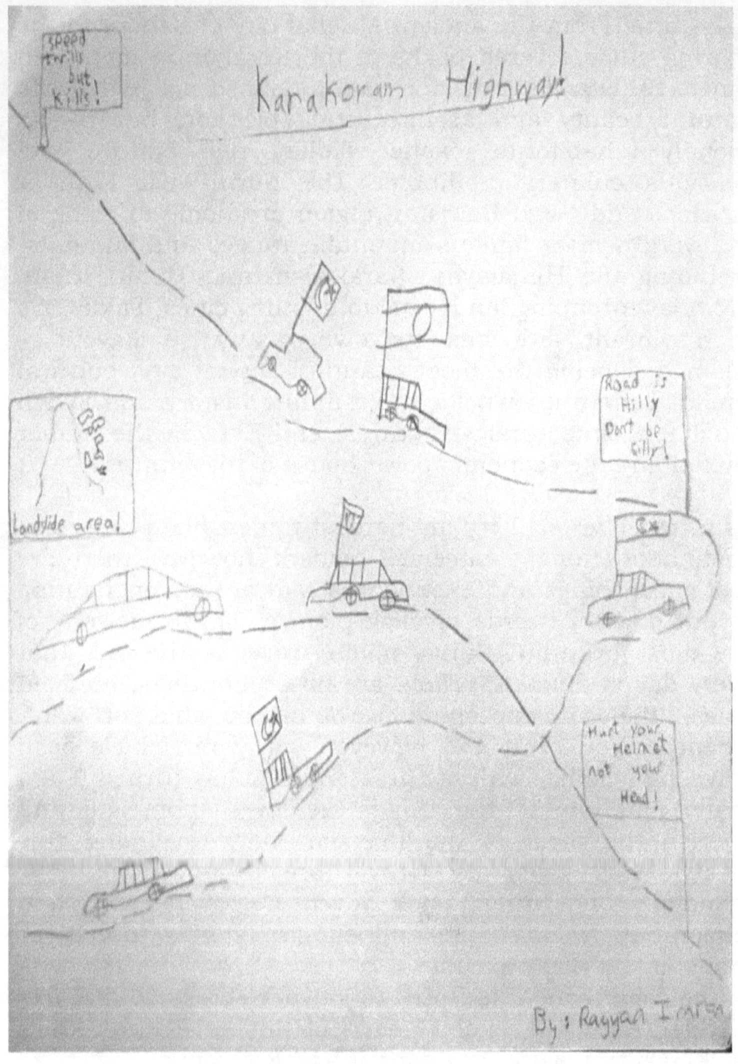

(Rayyan – 6 years old)

www.ingramcontent.com/pod-product-compliance
Lightning Source LLC
Chambersburg PA
CBHW020326160726
47992CB00004B/1723